Ari
May all of your
Bridges be very
"Successful!"

BRIDGING THE PM COMPETENCY GAP

A Dynamic Approach to Improving Capability and Project Success

Loredana Abramo, PMP
Rich Maltzman, PMP

Copyright © 2017 by J. Ross Publishing

ISBN-13: 978-1-60427-140-9

Printed and bound in the U.S.A. Printed on acid-free paper.

10 9 8 7 6 5 4 3 2 1

Library of Congress Cataloging-in-Publication Data

Names: Abramo, Loredana, author. | Maltzman, Richard, author.
Title: Bridging the PM competency gap : a dynamic approach to
 improving capability and project success / by Loredana Abramo
 and Rich Maltzman.
Description: Plantation, FL : J. Ross Publishing, 2017. | Includes index.
Identifiers: LCCN 2017023921 (print) | LCCN 2017032249 (ebook) |
 ISBN 9781604277876 (e-book) | ISBN 9781604271409 (hardcover :
 alk. paper)
Subjects: LCSH: Project management.
Classification: LCC HD69.P75 (ebook) | LCC HD69.P75 A293 2017
 (print) | DDC 658.4/04--dc23
available at https://lccn.loc.gov/2017011755

Direct all inquiries to J. Ross Publishing, Inc., 300 S. Pine Island Rd., Suite 305, Plantation, FL 33324.

Phone: (954) 727-9333
Fax: (561) 892-0700
Web: www.jrosspub.com

Contents

Preface

This book is about establishing a continuous, sustainable learning environment in your organization so that project management (PM) maturity and competency evolve in step with your business needs:

> "By 2020, 11 million PM roles will be added in 11 countries, increasing their gross domestic product (GDP) by $6.61 trillion across project-intensive industries (Project Management Institute Industry Growth Forecast 2010–2020)."
>
> "Organizations that are good at knowledge transfer are 20% better in meeting scope, 32% better at meeting schedule, and 27% better at meeting budget goals than organizations that are not effective at knowledge transfer. [...] When essential knowledge is captured and shared, organizations see improved results across the range of project metrics, including cost savings, time-on-task, error rates, and innovative solutions (*PMI Pulse of the Profession*®, March 2015)."
>
> "Eighty percent of global executives believe having project management as a core competency within their companies has helped them remain competitive (from *Closing the Gap: The Link between Project Management Excellence and Long-term Success*, Economist Intelligence Unit briefing paper, sponsored by Oracle, 2009)."

In any organization, project managers and their ability to lead projects are an essential element to successful delivery of business outcomes, and so is the competency of these project managers. However, the project managers' level of competency are often not equal to the challenges they encounter in their profession as the project environments in which they work (including tools, processes, and teams) are moving and evolving targets.

This book will provide approaches to establish a continuous learning environment, to foster project manager competency not only on a proven methodology and techniques, but also in emerging tools, cultural and leadership aspects of the profession, as well as business acumen.

Beyond classroom training and *lunch-and-learn* sessions, the book will describe tactical options for implementing competency development as part of organizational culture, leveraging internal and industry-based expertise, as well as tools to be used for virtual, collaborative knowledge sharing.

Next, focus will move on to delivery planning for the continuous learning environment selected and metrics to track effectiveness of the competency development techniques, from peer reviews and jury boards, to project key performance indicators and dashboards. The final part of the book will discuss methods to ensure that there is an established way to evolve the strategic approach as the project managers' maturity level and skill set in the organization change over time.

The book will:

1. Define the problem and explore the compelling reasons behind the need to fill this competency gap;
2. Help you assess your project managers' competency gaps to identify the most appropriate strategic approaches;
3. Aid in the analysis of your PM community and its specific traits;
4. Support your selection of the most suitable improvement options for your goals and audience, including implementation options, planning possibilities, and execution alternatives; and
5. Suggest ways to monitor progress and to continuously find opportunities to move beyond your current competency levels.

Leveraging over 65 years of combined experience in the industry, the authors will describe strategic approaches on how project managers' competency can be developed and sustained, with practical suggestions, real-life examples, and templates.

Foreword

I have been managing projects/programs for nearly 50 years, beginning with relatively simple sounding rocket and high-altitude experiments, and finally with some of the most complex space activities. These include the Compton Gamma Ray Observatory, the Hubble Space Telescope, and the Chandra X-ray Observatory. My deepest and most surprising learning experience came from losing a payload during the Space Shuttle Challenger explosion, and then launching the Hubble Space Telescope with a flawed mirror. The failure boards for both the Challenger and the Hubble identified flawed *social contexts* as the root causes of the failures. These findings motivated me to understand this phenomenon and develop a system, the *4-D System*, to measure and manage these social fields. Over 1,000 NASA teams and people in 75 countries have used this system to measure the social context of projects, and to enhance performance and reduce risk.

This book, which complements my work in the area of project management competency, investigates how to provide practical ways to improve project management—and in particular, project success rates. With the dynamic changes we face in the world of projects, this book is important and timely.

I hope you take advantage of the background, tools, and references that this book provides. The authors have taken an analytical approach to the development of project management competencies by starting with a problem statement (identifying the gap in competency), sharing best practice methods to bridge that gap, and more important, to sustain that bridge. As a scientist and project leader, I study and now convey—to project leaders around the world—the critical importance of the human element of projects.

This book gives you a unique opportunity to improve that element. You, your projects, and your enterprise will be better off when you enhance your project management competency!

Dr. Charlie Pellerin
Former Director, Astrophysics, NASA

Prologue

Establishing a continuous learning environment for the project manager is the main theme of this book and is developed right on target. It is good that Abramo and Maltzman are sharing their thoughts on a critically important topic. They are the right people to be doing that. That effort certainly requires senior management recognition and commitment but the project manager is the person who will actually make it happen. In most organizations, this will happen if and only if the project managers shift their thinking from a passive to an active participant in the learning process. For most project managers, that will be a challenge and will require a significant behavioral change. Let's dig into that behavioral change.

First of all, I am honored to have this opportunity to comment as it strikes close to home for a topic that has occupied me for several years. There are lots of reasons for this, but most reduce to the inability of our thought leaders to make inroads into reducing the historically unacceptable project failure rates. My fundamental premise is that the complex project is unique and that its best-fit project management approach will therefore also be unique. That uniqueness follows from the characteristics of the project; the internal organizational environment and culture; and the prevailing market conditions. All of these are continually changing and so the best-fit project management approach will also be subject to revision throughout the project life span. That may be seen as heretical to many thought leaders, but it is the reality one faces in the complex project landscape.

One further observation that should be mentioned is the role of the executive in establishing a continuous learning environment. It is a critical success factor. That is, to vest as much decision-making authority as possible in the project manager. In my experience, organizations that take this approach have shown increases in morale and have instilled ownership and commitment in the project manager and the team members as well. This increase of project manager authority will motivate him or her and the team to strive for maximal performance—hence, continuous learning.

As for the project management approach, it must be flexible and draw upon the project manager's creativity and problem-solving competencies for maximal benefit. As discussed before, the complex project landscape is dynamic, which requires a flexible approach that allows for the continual and adaptive best-fit alignment of the project management approach to what is an ever-changing situation.

Robert K. Wysocki
President
EII Publications

Acknowledgements

We would like to thank some of the individuals that have made this book possible, by providing encouragement, inspiration, and support all throughout the life cycle of this project.

We wanted to make this book as close as possible to real life, rooted in every day project management, rather than in theoretical statements. So we would like to start by thanking the 250+ respondents to our peer survey for their time and input on project management (PM) competency.

In particular, we would like to thank three colleagues who have contributed directly to our efforts. Helen Bull has shared with us her experience at Philips, and has agreed to share with our readers the approach used there in our Case Study. Charles Pellerin authored our Foreword and has inspired us with his focus on leadership competencies for project managers based on his experience at NASA. When we approached Robert Wysocki with some of the questions we had in our chapter called *Leveraging Expert Judgment*, he responded enthusiastically and wrote our Prologue.

Our sincere thanks to the many PM *thought leaders* who have responded (some instantaneously!) to our request to answer questions on PM competency. Their insights have provided confirmation—almost reassurance—that our focus on a dynamic and flexible approach to developing PM competencies beyond the standard triple constraint was valid.

We thank Diana Zarazua and Morse Shankman for their guidance and encouragement at our workplace.

Sarah Shah and John Alleman have helped us tremendously with style and consistency checks, and historical context for our Introduction, respectively. Many thanks to both!

We jointly dedicate this book to our spouses, Ellen Maltzman and John Alleman, and to our children, Sarah Shah, Daniel Maltzman, and Matteo Alleman.

About the Authors

Loredana Abramo, PMP, has over 25 years of experience in deploying telecommunication networks for international projects, with roles such as lead engineer, technical deputy, business operations manager, and project management competency development leader for emerging technologies.

On one of her more recent customer-facing assignments, she was the Deputy Director of the project management office (PMO) for a major telecom project in Australia. Loredana has worked and lived on assignment in North America, Europe, Asia, and Australia, and has presented at several Project Management Institute (PMI), Institute of Electrical and Electronics Engineers (IEEE), and International Project Management Association (IPMA) global events in North America, Australia, Malaysia, and Italy. She has published several articles and translated Peter Taylor's *The Lazy Project Manager* into Italian, (*Infinite Ideas*, Italian edition © 2013).

Ms. Abramo has a Master's in Electrical Engineering and is board certified as a Professional Engineer in Italy, as well as a certified Project Management Professional (PMP)®. Loredana has a Convergence Technologies Professional accreditation from the Telecommunications Industry Association, and a Certificate in Advanced Project Management from De

Paul University. She is a Member of PMI and a Senior Member of IEEE. Loredana is currently based in Naperville, IL, USA.

Rich Maltzman, PMP, has been an engineer and PMO leader for almost 40 years. His international project work has been diverse, including the integration of two large PMOs of merging multinational corporations. As a second but intertwined career, Rich has also focused on consulting and teaching at several universities in the U.S. and China.

Rich has also professionally developed PMP® exam prep courseware and has presented at international PMI and IPMA conferences in South Africa, the Netherlands, Costa Rica, Mexico, North America, and Malaysia.

Mr. Maltzman's educational background includes a BSEE from the University of Massachusetts–Amherst and an MSIE from Purdue University. In addition, Rich has a mini-MBA from the University of Pennsylvania's Wharton School and a master's certificate in international business management granted jointly by Indiana University's Kelley School of Business and INSEAD of France.

He has published numerous articles and coauthored three books— *Green Project Management*, winner of PMI's David I. Cleland Project Management Literature Award; *Project Workflow Management*; and *Driving Sustainability Success in Projects, Programs, and Portfolios*.

Rich is an active speaker at various professional conferences and an active blogger on projectmanagement.com.

At J. Ross Publishing we are committed to providing today's professional with practical, hands-on tools that enhance the learning experience and give readers an opportunity to apply what they have learned. That is why we offer free ancillary materials available for download on this book and all participating Web Added Value™ publications. These online resources may include interactive versions of material that appears in the book or supplemental templates, worksheets, models, plans, case studies, proposals, spreadsheets and assessment tools, among other things. Whenever you see the WAV™ symbol in any of our publications, it means bonus materials accompany the book and are available from the Web Added Value Download Resource Center at www.jrosspub.com.

Downloads for *Bridging the PM Competency Gap: A Dynamic Approach to Improving Capability and Project Success* include a:

- Self-Assessment Radar: Self-Management and Leading Others
- FACE Model Assessment of your Organization
- Success Predictor Radar: Vision, Skills, Motivation, Resources, and PM Discipline
- Competency Logger, using the ABCD-5E Model
- Roundtable Events Checklist
- Continuous Learning Opportunities Template
- High-level Planning Elements Template
- Phase Planning Template
- Audience Analysis for Communication Plan Template
- Planning for PM Symposium Template
- Agenda for PM Symposium Template
- FACE Model Elements Template

Introduction

Although the Project Management Institute's *Project Manager Competency Development Framework* was only first released in 2002, project management (PM) competency development has been a recurrent practical concern throughout history, specifically in the successful execution of large-scale military and civic projects—of course, not phrased in precisely these terms.

Concepts such as *project* and *management* have only emerged over the last 300 years, while the current articulated disciplines have evolved within the context of the Industrial Revolution and the emergence of scientific management principles in the 19th and early 20th centuries.

The use of the word *competency*, which roughly means *sufficient qualification for a task*, was first recorded in 1794 and did not emerge in its current human resources usage until appearing in an article by R. W. White published in 1959.

Competency as applied to PM really means possessing the practical and theoretical knowledge of technology, processes, and systems; interpersonal and social skills; and creative, tenacious problem-solving skills sufficient to manage projects of varying scope within a specific technology context. We will provide our definition of PM competency in Chapter 1. Interestingly, *competence* shares the same Latin root—*competere*—with *compete*. So, you might consider PM competency as the necessary and sufficient qualifications/skills to successfully compete in a specific PM environment.

The concept of PM competency may seem an artifact of the modern postindustrial world, but fundamentally, current practitioners are "*nanos gigantum humeris insidentes*" ("dwarfs standing on the shoulders of giants" as attributed to 12th century monk Bernard of Chartres). It is the accumulated experience of master builders, skilled tradesmen, military planners—or in other words, all of our predecessors who, in the process of putting teams of people together to attack the extraordinary tasks of engineering and organization, developed and refined the skills, processes, and tricks of the trades from which all of our *modern* PM practices can be understood to have emerged. Looking back at a few of such *projects*, as passed down to us through historical records, to understand the challenges faced and the methods of acquiring the needed expertise to successfully complete them, can give a context to the competency development challenges faced by our contemporary PM community.

A BRIEF HISTORY OF PM COMPETENCY

In 246 BC, outside of what is now Xi'an, Shan-xi, China, work began on a necropolis that was to be the burial site for the then young King Qin Shi Huang. The emperor-to-be was 13 when he ascended to the throne, and he was to become the first emperor of a united China before being buried in the necropolis in 210 BC. The tomb complex was scoped to be the largest ever built in China, in effect a full-scale city-sized habitat worthy of the first emperor. Modern radar soundings estimate the complex covers 98 square kilometers (38 square miles). Based on Chinese histories, at least partially confirmed through modern scientific tests and analysis, the necropolis of Qin Shi Huang contained everything needed to support the emperor in the afterlife, in even greater splendor than he enjoyed in his physical life.

There was, of course, the *Terracotta Army*, which was the first part of the project excavated in 1974, a small part of which now visits museums around the world. This army, buried in caverns with Emperor Qin, included roughly 8,000 foot and cavalry soldiers, with chariots in the hundreds and over 600 horses, both to pull the chariots and for cavalry soldiers to ride (see Figure I.1). There were also court officials to assist the emperor in running the necropolis, and entertainers (acrobats, musicians, etc.) for the needed diversions. Per the contemporary accounts, there were

Figure I.1   Terracotta Army

also over a hundred simulated rivers of shimmering mercury, all fitted into a complex of tunnels and caverns.

This was a public works project of extraordinary scope and complexity which eventually employed on the order of 700,000 workers. To produce the many life-sized figures, craftsmen built the arms, legs, torsos, and heads separately. There were at least 10 different face molds. The different parts could then be assembled, mixing and matching to maximize variety. After assembly, each was individually painted. To manage the end-to-end process of producing the 8,000 soldiers, something like a large-scale assembly line was likely used.

Technically, the work involved civil engineering (excavation and construction of caverns/rooms and connecting tunnels, simulated rivers, etc.), military engineering (functional weapons, including loaded and primed crossbows, were built for the army), arts/crafts (statues and related artifacts, kilns, paints, brushes, tools, etc.), and industrial engineering (mass production of the figures populating the necropolis). Organizationally, the master builder would have created a large, 700,000-person manufacturing facility in sustained operation for over a decade. Food, water, waste management, health care, supply chain management—all aspects of city management and PM—were required on a massive scale.

While the uncovered artifacts are works of great artistic merit individually, the real wonder of the Mausoleum of the First Qin Emperor is the extraordinary PM skill sets that must have been applied to create such a huge and diversified set of figures and the environment into which they were placed; as a single sustained project involving at its peak 700,000 workers, carried out over a less than 30-year period—and all without the benefit of *A Guide to the Project Management Body of Knowledge (PM-BOK® Guide)*. It was and is a wonder, but also part of what makes it a wonder is the fact that it was never repeated. The competencies developed on various skilled jobs over generations came fortuitously together in one place, for one generation, under inspired leadership to produce a single object of wonder.

The Hagia Sophia (*holy wisdom*) (Figure I.2) is a cathedral built in the sixth century AD on the other side of the world from Xi'an, in Constantinople (present day Istanbul, Turkey). Another public works project by another emperor, Hagia Sophia was built at the instruction of the Byzantine Emperor Justinian I—in part to reestablish imperial grandeur after the Nika riots that nearly toppled him; in part as an expression of his true Christian piety; and in part to establish the primacy of Constantinople, that is, reestablish the scope and dominance of the Roman Empire now ruled from Byzantium. The project had a short, sponsor-imposed end date constraint since the desired stabilizing effects on Justinian's imperial power were needed sooner rather than later. Therefore, the cathedral needed to be an engineering wonder.

Anthemius of Tralles and Isadore the Elder were selected to lead the building of the cathedral in roles that encompassed the modern ideas of lead architect, lead engineer, general contractor, lead designer, and lead project manager. Anthemius and Isadore put together a workforce of 10,000 men, divided into two teams of 5,000 each under 50 master builders. The cathedral was to be built on the footprint of the original Hagia Sophia, which was destroyed in the Nika riots, so they worked in a confined environment surrounded by preexisting structures that were susceptible to earthquakes.

Sixth century AD Constantinople was a different work environment than third century BC China. The project was run under a hierarchy of worker guilds on whose skilled laborers the project delivery schedule

Figure I.2   Hagia Sophia

depended. Another difference from the mausoleum of Emperor Qin was that the cathedral was primarily meant to be an object of public splendor and beauty dedicated to God, not the emperor—the accomplishment of which would also require an object of extraordinary engineering.

The project was completed in five years, compared, for example, to nearly a century required to build Notre Dame Cathedral in Paris (construction of which began in 1163 AD). The floor plan runs 82 meters (270 feet) in length and 73 meters (240 feet) in width, with a domed roof of 33 meters (108 feet) in diameter and a crown that rises 55 meters (180 feet). It was an extraordinary engineering accomplishment for a dome built without steel; however, it should be noted that the aggressive time constraints led to problems with the dome, which collapsed 20 years after completion. The domed roof was then rebuilt by Isadore the Younger. This dome, without further repair, has lasted until the present day (nearly 1,400 years).

Looking only at the PM aspects, it seems clear that the competencies required to complete such a grand project on such an aggressive, inflexible schedule were impressive. In this case, compared to Emperor Qin's mausoleum, the engineering tasks were formidable, requiring serious technical PM skills in addition to the scheduling, coordination, supply chain management, and resource management skills that would have been somewhat like the mausoleum project. In addition, the project managers would have been required to understand and work within the regulations defined by the various labor guilds. In summary, the work force was large, the regulatory environment complex, the sponsor very demanding, the stakeholders numerous, the schedule aggressive, and the technical aspects challenging. Sound *familiar*?

With the mausoleum of Emperor Qin, we highlighted the huge human resource and logistical challenges that the project managers would have dealt with when building a vast necropolis over a period of a few decades. With the Hagia Sophia, the project managers encountered a more complex regulatory environment, more aggressive time constraints, and more central engineering challenges, as well as significant human resource and logistical challenges. The final preindustrial-age example we will detail confronted the significant architectural and PM challenges of a multicultural, multilingual cathedral building project from the 12th century AD.

The third of the Norman kings of Sicily, William II, ascended to the throne of Sicily in 1172 at 18 years of age. He had inherited a kingdom only just wrested from the Arabs by his great grandfather, Roger I, 70 years earlier.

The island of Sicily had been populated by a multicultural, polyglot mixture of peoples for centuries, if not millennia. At the time of the Norman conquest of Sicily (1068 AD) by Roger d'Hauteville, the island's Byzantine Greek, Roman, Apulian, Venetian, Jewish, and Pisan inhabitants had been ruled by Muslim Arab chieftains for 200 years, to that mixture was now added the Norman French.

The Normans had, from the start, been inclusive leaders who fully integrated the various genius of the different peoples to build a society greater than the sum of its parts. As such, William II unified elements of Norman, Byzantine, Latin, and Islamic cultures in the architectural design of his cathedral at Monreale, located outside of Palermo in north central Sicily. The vast trade routes established by the Arab traders who preceded the Normans were reutilized to acquire the building materials, and

Figure I.3   Monreale, interior

through the associated contacts, he could acquire various artists, crafts-men, builders, and laborers from throughout the Mediterranean region. He utilized the d'Hauteville fortune to finance the project.

Construction started in 1172 AD on the main building of what was to become the monastery complex of Monreale. The work on this building was completed in four years. The cathedral is 102 meters (334 feet) long and 40 meters (131 feet) wide. The exterior is a mix of Norman and Islamic elements. The interior structurally merges Roman basilica and Byzantine cathedral elements, but most spectacularly contains 6,500 square meters (65,000 square feet) of exquisite wall-to-ceiling Byzantine glass mosaic work (see Figure I.3). The resulting complex is still intact, but sadly very little has come down to us regarding the master builder (unknown) or the details of the staff or their organization.

However, we can infer from the perspective of the project manager that there was an aggressive time constraint imposed in this case by the new king, establishing himself in a tricky political relationship with the pope and the local aristocracy—a complicated supply chain, a series of multicultural technology dependencies, and challenging communications constraints. The stone construction materials were probably locally quarried, but gold, glass, and precious stones would have all been imported. Local tradesmen may well have been utilized for the stone work, but there may have been French-speaking Norman and Arabic-speaking Muslim artists/craftsmen imported to decorate the mixed motif exterior, while Greek-speaking Byzantine artists created the interior mosaics, and Arabic-speaking Muslim boat builders constructed the interior wooden ceiling in the form of an inverted ship's hull.

Different from Emperor Qin's mausoleum and Justinian's Byzantine cathedral, the lead designer at Monreale needed a *broad* enough understanding of the diverse artistic/architectural styles, reflective of the 12th century Sicilian reality and the cultural/religious foundations of these styles, to merge them into a harmonious architectural whole. William II's project manager and architect needed a broad *enough* understanding of the technological and cultural/religious foundations of the diverse building practices, material sourcing, and labor pool to merge them all into an effective project team and supply chain. It comes remarkably close to the diverse workforce and technology that typify the modern global project environment.

From these three examples, it is clear that there have been extraordinary practitioners implementing PM principles around the world throughout the history of organized human activity. It must be so, or nothing on the grand scale we so admire would ever have been accomplished. However, there is also something critical missing from the historic PM accomplishments that we have reviewed in this introduction: instructions passed on to others to share the lessons learned and the tools and techniques that worked as a foundation to train the new project managers needed to manage subsequent projects. If we are to gain the benefit of two or three thousand years of effective (and ineffective) application of PM principles, we must dig relentlessly through historical records in search of some scattered, accidental reference as to how things were organized to work in each case—since no one bothered to prepare, systematically, in writing, for the next project.

This is why we see the great accomplishments of PM in the past (the past, in this case, probably not starting to change until just 40 years ago) as *inspired acts of genius combined with generational skills*, rather than

Table I.1   Through the years

Attributes	Year 0 through 1970 AD	Post *PMBOK® Guide*
Skill conveyance	On-the-job	Formal training and knowledge transfer
Project duration	Decades to centuries	Months
Recognition of PM	None	Formalized
Talent provided by	Serendipity	Competency development

exemplary testaments to good training and discipline (see Table I.1). Try to imagine the disasters that might have been avoided and the extraordinary projects that might have been undertaken and completed by well-trained but ordinary people if someone had just passed on the quality control, supply chain management, multilingual communication, and cross-cultural resource management insights that these inspired geniuses learned while building the Great Pyramid of Giza or Emperor Qin's mausoleum or the cathedral at Monreale or—well you get the point.

FAST FORWARD TO THIS MILLENNIUM

In a very nice article in the September 1, 2008, issue of APPEL magazine on PM development at NASA, Dr. Edward Hoffman noted that prior to the 1986 Challenger disaster, all PM professional development at NASA was achieved through on-the-job training (OJT)—there was no formal PM training program. The Challenger accident was a stimulus to set up the NASA Program and Project Management Institute that became the Academy of Program/Project and Engineering Leadership (APPEL), which was tasked specifically with providing structured training programs to transfer basic knowledge and competence to the PM and engineering communities at NASA.

NASA was thus one of the canaries in the global coal mine that warned us that the pace and scope of technological growth, along with the fierceness of competition, could no longer be managed through intuition, OJT, and individual, inspirational genius. It was time to put disciplined PM competency development programs in place to prepare the army of talented, well-trained-but-ordinary project managers that could navigate the projects' seas safely in the rapidly evolving, global, high-tech world.

PM ACHIEVES UNANIMOUS CONSENSUS
IN THE U.S. SENATE

As this book was being written, the U.S. Senate unanimously passed S.1550—a bipartisan bill sponsored by Senator Joni Ernst of Iowa and Senator Heidi Heitkamp of North Dakota. A statement from Senator Heitkamp's office said:

> "Making sure federal programs are well managed is key to creating effective and helpful relationships among federal agencies, communities, and businesses, whether it's in energy, agriculture, or any other field. This bipartisan bill aims to give federal agencies a framework for better managing their programs—helping us reduce waste and promote effective management practices."

The Program Management Improvement Accountability Act establishes additional requirements of the Deputy Director for Management of the Office of Management and Budget to:

- Adopt and oversee implementation of government-wide standards, policies, and guidelines for program and project management for executive agencies;
- Chair the Program Management Policy Council (established by this Act);
- Establish standards and policies for executive agencies consistent with widely accepted standards for program and project management planning and delivery;
- Engage with the private sector to identify best practices in program and project management that would improve federal program and project management;
- Conduct portfolio reviews to address programs identified as high risk by the Government Accountability Office;
- Conduct portfolio reviews of agency programs at least annually to assess the quality and effectiveness of program management; and
- Establish a five-year strategic plan for program and project management.

- The Office of Personnel Management must issue regulations that: (1) identify key skills and competencies needed for an agency program and project manager, (2) establish a new job series or update and improve an existing job series for program and project management within an agency, and (3) establish a new career path for program and project managers.

So, it is now law in the U.S. that key PM skills and competencies must be identified, and that this be codified in terms of a *series* of jobs (meaning job descriptions) and an accompanying career path. This helps underline the importance of the opinions, findings, and guidance provided in this book. We can't say that it's illegal not to read this book, but we can say with confidence that there is legal encouragement for you to do so.

NOTES

1. Figure I.1—Terracotta Army
   https://en.wikipedia.org/wiki/Terracotta_Army#/media/
   File:Terracotta_Army,_View_of_Pit_1.jpg
2. Figure I.2—Hagia Sophia
   https://en.wikipedia.org/wiki/Hagia_Sophia#/media/
   File:HagiaSophia_DomeVerticalPano_(pixinn.net).jpg
3. Figure I.3—Monreale, interior
   https://en.wikipedia.org/wiki/Monreale#/media/
   File:MonrealeCathedral-pjt1.jpg

Problem Statement: In Other Words, *The Gap*

Project managers are accountable for the delivery of business objectives. Rapidly evolving technologies, a set of ever-changing customer requirements, and increasing global business interdependencies all demand that project management (PM) competencies are adequately improved to enable delivery of successful project outcomes. At the same time, the PM discipline as well as related tools, credentials, methodologies, and processes is undergoing some substantial transformations.

Let's approach this issue as we would approach a project. The first and most important step in a project is identifying and expressing the need for the project in the form of a project charter. The charter provides a brief business case, which describes the need for investment—the need for change in the first place. It is a source of authority for the project manager and, equally important, it lets all stakeholders know what the project *is all about* and what success looks like, so that the project team will know what it means to be *done*. Remember: a project exists *only because some sort of change is being made*. A project exists only because the status quo is just not good enough. In effect, *every project is about a gap*. More accurately, every project is about *filling* that gap and achieving an important outcome. As to the gap, it could literally be filling a gap, for example, building a bridge over a ravine, or, more likely, it could be more sublime; for example, a new app to match adoptive *pet parents* with pets who need adoption, which is bridging a very different sort of gap, in that case—an

13

emotional one. Here we apply the very same foundational idea of gap-filling to the initiative to improve PM competency and the resulting success of projects. To do so, we need to describe the current situation and the shortfalls we see as longtime proponents of PM excellence and continuous improvement. So, what is this PM competency gap? We express this gap as a problem statement:

> *A project manager's level of competency is often not equal to the new and dynamic challenges encountered in his/her profession.*

As a result, we see ineffective use of tools and technology, and insufficient communication and engagement in project teams, which leads to suboptimal delivery of business objectives.

Considering how fast the landscape of platforms, methodologies, and team dynamics is changing around us, it is not surprising that PM courses attended just a few years ago are now obsolete, and that even the *soft skills* learned during the last training courses are no longer working for us. If we try to maintain our PM competencies by using the traditional approach of courses and tests, we find ourselves and our project managers unable to keep up with this rapidly changing environment. The project managers' ability to deliver business outcomes is thus severely impacted, and that is a major threat to any organization.

The answers we will explore in the next chapters are centered around the concept of *establishing a continuous learning environment*, self-propelled and adaptable, therefore able to evolve with our projects and profession. To leverage an eminent, state-of-the-art approach to this improvement methodology and solid PM best practices, we recommend following these steps:

1. Define the problem: we start with a problem statement and we will continue to explore the compelling reasons behind the need to fill this gap in Chapter 1.

2. Assess your project manager's competency and identify your PM competency gaps: you need to be able to baseline the current status as well as measure progress. We will discuss this phase and the related strategic approaches you can plan in Chapter 2.

3. Study your PM community and its specific traits: whatever competency development bridges you decide to build, they must be based on who will be using them. There is no *one-size-fits-all* approach that will work for any group of project managers. We will discuss this aspect in Chapter 3.

4. Choose and implement the most suitable improvement options for your goals and audience: we will share what we and other respected colleagues have learned that have worked for many years in this field. We will describe possible implementation choices, planning possibilities, and execution alternatives in Chapters 4, 5, and 6.

5. Monitor progress and continue to improve while implementing your plans and assessing progress which has a beginning and an end with specific deliverables and timelines: you need to consider how to continuously find opportunities to move beyond your current competency levels. We will address these last (but not least!) aspects in Chapters 7 and 8.

THE VALUE OF PM AS A DISCIPLINE

A prerequisite to building competence in your PM staff is the recognition that PM is indeed a discipline of its own. As a testament to this concept, observe the growth of PM in the academic world.

According to a database maintained by the Project Management Institute (PMI)® Academic Programs Group, the number of PM-related degrees has grown from two Bachelor's degrees and nine Master's degrees in 1995—which frankly does not seem that long ago—to 206 Bachelor's degrees and 710 Master's degrees in 2015. There are now 100 times more Bachelor's degrees and 80 times more Master's degrees in the past 20 years, as illustrated in Figures 1.1a–d.

Before you go writing off these statistics as being *just an academic exercise*, remember that colleges and universities are also businesses, and they're offering these degrees not because they choose to follow that academic path: they are offering these options because of real demand for PM competency! Just as in the world of academia, the acknowledgment of project management as a distinct discipline in an organization is the

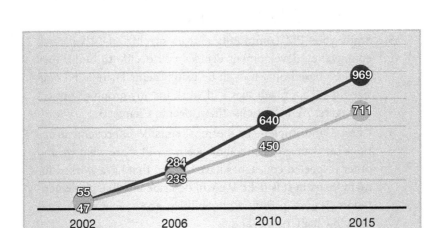

Number of identified project management focused degree programs:

- 2002: 55 degree programs in 47 universities
- 2006: 284 degree programs in 235 universities
- 2010: 640 degree programs in 450 universities
- 2015: 969 degree programs in 711 universities

Adapted from: PMI Academic Programs Group, March 2016

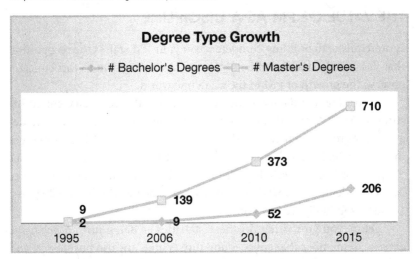

- 1995: 2 Bachelor's degrees; 9 Master's degrees
- 2006: 9 Bachelor's degree programs; 139 Master's degree programs
- 2010: 52 Bachelor's degrees; 373 Master's degrees
- 2015: 206 Bachelor's degrees; 710 Master's degrees

Adapted from: PMI Academic Programs Group, March 2016

Figures 1.1a–d   Project management degree programs

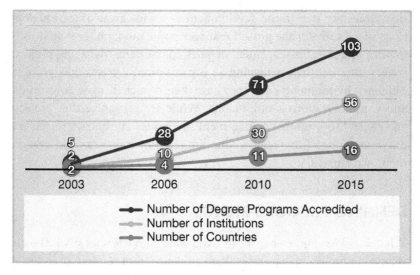

- 2003: 5 Programs in 2 institutions, in 2 countries
- 2006: 28 Programs in 10 institutions, in 4 countries
- 2010: 71 Programs in 30 institutions, in 11 countries
- 2015: 103 Programs in 56 institutions, in 16 countries

Adapted from: PMI Academic Programs Group, March 2016

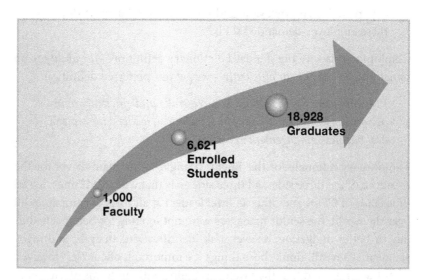

- Over 1000 faculty teaching in PMI's Global Accreditation Center (GAC) programs.
- 6621 graduates of GAC programs in 2015.
- 18,928 enrolled students in GAC programs.

Adapted from: PMI Academic Programs Group, March 2016

first, necessary step in the development of a wide array of learning options specifically for the project manager population, rather than directing PM to general management or sales courseware. Managing projects is very different than managing an organization. Projects take place in different environments since they have their own challenges, constraints, and communications requirements. While we recognize that projects and general (operations) management share *some* attributes, projects are different enough (uniqueness, time-limited, PM framework) to deserve their own curricula.

DEFINING PM COMPETENCY

What does PM competency mean? And what competencies should be developed in project managers? Is there guidance from research or industry associations? With regards to the definition of PM competency, we rely as a starting point on the definition from PMI that relates to the Talent Triangle®, shown in Figure 1.2:

> "The ideal skill set—the PMI Talent Triangle®—is a combination of technical, leadership, and strategic and business management expertise. To stay relevant and competitive, you must develop these employer-demanded skills."

Combining this with the standard dictionary definition—*the ability to do something successfully or efficiently*—we get our preferred definition:

> *PM competency is the ability to successfully and efficiently manage projects with a combination of technical, leadership, strategic, and business management expertise.*

The primary rationale for the Talent Triangle®—the main driver for the existence of the three sides, all three sides—is that when PMI interviewed thousands of CEOs and other C-level leaders at all sorts of companies all over the world, the senior managers were not looking for better scheduling, or better budgeting, or even risk identification, analysis, and management. They still think those things are important, of course. However, what they indicated that they were struggling with, in terms of capability and talent, was the more human side of our discipline—dealing with ambiguity and change, interaction with people, influencing stakeholders, and

PMI Talent Triangle®

Figure 1.2   The PMI Talent Triangle®

negotiating. They were looking for a better balance between the technical PM skills and the increasingly important human interaction, leadership, and strategic skills. Let's look at each of the sides of the Talent Triangle®.

Technical PM

PMI's *Pulse of the Profession*® report (PMI, 2013) showed that for 66% of surveyed organizations, project managers with the appropriate technical skills were very hard to find. (See also: *Pulse of the Profession*® In-Depth Report: The Competitive Advantage of Effective Talent Management, 2013.) The root cause, however, is not a simple lack of project managers, but rather the fact that the project managers in the organization often simply don't possess the necessary technical PM knowledge.

What is this *technical* side? The term *technical PM* can best be understood if you think of the *technician* project manager, that is, one who is an expert in the science of PM—applying methods and tools, such as the

Gantt chart, earned value management, RACI (responsible, accountable, consulted, and informed) matrices, and so forth. This is distinguished from the technical components of the practice area; so, for a construction project manager, the focus of the technical side of the triangle is not on new carbon composite building materials, but rather the technical components of planning for, assessing the risk involved with, and scheduling the assembly of those composite building materials.

Required competencies in the technical side of the triangle include (but are not limited to):

- Techniques for requirements analysis and definition
- Project planning and controlling
- Risk management
- Scope management

PMI advises that the competencies in the technical side of the Talent Triangle® can best be learned via seminars, webinars, online trainings, etc., due to the structured nature of this type of knowledge. In contrast, the elements which must be learned on the *leadership* side are developing and fine-tuning the soft skills of the project manager and likely requires training experiences which have an experiential element.

Leadership

Another *Pulse of the Profession*® survey (Navigating Complexity, 2013) showed that 71% of organizations indicated that they considered leadership skills and talent most important for long-term success, and 75% of survey respondents considered leadership as *very important* for the successful management of complex projects.

Consciously naming and designating *leadership* as its own area of competence emphasizes that the successful management of projects not only requires technical/methodical knowledge, but also leadership skills. As the project level becomes more complex, project leadership skills become—perhaps exponentially—even more important.

Leadership is the sum of soft skills as well as the ability to demonstrate referent power. This side of the triangle is about the *ability to lead and develop a team* and to demonstrate the use of appropriate behavior in dealing with the various stakeholders in wildly differing situations over time.

While a project manager with expertise in the technical PM area can plan and execute the project, his expertise in the field of *leadership* will help in dealing with the handling of the various stakeholders in the project. It involves inspiring, leading, and serving the project team—helping them stay focused on the project's end goal and understanding the benefits that the project will realize for its clients, for the organization, and for the team members themselves.

Leadership talents include (but are not limited to):

- Negotiations
- Conflict management
- Motivation of employees
- Feedback techniques
- Ability to influence stakeholders
- Active listening
- Team development
- Emotional intelligence
- Change intelligence

Strategic and Business Management

PMI's research (PMI, 2013) has revealed that organizations which have their talent aligned with strategy have a 72% success rate in their projects (meeting original business goals) versus 58% when this connection is misaligned. That's a 14% increase in success rates and literally billions of dollars of difference (to say nothing of the morale, brand, and other hard-to-measure attributes). This explains the rationale for PMI to include a side of the triangle dedicated to this focus.

Strategic and business management competency is focused on the connection between the project and the business environment in which it *lives*, including the organization's internal environment (the mission, vision, values, and strategy of the organization) as well as its external environment (customers, suppliers, competitors, and regulatory agencies).

This means specifically that project managers implement and execute their projects according to the strategy of the company, as well as acting with an entrepreneurial spirit and having knowledge of the industry they are working in.

These include (but are not limited to):

- Entrepreneurial activity
- Marketing and law
- PESTEL (political, economical, social, technological, environmental, legal) and SWOT (strengths, weaknesses, opportunities, threats) analysis
- Strategic planning and alignment of multiple projects
- Contract management
- Management of complexity

(*Competitive Advantage of Effective Talent Management*—http://www.pmi.org/-/media/pmi/documents/public/pdf/learning/thought-leadership/pulse/talent-management.pdf)

One of the more interesting findings in our research on the Talent Triangle® was that 90% of companies surveyed stated that the technical and strategic/business skills are teachable (PwC and PMI, November, 2014), but not so for the leadership skills. That is precisely why we put so much stress in this book on alternate ways of assessing and improving leadership skills, rather than relying on traditional classroom training as a way to improve capability on this side of the triangle.

DEVELOPING PM COMPETENCY

Project managers, those who have been in this profession for many years, are a tremendous benefit to any organization. They possess general PM experience, know the organization's methodology very well, and understand the best approach to manage a difficult delivery. But does this experience always benefit the organization? Sometimes, being good at something leads to confidence, and often that same confidence that helps resolve issues also blinds us to shortcomings related to advances in methodology, soft skills, and technology.

Maintaining an open mind and a willingness to learn becomes a critical skill, in and of itself, for the whole community (catching up with the latest version of the *PMBOK® Guide*, learning about Agile, or how to use a new desktop sharing tool, etc.) and can make the difference between a good enough project manager and an outstanding one—one which can serve as a differentiator for an organization.

One of the most important themes of the project manager's day-to-day work is *advancing* data into information, into knowledge, and into wisdom. In the *PMBOK® Guide*, this is presented as transforming *work performance data* into *work performance information* and *work performance reports*, but it is the same principle. Over the years, the authors have seen time and time again that one of the underlying functions of a successful project manager is to clarify, unify, and show the significance of apparently unrelated facts (data) to the more contextual intelligence (information) as the basis for quality decision making (knowledge). Let's look at a model often referenced to understand this process: the *data, information, knowledge,* and *wisdom* (DIKW) model illustrated in Figure 1.3. For more information on this model and its author, see Appendix 1.

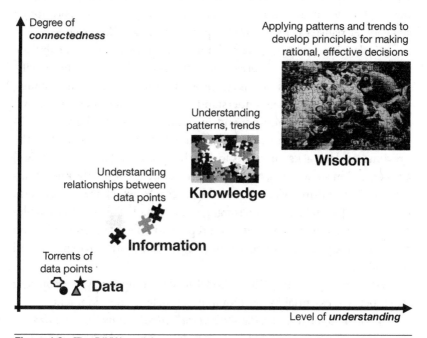

Figure 1.3   The DIKW model

Data is raw. It simply exists and has no significance beyond its existence (in and of itself). It can exist in any form—usable or not. In computer parlance, a spreadsheet generally starts out by holding data. For a project manager, this could be a list of experts, which could be related to the project or not.

Information is data that has been given meaning by way of relational connection. This *meaning* can be useful, but does not have to be. In computer parlance, a relational database correlates information across the data stored within its tables. A project manager uses a stakeholder register for his or her project, and that's information.

Knowledge is the appropriate collection of information, such that its intent is to be useful. Knowledge is a deterministic process. When someone *memorizes* information (as less-aspiring test-bound students often do), then they have amassed knowledge. This knowledge has useful meaning to them, but it does not provide, by itself, an integration which would allow development of further knowledge. In computer parlance, most of the applications we use (modeling, simulation, etc.) exercise some type of stored knowledge. The sustainable capability to combine information such as templates, organizational roles, and prior experience into a stakeholder register is relying on the project manager's knowledge.

Wisdom is an extrapolative and non-deterministic, non-probabilistic process. It calls upon all the previous levels of consciousness, and specifically upon special types of human programming (moral, ethical codes, etc.). It beckons to give us understanding about which there has previously been no understanding, and in doing so, goes far beyond available knowledge. It is the essence of philosophical probing. Unlike the previous levels, it asks questions to which there is no (easily achievable) answer, and in some cases, to which there can be no humanly-known answer, period. Wisdom is, therefore, the process by which we also discern, or judge, between right and wrong, good and bad. This is what enables an experienced project manager to prepare an effective communication plan—an inherent sense of how to best reach stakeholders when standard methods fail.

When we apply the DIKW model to PM competency, we consider two aspects as essential for harmonious competency development.

- *Developing the specific skills of individuals allow the organization to advance data into knowledge.* Projects, due to their very nature of uniqueness and exposure to uncertainty, require problem-solving and decision-making skills. Project managers who develop the ability to work with contextualized information can solve problems more efficiently and effectively, and make better decisions more reliably. This is the individual growth required to deliver projects.

- *The project managers, as a community, collectively develop an environment that supports an adaptable and evolving advancement of data into knowledge and wisdom.* Note: this does not happen automatically—in our experience there needs to be at least one *catalyst*; an advocate for building and energizing this community. As a PM community builds appreciation for this flow of data-to-information-to-knowledge-to-wisdom, the project managers—as a community—become more capable of, and interested in, sharing knowledge, so that findings from Omaha, Nebraska, USA, for example, can be used in Kuala Lumpur, Malaysia for a similar project problem. This is the *collective growth* required to build a continuous learning environment.

PM COMPETENCY AS A MEANS TO BE RESILIENT TO CHANGE

A competent project manager adapts better to organizational changes; and an organization with competent project managers is better able to adapt to business changes.

Organizations in any industry are frequently undergoing changes to adapt to new business models in order to improve efficiency and reduce costs. Project managers who are used to continuously learning new techniques and methodologies are more likely to take organizational changes in stride. In a complementary fashion, an organization's ability to leverage the opportunities triggered by business changes, and to mitigate any negative impacts, is strengthened considerably by a PM community that promotes a continuous learning environment.

Due to the nature of their role, project managers have to be able to move seamlessly through several management layers (to secure resources, gain consensus, etc.), across functional/technical silos (to reach experts, for example), and at the same time overcome geographical and cultural barriers (think of virtual and/or international teams!) as illustrated in Figure 1.4. Working across these different dimensions (management, technical, and cultural) helps project managers develop skills that are useful beyond project delivery: these are the skills needed to adapt to any type of professional change.

One of the reasons many people find PM intriguing as a career is the fact that although it is obviously important to know the *science* of your practice area (financial management, telecom, insurance, and so forth), the *art and science* of PM is almost always transferable across practice areas. In every case, projects are the single connection point between strategy and steady-state operations. In Figure 1.5, note the location of projects, programs, and portfolios as this connection point. This connection point is key. Without it, there is a gap (there it is again) between what the organization believes (mission, vision, values), what they want to do strategically, and their ability to execute day-to-day. The point here is that PM is *portable* as a profession and PM competencies will naturally be similar across industries.

An accomplished telecom engineer with several patents under his belt had transitioned to a career in PM, achieving his Project Management Professional (PMP)® credential after a few years of practice. When massive downsizing led to the company laying him off, it was not too long (actually, it was just a few weeks) before he jumped industries, and became a project manager in a leading pharmaceutical company—and ironically became director of their PM office within just a few more years. He told us that his competencies in PM were what made the difference in that not-so-radical career shift. No organization is greater than the sum of the people whose daily dedication and performance maintain the health and vitality of that organization.

This is the first of many examples that we will use throughout the book to support our statements. These examples are drawn from our experience, and some have been shared by other professionals as we have discussed competency development with them. We will be leveraging such examples to provide you the benefit of our combined experience in this field and that of our colleagues.

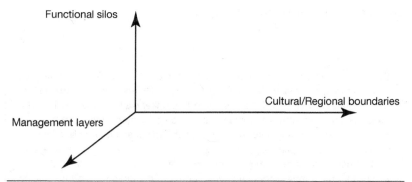

Figure 1.4 Maneuverability space: navigating across multiple dimensions as a project manager

The Strategic Execution Framework (SEF)

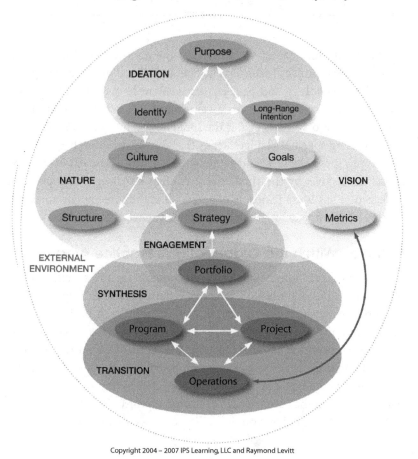

Figure 1.5 A strategic framework developed by IPS Learning and Stanford University's Advanced Project Management Program

One of the authors spent 25 years of his career at a 2,000,000 square-foot manufacturing and research and development (R&D) facility in the northeastern United States. Today, this facility is home to a bakery, a laser-tag arena, and a dance school, among other things. Other than cinnamon bread, not much is manufactured there anymore, even though the manufacturing facility formerly located there, at its peak, employed over 11,000 people—a small city in and of itself. When these sorts of major global shifts take place, it is the PM staff in the manufacturing company that can help it adapt to the change. The outsourcing or insourcing of jobs—well, that's a project. Relocating the R&D teams to another facility in the area—that's a project, too. Building a new business model for supply chain—that's a major transformational project. Establishing a video conferencing service to allow a global company to convene easily—yes, that's another project.

Earlier in this chapter we referred to the rapidly changing environment in which project management operates. None of these changes is a novelty: technology and project management knowledge evolve continuously, and have done so for a very long time. What is different today, compared to 20 years ago, is the *speed* at which these changes occur. An increasing speed of change means that the organization has less time to adapt to these changes, and renders the classical approach of *training classes* ineffective: by the time course content has been developed and packaged, it has become obsolete. Let's look at the three major areas impacting PM competency and generating the *gap* we plan to address.

Evolution Within the Organization's Practice Area

The technical, economic, and social knowledge for the specific industry in which the organization operates requires constant improvement. The project manager does not work in a vacuum: each project delivers in a community and uses technology to produce business outcomes; any changes in these areas has an impact on the success of the project. Experts whose knowledge is no longer accurate provide less accurate estimates and solutions; budget calculations are impacted by the political and financial health of the community in which the project is delivered, and so forth. Your PM staff gives you the ability to be resilient to change.

Evolution of PM Capabilities

PM itself has changed significantly since the pyramids, and even since the first edition of the *PMBOK® Guide* in 1969. In addition to the standards, the tools—especially the online, collaborative tools—that are available to project managers have improved. Enterprise PM software, which provides the project manager with amazing insight—for example, how a supplier being late by a week *ripples through* the entire network diagram, showing the project manager in real time how this affects resource needs, and even how it moves the end date of the project. None of this matters, though, if the project manager does not grow along with the profession to take advantage of such features.

Evolution of a Global Mindset

Our world is constantly getting smaller: we see increasing dependencies on the global economy, and our projects have stronger links to data and deliverables that are available from teams operating abroad. Project managers are not always attuned to the cultural and geographical realities of stakeholders, team members, and contractors located beyond their surroundings.

Traditional learning opportunities for project managers rarely provide recommendations and guidance on how to relate to a global team. More important, project managers might not even be aware of how such diversity can be leveraged for project success, or how they can create deadly pitfalls. Overlapping time zones might be difficult for team meetings, but may work wonders for handing over issues to those who can make progress while folks in our time zone are (generally) asleep.

A MATTER OF SCALE

What we will discuss is organizationally agnostic. Most of the concepts we illustrate are applicable regardless of the size of your company or organization. Our recommendations and suggestions, however, will necessarily have to be based on some assumptions regarding the size and breadth of the PM community we are targeting.

When you see the ladder symbol throughout this book, there will be suggestions on how to scale up or down these recommendations, so they can be applicable to smaller or larger communities.

2

Wanted: Bespoke Strategic Approach

For project management (PM) competency to be considered important, to be supported, and to be bought into by the project managers themselves, what overall strategic approach makes sense? Should this be a top-down effort, led by an overarching, global project management office (PMO), or a top executive leader of the organization? Should it be a grassroots groundswell of momentum and a collection of real, *from-the-trenches* assessments of what is needed for success? Should middle managers—for example, supervisors of project managers—be driving this effort since they have responsibility for the project managers? Should we focus on immediate results (three to six months), or develop a plan for the next three to five years? Should we spend more energy on developing a PM framework in the organization, or in improving the leadership skills of our project managers?

Yes, we say. All of the above. There are as many different answers as there are PM organizations—each situation is different; each organization has a different culture, population, geography, and set of needs, and so each organization requires a tailored strategy to address its specific requirements. Just as you might need to see a satellite map, or a street-level map, or a graphic representation of the terrain around you when trying to find something new; that's why we offer different types of *maps* with answers for you to consider and use based on what resonates with the organization you want to grow and its specific requirements, instead of outlining any *single path* to competency development.

In this chapter, you will find insight into what has worked in terms of the possible approaches based on solid theories on learning and behavior. We have leveraged our own *feet on the street* PM experience and that of other veterans of the practice. Although we respect and refer to theory, we write this book from our perspective of practice in PM competency development.

TOP DOWN, BOTTOM UP, OR MIDDLE OUT?

Since we want the building of competency for our project managers to be a long-term, sustainable, and supported endeavor, there must be top leadership endorsement of the importance of PM. It is important that organizational leaders appreciate the fact that PM connects the vision, mission, culture, and strategy of an organization to its operations. In fact, we particularly like the Strategic Execution Framework view of project (and program, and portfolio) management as the single connection point between all of the creative energy of the company and its day-to-day operations, as referenced in Figure 1.5. Leaders can use a large organizational meeting to convey not only to the project managers but to the entire staff their view of the importance of PM as a key discipline within the organization.

This periodic endorsement of the PM discipline in your organization is the fundamental *heartbeat* of your PM community. In Chapter 5, we will provide a very specific example of such an endorsement that has worked—not just for a year or two, but for a decade—in a highly changeable business. We strongly believe that leadership must publicly recognize the importance of PM and follow up with support for PM competency development.

But this leadership *push* is not enough in and of itself. To *maintain* the push from top management, it is imperative that the project managers *themselves* are aware of their needs and *own* their development. Were you to set up the best possible training programs, they would be effective only when the continuous effort of renewing and improving competencies is inherent to the organizational culture and when the project managers become self-directed learners. We've seen situations in which well-intentioned efforts to develop competency fell flat when the project managers themselves either didn't see a gap, or even worse, saw the gap and lacked the motivation to fill it. Perhaps, even if top management is pushing for it, the message is not getting through; the message is being *diluted* by the ever-present mandate to complete key project deliverables urgently (for an end-of-quarter reconciliation, for example), or lost altogether in the midst of overabundant organizational communications. The project managers need to exercise a continuous *pull* of the competency improvements they require in order for any efforts to set up a learning environment to be successful.

This leads us to the critical role of middle management as an enabler of any competency development initiative. Typically, these are line managers operating between executive directives and overworked project managers, especially in the case of a middle manager who oversees additional functions, so that PM as a discipline gets only part of the middle managers' attention and appreciation. To make competence building an ongoing, active contributor to project success, it takes a very strong middle-out effort. That is, middle managers and regional or divisional PMOs must grab on to the (hopefully) strong support of top leadership and convey that to their PM staff, while simultaneously listening carefully to and observing the behavior of their PM staff to look for specific areas for improvement in PM competence.

LONG TERM OR SHORT TERM?

Another dilemma surrounds expectations on the outcomes of competency development initiatives. While we all want to look at the long-term benefits of any effort to build a solid competency development framework, we must also consider that both our sponsors (senior management) and our intended audience (project managers) need to realize short-term gains. Without quantifiable results, sponsors will start channeling some of their resources and budget to more pressing issues. Without success stories and tangible artifacts, the PM community will not respond to training course offerings and other initiatives. After all, project managers are results-oriented people!

That's why our response to the long- or short-term question is another *yes*! As we will discuss in more detail in Chapter 5, we propose a framework in which multiple initiatives (our competency bridges), each with its own short-term goals and measurable results, be combined to deliver a comprehensive, long-term competency development program to establish a continuous learning environment.

ASSESSING COMPETENCY: THE PEAKS MODEL

We like to look at PM competency assessment using a model called the PEAKS model from Project Management Institute (PMI) Fellow Dr. David Hillson and respected colleague Ruth Murray Webster. Summarized in Table 2.1, this model defines competency as the combination of five core elements: personal characteristics, experience, attitudes, knowledge, and skills—creating the handy acronym PEAKS. The PEAKS model is based on these principles:

- Competence must be demonstrated and observable (in a specific context)
- Competence is demonstrated through behavior(s)
- Behavior (which is all we can observe) is influenced by the PEAKS elements

As you know, you cannot improve what you cannot measure. So we need some way to assess the observable behaviors in order to assess PM competence. Table 2.2 illustrates the PEAKS elements along with ways of assessing them and provides improvements and development suggestions based on that assessment. There is significant value in this model and this table shows how you can put this theory to work in looking at individual PM competencies.

One way to do this is to assure that any PM assessment program measures the candidates not only on the qualitative judgment by their supervisor, and not only by the score on an exam, but rather by a combination of assessments—for instance, how the project manager behaved on prior assignments, feedback from customers and team members, and quantitative results of knowledge accrual such as a quiz or exam.

In terms of development, an assessment using the PEAKS elements can go beyond measurement—it can help diagnose and recommend more effective training or capability enhancement. For example, let's say an individual has been assessed using PEAKS elements and has great results

Table 2.1   The PEAKS model

PEAKS Element	Question at Hand	Summary Description
Personal characteristics	"Who am I?"	Natural preferences and traits; e.g., self-confidence, pragmatism, or a need to be well-organized.
Experience	"What have I achieved?"	Acquired as an outcome of practicing PM in the context of an organization and measured by relevant achievements.
Attitudes	"How do I act and respond?"	These are the individual's chosen responses to PM situations. Some are deeply rooted in their value system, others are more changeable. An example: strong concern and care for stakeholder needs.
Knowledge	"What do I know?"	Gained on the job or via training, these are codified (for example) by PMI into Knowledge Areas such as Time, Scope, Cost, Stakeholder, HR, Risk, and Communications Management.
Skills	"How ably do I apply knowledge?"	This is application of knowledge, which must be learned experientially. Skills will bring the P, E, A, and K above into play, by (for example) combining a characteristic to need to be organized with the experience of doing project planning, the attitude that planning is important, the knowledge of planning methods, and the skill of using a particular planning software package.

in terms of all but the *knowledge* (K) element. This could be an outcome related to poor test-taking ability.

From our experience in Project Management Professional (PMP)® exam preparatory training, we've observed people who are top-performing, very capable project managers have extreme difficulty with the exam. This can be remediated with training in test-taking skills and can be overcome. Or, if *experience* (E) is the only element missing, clearly this can be resolved with on-the-job training or mentoring.

So, What's the Best Approach to Use?

We suggest applying the PEAKS model when preparing your strategic approach to the design of competency assessments. Once you determine what needs to be improved for the project managers in your

Table 2.2 Assess and improve PEAKS elements

PEAKS Element	How to Assess	How to Improve and Develop
Personal characteristics	• Personality or preferences tests (i.e., 4-D, MBTI, DISC) • Emotional quotient, change quotient profiling tools • Self-reflection • 360-degree feedback session	Not always developable because some traits are inherent and innate. If the characteristic is developable, coaching and mentorship is ideal, but this also requires self-discovery on the part of the individual project manager.
Experience	• Interviews • Comparing CV/resume against organizational needs • Simulations • Project reviews and audits • Quarterly and/or yearly reviews • Demonstration of relevant achievements	• Relevant project contribution, day-to-day • Job rotation to give wider experience and empathy • Structured PM career path with support from the organization
Attitudes	• Observation • Feedback from peers and customers • Self-reflection • How issues are escalated	• Coaching and mentoring • Strong, supportive leadership from line management, based on quarterly and yearly reviews
Knowledge	• Examination/testing • Internal certification • Completion-of-course knowledge checks • External certification (e.g., PMP® and PRINCE2)	• Self-directed learning (depends on attitude) • Training courses (virtual, instructor-led, in-class) • Active participation in PM online community • On-the-job learning • Professional seminars/webinars • Participation in professional organizational meetings and governance (e.g., PMI local chapters)
Skills	• Role play • Job simulation • Mentorship/observation • Project reviews and audits	• Mentor/mentee programs • Courses that include experiential learning • PM coaching

organization—in other words, once you have a clearly defined *gap*—you need to think about how you will measure your progress in filling this gap before implementing any improvement initiative. A baseline of the current competency levels, followed by periodic assessments of your progress, must be part of any strategic approach you choose to take.

Thinking about how to track progress later on in this process, for example, when you have already started to implement training programs, is not effective. Unless you have decided ahead of time how to assess progress, you will not have a reference—a *before* status—as a comparison between where you were and where you are. Once again—and it is worth repeating—you cannot improve what you cannot measure! Basic training in the PEAKS model is an important addition to the competency development for project management mentors and direct supervisors who do real-time, one-on-one coaching of project managers because it helps provide a clearer picture of what makes up competency, and thus provides a better opportunity for improving it.

WHERE TO START: USING THE FACE OF KNOWLEDGE

In order to look systematically at the areas to consider when planning your strategic approach to PM competency development, we propose a model we call *The Face*. We also apply framework, application, community, and expertise (FACE) as our method for the identification of competency gaps. The idea is that, in general—just as in a human body—there is knowledge stored up near the top of the system (the head—and the brain in particular), but it is ineffective unless it can be put into words and actions, and improved by observation and listening (see Figure 2.1).

In general, and in very simple language, the model starts at the top with *knowing stuff*, and advances to *getting things done* when several drivers, such as expertise, attitude, and a supportive PM community are present to enable and activate the knowledge. In this model, basic *PM framework* knowledge is shown in the left eye, and the *general methods (practices) and tools* (using a Gantt chart, for example) are shown in the right eye.

The nose takes what the project manager *knows* and brings it closer to reality: this is the effect of *expertise and attitude*.

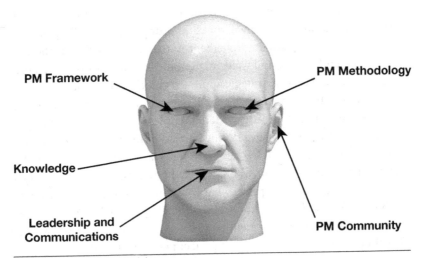

Figure 2.1 The Face model

Thinking of the expression, *keep your ears to the ground,* or *vox populi,* the ears represent access to the amassed knowledge and wisdom of other project managers in your organization—the *PM community.* The project managers have a lot to say and anyone working to improve PM competency should be listening and leveraging this cumulative experience.

A project manager does not work in a vacuum. He or she *must get work done through others.* So on top of the knowledge, the tools and practices, the drivers of expertise and attitude (the eyes and the nose), and attention paid to colleagues in the community (the ears), the project manager must bring heart and soul (leadership) to the project team and its full set of stakeholders.

At this point, it's no longer about what the project manager knows, but rather about the *application* of the knowledge and framework and the basic methods to real projects—the day-to-day leadership of projects that result in benefits being realized, which after all, is the real contribution of project managers to their organization. The mouth of this model represents the importance of *leadership and communications* in the project manager's job. We like this definition of leadership from former U.S. President Dwight D. Eisenhower:

"Leadership is the art of getting someone else to do something you want done because he wants to do it."

Leadership and the effectiveness of communication are rooted in hard-earned and successful experience, in communication skills, and in a solid support network. A project manager who has these traits, and who can communicate clearly and crisply, will get others to do things, not because the project manager said so but because they'll be motivated to do so. In other words, this gives the project manager the single most important capability they need: the ability to influence without authority. Once you look at the PM competency in terms of these areas of focus, you can identify what needs to be improved, and what approach can be effective.

How can we use this model? Let's say that the project managers in your organization have solid PM framework knowledge, but are not effective in the use of PM tools for scheduling, risk management, etc. In our FACE model, this means there is a *weak left eye*. So, we need to determine what type of intervention would be more effective to improve the situation: do we need to *fix* vision (eye surgery) or *support* it (use of a corrective prescription) or both? Let's examine both approaches.

Fix: we improve tool competency of project managers so they can become efficient tool users. This works well if there is a small PM community and/or the project managers deal with relatively simple projects, so that, for example, using spreadsheets or entry-level PM platforms might be good enough to effectively track all project aspects. Learning how to leverage built-in functionality in standard office applications, such as pivot tables and data lookup, would be an appropriate strategy in this case. If you want to develop knowledge of more complex, enterprise-level tools, then you would need to plan different learning paths, and also look further than PM competency development to include improvements in your office information technology (IT) infrastructure (e.g., accessibility of these applications via servers or cloud agreements, licenses, etc.).

Support: we plan to develop a group of specialized back-office personnel who will provide the project managers with expert support in PM schedule control. This group is highly trained in the advanced capabilities of software tools and can implement (working in conjunction with the project manager) complex updates to the project schedule in the tools, for example. Based on the size of the organization and its projects, this could be a very small group or a very large one. The advantage of such a group is that it will enable the project managers to focus on the effective use of their expertise in critical areas such as communication and leadership, rather than the intricacies of enterprise-level platforms and tools. This approach will require establishing a career path, if not yet in place, for the back-office personnel (aka, the PMO, whether distributed or as an actual entity), as well as the IT infrastructure mentioned earlier.

Once we decide the strategic approach that would work best in the organization, then we can plan the best way to do so: prescription glasses or contact lenses? These are the tactical options we will examine in Chapter 4. Do you see the difference? In the *fix* remedy, we are trying to bridge the gap by adding new *tissue*—or new capability to the project managers. In the *support* remedy, we are easing the use of the tool by providing expert schedulers or tool specialists who will support the project managers in the day-to-day activities requiring the tools. Of course, you may need to combine these approaches, and likely will need to, in the case of a major deployment of an enterprise project management (EPM) software system.

We will now look at each element—the *features*—of the FACE model and at the ways in which you can design a tailored, *bespoke* strategic approach to bridging your PM competency gaps.

PM FRAMEWORK: THE LEFT EYE

None of the PM competencies make any sense or have any use if they are not in tune with a general framework of PM knowledge. *A Guide to the Project Management Body of Knowledge (PMBOK® Guide)* provides this framework. Note that its very name indicates that it is (literally, and thus stated on its cover) a guide to a body of knowledge—not a methodology. In PMI's *PMBOK® Guide*, for example, you find a common vocabulary and a common structure of 10 knowledge areas (such as project scope, time, and cost management), and 47 processes tucked neatly into five process groups (not phases, but groups of somewhat overlapping processes—initiating, planning, executing, monitoring and controlling, and closing). This framework provides a basis for the conveyance and use of the knowledge.

Other frameworks, and in some cases methodologies such as PRINCE2, IPMA, and others, contribute to this basis. There is even a Sustainability Wheel™ (see *Driving Project, Program, and Portfolio Success: The Sustainability Wheel* by Richard Maltzman for more details) framework to help project managers understand how to embed long-term thinking and benefits realization in their project planning.

As described in Chapter 1 in the discussion of the data, information, knowledge, and wisdom (DIKW) model, these frameworks allow the project manager to advance (or *promote*) the plethora of their project *data* into PM *wisdom*. Importantly, the PM framework allows project managers, across the organization and even outward to suppliers and customers, to use a common vocabulary and *way of thinking* about their projects. The use of the word *framework* is not coincidental here. We have seen from experience that without this framework, any building of PM competency will quickly collapse under its own weight.

Your bridge, if the PM framework represents a gap you need to address, could be built on establishing a core competency based on industry credentials and adopting internal methodologies based on this framework so that you institutionalize the use of terminology and best practices in the PM community and its key interfaces. This means working out a way to support your project managers in obtaining and maintaining the credentials, but also, for example, working with your human resource (HR) partners to ensure there are recognition programs in place.

METHODS AND TOOLS: THE RIGHT EYE

We know that the PMP credential is not about methods and tools. It's based on being able to prove three to five or more years of experience leading projects, combined with the passing of a very picky 200-question multiple-choice exam that is based in great part on the *PMBOK*® *Guide*. Over the years, both of us have heard, dozens of times, a sentiment expressed that goes something like this: "Sure, she has her PMP, but she couldn't project manage her way out of a paper bag." Indeed, there are project managers who are able to understand the framework and pass the exam, yet still cannot really manage projects. One reason for this may be the reality of managing a project in the context of an organization that has *its own project management methods and tools*—and these people, who have all the correct foundational knowledge, cannot apply it to managing projects delivered in/by that organization. So yes, the element of methodology is key. This is why many organizations have *internal certifications* (more about this in Chapter 7) that qualify the framework knowledge with further evidence that a project manager can take a project through to completion using the methodology of that particular organization.

Done correctly, this is a valuable certification—not only for the organization, but for its customers. Why would an internal certification be important to an external customer? In our experience, and as a matter of pragmatism, it shows that the project manager will be able to work across the full breadth and depth of the providing organization on the customer's behalf. For example, a project manager who is well versed in how the organization's purchasing and delivery tools work will be able to provide status to the customer and to escalate delivery delays of their particular product or service.

As per the discussion of the FACE model, the methods and tools are better deployed if they have been customized and propagated through the organization for the specific use in that practice area. For example, knowing how to use a Gantt chart is basic knowledge of a method. However, an organization with a more mature approach to PM will have an enterprise-level scheduling tool that links the inputs to the Gantt chart tasks to information coming from suppliers, customers, and contributing team members. This will ensure that a delay in installation of a product will automatically cascade through the scheduling system and alert the project manager to the new critical paths and a revised end-date. Using a system like this takes discipline and training, but yields much better and more consistent results because of the level of integration and the advancement of data into knowledge and wisdom for better decision making. It's about what we like to call *holistic intelligence*—a systemic view of the project in its broader environment. This capability also allows the project manager to serve more as a leader and communicator and to spend less time in the guts of a large Excel worksheet or a freestanding Gantt chart working out the details.

KNOWLEDGE: THE NOSE KNOWS

Knowledge: Business Competencies

Is the project manager a business manager? Well, ask yourself: is a project a business? Not technically, because a project has a definitive ending and (hopefully) that is not true for a business. However, a project manager is indeed very much like a CEO of a time-limited business. In fact, one could argue that a project manager has a more difficult job than a real CEO because they are running this business without the full-fledged title of CEO and must influence without authority. In fact, because running a project is a little like running a mini-business, it's hard to define strong borders around business skills.

Knowledge: Writing and Understanding a Business Case

Projects need to be launched with a project charter and at the core of the charter is the *business case*. The project manager may or may not be the one creating the business case, but either way he or she must be able to espouse that business case to stakeholders. Also, keep in mind that along the way there will be decisions to be made (for example, hiring an outside firm to take on a specialty task), and each of these decisions will need to have a proponent. Once again, the business case will become important—even if not created as formally for these decisions—and the skill of writing and understanding a business case will be needed.

Knowledge: Budgeting and Cost Control

The financial aspect of a project—the level of ownership that the project managers have for their project budget and the direct control of this aspect by the project manager—varies significantly depending on the organization and its culture, the practice area, and perhaps the project manager themselves. Totally disconnecting the financial aspect of the project from the project manager seems wrong, yet we're familiar with many cases in which a project manager had a project land on him or her after it had been *thrown over the wall* without any chance for the project manager to assess the overall or time-phased budget—and was then told to execute with someone else (in this case a product manager) worrying about the budget.

In this case, the project manager was overseeing the schedule and scope, but was not even given visibility to the finances of the project. Aside from not being very high up on the PM maturity scales, this type of organizational reality changes the competencies needed around net present value, internal rate of return, and sensitivity analysis. That approach, as we have seen, leads to a gap in not only financial competency but to a propensity to focus only on scope and time while leaving out the financial aspect. This can happen in a technical environment where the project managers tend to have an engineering or science background—and in that culture, money seems to always take a back seat to features, functionality, speed, and the general *coolness* of a project's outcome.

Knowledge: Contract Management

In some organizations, the project manager never gets involved with, never sees, or in fact, is not even aware of the contract. This is a dangerous situation. Since managing scope is fundamental to PM, and since the contract is where one finds the legal definition of scope, the project manager who has no knowledge of the contract is managing scope based on their own (or perhaps someone else's) perception of what needs to be provided to the customer.

> A systems controls provider allowed one of their project managers to write, on behalf of their company, an addendum to a contract which stated that they would provide the customer (a utility operating company) "all cables, test equipment, connectors, etcetera, as needed."

Etcetera! We know that project managers rarely create the contracts, but they can, and if possible *should*, be involved in the early stages where statements like this can be questioned, and if caught early enough, corrected. Project managers should have basic contract knowledge: they should have a working knowledge of contract types; they should know the meaningfulness of various types of clauses; they should at least be familiar with contract resolution techniques; and they should know the difference between mediation, arbitration, and litigation.

Knowledge: Business Analysis

According to the International Institute for Business Analysis (IIBA), business analysis is the practice of enabling change in an organizational context by defining needs and recommending solutions that deliver value to stakeholders. The set of tasks and techniques that are used to perform business analysis are defined in *A Guide to the Business Analysis Body of Knowledge (BABOK® Guide)*.

The relationship between the project manager and the business analyst (BA) is complementary—or at least it should be. Knowing more about the BA role facilitates this complementary relationship. Whereas the project manager leads the solution, the BA ensures that the project itself is indeed aligned with business objectives. The BA assures that the project is justified and establishes the business requirements. In short, the BA is making sure that the *front end* of the project is connected to the organization's strategy. If this role exists in the organization, it's imperative that the project manager works well with the BA. If the role is absent, the project manager often takes on this role—which means that they need to understand it. Either way, you can see the need for business analysis as an important competency for project managers.

Lacking capabilities in the areas of business analysis leads to poor judgment when identifying stakeholders, establishing/approving timelines for requirements definition, misunderstanding stakeholders, and most important, a gap in connecting the project to the strategy of the organization.

What's the Approach to Consider?

Let's consider the possible ways in which we can enhance the business competencies in our PM community. As seen in other sections, we can *fix* and/or *support*.

Fix: we can mend the gap in business knowledge by providing opportunities to grow that knowledge, which may also require an increased drive to gain that knowledge and to describe why it's important for the PM population. The *fix* may require senior executive *support*.

How do you develop this business sense in those who are money-agnostic? Aside from basic financial courses, challenge the engineers and scientists who have become project managers with the science of *moving money around in time* (which is what, for example, net present value really is). Sometimes simply rephrasing what appears to the technical mind to be *accounting* and *arithmetic* into a term like *engineering economics* can make a difference. We have seen technical people become much more interested in finance when it takes on this angle.

An additional and powerful instrument to fix the gap is an internal certification program. When paired with appropriate career steps and recognition (of completion of the certification), it helps establish a knowledge base around best practices in business and contract management. For example, a senior certification in PM within your organization might require that the candidates demonstrate, after appropriate training, that they can:

- Prepare, gain approval on, and deliver the project business case;
- Derive contractual obligation to the customer (internal or external) and map them to the project work breakdown structure (WBS); and
- Work collaboratively with the business analysts in the organization

Developing internal PM certifications might provide a way to ensure that at least a portion of your PM community develops these essential skills, and as a necessary step for the next advancement, are able to share them in the community with other project managers as mentors or internal consultants.

Support: an option to consider is to provide a *surrogate*, a support infrastructure of business expertise in the organization that project managers can leverage on when needed. If your PM methodology includes gates at critical points in the life cycle of your projects, a business or contract review with appropriate experts could be a mandatory step. Once the project managers understand what the issues and elements are that they need to pay attention to, these reviews could be quite fast and only serve as a final check before moving on to the next phase in the project.

Another form of a support-based strategy would be to promote certification in business analysis. Both PMI and the IIBA offer credentials in this field. Increasing the number of *co-certified* project managers not only increases the level of competency in this area, it also sends a message to the rest of the PM population that these business competencies are valued, and it tells customers that you are serious about understanding requirements.

A blend of fixing and supporting project managers would be to allow for *cross-pollination* in business awareness and contract management.

Consider the strategy of including a contract management specialization for experienced project managers, or a tactic as simple as a series of workshops or webcasts in which contract managers give real examples of contract faux pas from their experience, and how they think the project manager could have avoided these situations had they known the possible consequences in advance.

Knowledge: Technical Skills (and the Debate . . .)

There has been a debate about this as old as the pyramids (which some say was the first true application of PM). On one side of the debate are those who say that a project manager must have practice area knowledge firmly implanted in their head and must know the full *science* behind whatever industry they're in. We know from consulting with the pharma industry that some firms require a Ph.D. in a hard science for any project manager involved with a drug introduction. On the other side of the debate are those who wave the flag of PM so wildly that they believe that almost no knowledge of the practice area science is required at all—and that solid PM skills, knowledge, and attitude solves all problems. Of course, the truth is somewhere in between.

> A woman joined a PM organization that dealt with deploying large networks made from sophisticated fiber optic cross-connect and multiplex equipment— leading edge stuff. However, her background was in English literature and history, and her career path had taken her from administrative assistant to a position of project manager. She had her PMP credential and had been active in her local PMI chapter. The flag-waving PM person in the debate says that she can jump right in. Those on the other side of the argument would say that she doesn't have a chance. We can speak from real experience when we say that with a little bit of training in the purpose of the equipment, the key acronyms and functionality of the systems, and the network it provided for customers—in short, providing this project manager with a basic conversancy in the field—she was one of the most effective project managers we ever saw in deploying these networks. As often is the case, it is about balance—not taking sides.

What's the Approach to Consider?

Once again, we look at a *fix* and *support* thread.

Fix: your strategy should include creating a curricula specific for the PM population with *just enough* technology from your practice area so that project managers develop the proper conversancy in the technology. They do not need to be experts, and yet they must be able to talk intelligently about the products and services they are enabling. We also recommend that you establish a mechanism for cross-pollination with technical learning, such as job rotations through sales engineering or product management positions.

Support: one strategy we suggest for supporting project managers in the area of technical knowledge is to assign a technical deputy to the project manager to advise the project manager on technical matters. It is, of course, important that this technical deputy, in turn, is familiar with basic PM concepts. Some organizations create a *technical project manager* position—and this is a good strategy when the technology is multifaceted and particularly complex.

LEADERSHIP AND COMMUNICATION: THE MOUTH

Leadership and communication—the *mouth* of our FACE model—is where the project managers demonstrate their capability to transform project objectives into action and delivery. Let's take a look at these closely related areas together.

These competencies are far and away the most important since a vast majority of what project managers do is to convey information in a timely fashion, with the right media, to the right stakeholders, and to influence others to achieve project objectives. Some (we assert, a small part) of what makes project managers excel in leadership and communications capability is, of course, *talent* or inherent ability, but much of it can be learned, and vast improvements can be made with the use of an appropriate development strategy.

We combined research in these areas with our own experience from leading projects and managing PMOs, and from this combination of research and experience, we have derived what we see as the key PM leadership qualities: four simple, two-word statements which we hope are self-explanatory (but we'll discuss them a bit anyway).

We have provided practical references that assist in the development of leadership and communications skills in Appendix 1.

1. *Holistic thinker*—The ability to look at the long term and broad-reaching effects of what appear to be great project decisions at the time. For example, a holistic thinker would speak up if a project subteam was choosing to bypass a regulatory agency's requirements to get a project's product through an approval stage. A holistic thinker would realize that this may expedite the project at the moment, but may have far-reaching, negative consequences later (for an example, consider Volkswagen's engineers who, for a while, fooled the U.S. Environmental Protection Agency's carbon monoxide testing then ended up costing the company tens of billions of dollars). This type of thinking requires cross-disciplinary cognition, thinking like an accountant, an engineer, an architect, a designer, and a craftsperson—all at the same time. Holistic thinkers will keep their eyes on the prize. The quality of leadership here is one of laser focus on what the project charter says the project is all about, keeping the team on point while the project manager casts a wide net to get the resources the project needs and identifies the full set of stakeholders, the full set of risks, and the full array of issues that face the project. It's important that communications to the team always reinforce what the project is all about; that the individual pieces of work do, in fact, all yield the final deliverable and that everyone knows how these pieces interlock.

2. *Team enabler*—Not enough can be said about this quality. The key to this is the very learnable communication skill of active listening (which means not talking for long periods of time!) and knowing the audience and the best channel for conveying the multiplicity of project messages that have to be sent—and properly received—in any project. Think of this as being the conductor in a technical symphony. Although the project manager is not playing any instrument, you know the capabilities, volumes, pacing, and talents of each member of the orchestra and you get the most out of each for a better result. One of the most fundamental requirements for this quality is the letting go of any former technical role. This is easy to say, but very hard to do, especially for engineers and scientists. Both authors have direct experience with technical

people who just could not stop *playing the violin* enough to conduct the orchestra. One trick that we have found here is to ask them to imagine reversing the roles with the technical person whose work the project manager is taking. "Think back to when you were an engineer," we implore, "how would *you have felt* if your work was being done by some . . . some . . . *project manager?*" As in the above example, the project managers must know that they have given up the cello, the piano, the French horn. They are the conductor—they let the project team members do their work and do not hover.

3. *Pragmatic optimist*—The project manager must be able to keep a positive attitude. They are realistic and know when *the ship is sinking*, but they are not constantly bailing out a puddle. They already know that boats sometimes take on water. These project managers are fully aware that attitude is contagious, and for this reason, they set project-positive ground rules and live by them, exemplifying them. Part of this quality is simple diligence—remembering to set expectations at the start of a project. The other part is being fully conscious of their own behaviors and the fact that their team is watching. Pragmatic optimists are caring, knowing, engaging, and helpful leaders that demand respect and deserve the authority needed to get project work done. You can learn more about the capability to develop this quality by referring to the *cultivator* personality type mentioned in Chapter 3.

4. *Panic-averse*—All project managers get bad news in projects. Since projects are, by definition, unique and you cannot possibly have captured every possible threat during risk identification, some of these threats *will* negatively affect project objectives, even threatening the final deliverable itself, the date it's delivered, and/or the amount of money it takes to deliver it. When an identified or unidentified threat turns into an issue, the project manager's job is to keep a level head and bring the project team together to solve the problem. Consider the excellent scene in the film *Apollo 13* in which the project team had to deal with a workaround involving the air ducting to keep the astronauts alive. Key skills to develop here are thorough risk

identification, and in particular, use of issue management and stakeholder engagement tools and skills.

So, What's the Best Approach to Use?

Leadership: it's not an easy thing to teach, and it's even more difficult when the learner is a project manager who likely already considers himself a leader and perhaps already a *fully capable* leader. On the other hand, there is (hopefully) the chance that project managers will recognize how important these skills are to successful projects—and perhaps to an accelerated career path. The strategies (in this case, a blend of *fix* and *support*) that we suggest are the following:

- *Embed leadership in the career path.* Have stringent descriptors of projects in terms of size, complexity, scope of geography, technology, uniqueness, and strategic importance. Then, use these descriptors to delineate which job profile a project manager can take on projects in the categories defined by the descriptors. Doing this allows a progression of increasingly expanded accountability, and thus, further exercising of the project manager's leadership abilities. At the top of this career path, we recommend establishing a program director or portfolio leader—a position limited to just a small percentage of the project manager population and meant for project managers who are acting more like a portfolio manager and a role model project leader. Project managers with promising behaviors and a trail of successful projects, and who have already started to demonstrate leadership skills, can be targeted and perhaps groomed for this position in the future. It is beneficial to state in the job profile that it will include *giving back* or, in other words, coaching *rising star* project managers via specialized PM mentoring programs.
- *Include job rotation through the PMO as part of leadership development.* Project managers who have been planning and executing projects in the field can get good exposure to managing project managers and their development by taking a stint in a PMO or Center of Excellence (COE).
- *Develop a mentorship program focused on PM development.* Both mentor and mentee will gain tremendously from this relationship, and although general PM skills will be improved,

leadership skills get the biggest boost. As previously mentioned, higher level job profiles can be asked to take on this role as an expectation of the position.

- *Promote participation in local and global leadership of PM professional organizations.* Local chapters of professional organizations, such as PMI and the International Project Management Association (IPMA), are excellent opportunities to develop PM leadership skills. This is a way to have your organization give back to the profession and it benefits the project managers who serve. We can speak from direct experience here. One of the authors served as a volunteer VP of professional development for a local PMI chapter. It was an invaluable opportunity, and in particular, honed leadership skills. Keep in mind that while working in a role like this the project manager gets exposed not only to leading other project managers, but will be working with project managers from all sorts of different disciplines—and that yields opportunities for new ideas that may not be accessible within your organization. Aside from leadership positions, simply participating in PM conferences and symposia will be valuable. Keep in mind that PMI, for example, runs a specific session for its officers called the Leadership Institute Meeting (LIM), concurrent with its PMI Global Congresses. The LIMs are highly valuable learning opportunities where PMI volunteers interact with over 1,100 other leaders (that quantity is drawn from the 2016 North America Congress in San Diego). This can be taken to another level with PMI's Leadership Institute *Master Class,* which is a year-long program that helps participants hone the leadership skills they already possess and provides the knowledge needed to become a more effective leader. Again, we have direct experience with this session and can recommend it as a great opportunity to develop leadership skills.

Global/Cultural Awareness

The following list of bulleted items was taken from a July 2016 job posting for a PM position for a multinational pharmaceutical company:

- PM qualifications such as PMP/PRINCE2 preferred
- Five-year cross-functional, *cross-disciplinary PM* and business analysis experience, preferably within healthcare insurance or financial services
- Knowledge of key components of PM (e.g., scope, time, costs, quality, human resources, communication, risk, integration) and associated tools and methodologies
- Experience of managing projects *across multiple locations*
- Strong stakeholder identification and management
- Experience working within a PMO governance framework
- Strong communication skills and *the ability to tailor communications to specific audiences*
- Proven experience working on *multiple business* and IT projects with an understanding of the software delivery life cycle, as well as operational adoption of new processes
- *Cultural competency*
- Team working—*internal/external*
- Customer focus—internal/external
- Good business/product knowledge
- Organizational skills
- Good time management
- Negotiation skills
- Decision-making skills
- Advanced Microsoft applications—Word, Outlook, Excel, Project, Visio

Note the phrases we have placed in *bold italics*, all of which speak to global and cultural aspects of project management. We assert that *culture* is not necessarily ethnic or geographic in nature. An accounting department has a different culture than an engineering department—and this is true in Boston or Lagos. That is not to speak lightly of ethnic and geographical cultural differences, which certainly also affect projects and thus demand competency in the project manager.

One of the leading experts in this area, Geert Hofstede, has an excellent website on which a user can compare the cultural dimensions he's identified between any countries. The site https://geert-hofstede.com/ can provide an output such as Figure 2.2, which compares Australia, the Czech Republic, and Angola. Note the differences, for example, between Australia and Angola in *individualism*. Or, you could ponder the distinction between both Australia and Angola and the Czech Republic in terms of long-term orientation.

If you have a geographically diverse project team, wouldn't it be good to understand the propensities of the project team members and other stakeholders? A perspective on global PM is provided by Will O'Brien, Associate Professor of Practice, Clark University, Graduate School of Management. Professor O'Brien says:

"In a recent article in the Boston Business Journal (August 25, 2016) entitled "Cultural Agility Critical to Business Understanding," the author describes cultural agility as the knowledge, skills, and savvy to operate effectively in different countries with people from different cultures. Given the common and growing practice of corporations engaging in projects which involve teams with

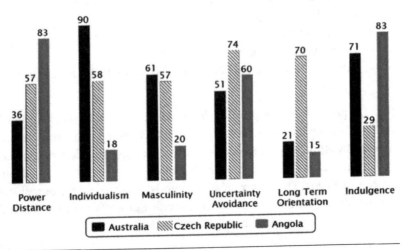

Figure 2.2 Comparison of cultural dimensions

members of different cultures, it is essential that project managers develop competence in cultural agility as well as global project management."

Professor O'Brien also notes this from Cleland Award-winning author Jean Binder:

"Ongoing research shows that whilst 90 percent of large companies are conducting global projects to take advantage of distributed skills, around-the-clock operations and virtual team environments, less than one third of them have effective, established practices to help project managers and team members working over a distance. Consequently, most organizations struggle to reach the required levels of quality and effectiveness from these projects because their methods and practices are not adapted to a global multi-cultural environment, where most communication is in writing and asynchronous."

As we illustrated with the *Maneuverability Cube* in Chapter 1, the project manager must navigate among and between management layers, national cultures (as discussed previously), and organizational culture as well.

Hofstede's site also has resources in this area. It defines organizational culture as the way in which members of an organization relate to each other, to their work, and to the outside world in comparison to other organizations. The Hofstede Multi-Focus Model on Organizational Culture is a strategic tool aimed at helping the organization become more effective.

The dimensions of organizational culture are:

- Means-oriented versus goal-oriented
- Internally driven versus externally driven
- Easygoing work discipline versus strict work discipline
- Local versus professional
- Open system versus closed system
- Employee-oriented versus work-oriented
- Degree of acceptance of leadership style
- Degree of identification with your organization

Think about your own organization. Where does it fit along the scales of each of these dimensions? You can actually go to this site and determine where you fit: https://geert-hofstede.com/culture-and-strategy.html

Let's connect the organizational dimensions to our world of PM by looking at a spectrum in which the extremes are indicated on the left (project dominant) and right (organizational dominant). We've mapped a selection of six organizational dimensions to project and organizational dominant extremes to illustrate this point (see Table 2.3). Readers of the *PMBOK® Guide* may recognize this as a scale somewhat along the lines of *projectized* to *functional* organizations.

What's interesting about this table—and a discovery for us as we wrote this book—is that with project dominance, it's not really a matter of one end of the spectrum or the other. A projectized organization, or any with a high level of maturity and sophistication around PM practice, takes advantage of *the best of both worlds*. It's almost as if, rather than a linear scale, it's actually a circle with no *extremes*.

For example, a mature project organization—one that has a strong project culture—is connected to the organizational goals and to the specific goals and objectives of the project. That's why you see *externally and internally*; *goals and means*; *work and employee*. A competent project manager, working in a project environment that enables her or him to be the best possible project manager, is capable of *pairing* these cultural differences, realizing that they are sometimes complementary rather than choosing between them.

Table 2.3   Organizational dimensions map

Project Dominant	Organizational Cultural Dimension	Organizational Dominant
Goals and means	Means versus goals orientation	Means
Externally and internally	Internally versus externally driven	Internally
Open	Open versus closed system	Closed
Work and employee	Employee versus work orientation	Employee
High	Leadership style acceptance	Low
Medium	Degree of identification with organization	High

What's the Approach to Consider?

Our strategy for improving these skills is organized into *fix* and *support* threads.

Fix: make training and coaching available in the cultural and organizational dimensions. There are dozens of vendors selling programs aimed specifically at improving skills in this area.

Support: in addition to training and coaching, there is quite a bit to be gained by simply assuring a higher level of focus on the global nature of business. It is important for senior management to demonstrate that an organization in which individuals are more capable of dealing with a variety of different cultures are more successful, and that the increasingly global nature of business is something to be embraced and not to fear.

 Leveraging on the opportunities offered by long- or short-term international assignments, when applicable, or by rotational assignments in different organizations can be a way to bridge these gaps as it allows your project managers to walk in someone else's shoes for a while.

THE PM COMMUNITY: THE EARS

We've talked about the eyes, the nose, and the mouth. Now it's time to cover our ears. Not literally, of course, but using the FACE model. The ears represent the PM community and your chance to build competency by taking advantage of the important conversations and messages among the project managers in your organization. This element of tacit knowledge transfer serves you much better if it is made explicit and widely-shared.

Even in a small organization, bringing together the project managers and encouraging them to share best practices and lessons learned gives your organization an increased level of maturity. This will allow quantum leaps in capability since the project managers are less likely to repeat common mistakes, or miss out on a great practice that worked wonders in a different business or region. Of course, in a larger organization, a *community* is even more of a benefit because of the sheer numbers of participants and the diversity of thought and practice that is being shared. There is also a huge benefit in terms of morale-building for your project managers. The sense that the organization has a *home base* for discussing PM-related topics has value in and of itself. The following are some examples of benefits from an active PM community.

> A project manager in Kansas notes that a certain globally applied component has a high failure rate during installation and shares this, thus preventing hundreds or thousands of other incidents of project delays (in the rest of North America, as well as in Europe, the Middle East, Africa, Oceana, and Asia) by avoiding its use altogether.
>
> • • • • • • • • • • •
>
> PMP candidates share their successful practices and experience in preparing for and taking the exam, thereby decreasing the anxiety for your organization's test takers and increasing the chances of their success.
>
> • • • • • • • • • • •
>
> A project manager in Malaysia develops a macro-empowered responsibility assignment matrix that facilitates the answer to the *who's doing what* question on his project, and it is shared, is used by others, and eventually becomes part of the organization's methodology.
>
> • • • • • • • • • • •
>
> A soon-to-retire project manager shares her top 10 tips for managing projects within the organization, giving specific advice about what has worked and what has not worked for her in hundreds of projects.

These real-life examples, as well as significant research, show the advantage of building, energizing, and supporting a community; and working hard to convert tacit knowledge to explicit, immediately usable knowledge, templates, and practices.

Some quick statistics in comparing organizations that are effective in enabling knowledge transfer in PM:

- 82% of those most effective at knowledge transfer *met their projects' original business intent* versus 62% that were least effective at knowledge transfer

- 74% of those most effective at knowledge transfer *kept projects on their original schedule* versus 42% that were least effective at knowledge transfer
- 75% of those most effective at knowledge transfer *stayed within their projects' original budget goals* versus 48% that were least effective at knowledge transfer

All in all, a more effective knowledge transfer mechanism (a community) helps explain a set of striking improvements (20% to over 30%!) in the all-important measurements of project success—scope, time, and cost. Further, these are only the *measurable* components and does not consider the morale and career growth aspects of the community.

What's the Approach to Consider?

The strategy here is actually relatively simple since the tools to create online communities are getting easier to deploy every year. Without a lot of effort, you can build a very active online community of project managers, using an off-the-shelf platform that allows blogging, file sharing, and threaded discussions—all very easy to create, respond to, and track, without an inundation of e-mails from the system (one of the bigger complaints of such systems).

So, our recommended approach: use a system—it can be as simple as deploying Yammer or SharePoint, or it can be a proprietary system. Promote it heavily and make sure it is part of the larger system of knowledge sharing in the organization, but devote a *branch* to PM. Beware of *splintering*—that is, having many (well-intentioned) individuals start their own PM communities, which will actually squelch the effort because people don't want to have to participate in 20 different communities to get the benefits that should be in one optimized community with the maximum number of contributors.

Think of LinkedIn where we've seen alumni of a university try to establish one community, only to find that there were 15 other similar groups, each of which only had 10 members. There needs to be a higher level of coordination. The global PMO or COE should take charge of this. There can (and should) be some specialty groups under the larger umbrella of the PM organization. For example, there can be communities set up that are focused on PMP exam preparation. The key is to assure the largest possible membership of a central PM community, and to encourage active communication and contribution of value from more than just one or a handful of individuals.

A slight *twist* to a PM community—not a substitute but an additional strategy—is to have an award or recognition program for project teams (not project managers, but teams) who have overcome amazing odds to achieve success, have worked on a project of particular strategic value, or have worked on a project that supports the corporate social responsibility objectives of the organization. Teams can be nominated for this award and the key *community* element of this recognition program is the fact that the nominated teams can be featured in periodic organizational newsletters or other communications. In this way, even the nominated teams get recognized and there is a *stream* of sharing of best practices and lessons learned from these stories of team success.

3

Know Thy Audience

So far, we have looked at the terrain: what are the topographical and morphological traits in the area in which we operate and where is the best spot in which to start building a bridge (or the first of many such bridges) to overcome existing gaps? Now we have to consider for *whom* we are building this bridge. A gap in project management (PM) competency—say, the PM framework—will have to be bridged differently if the project managers in your organization are mostly Millennials, or if they are a mix of Baby Boomers and Millennials. Having a large number of project managers with *directing* personalities in comparison to *creative* ones will determine what tactical options you choose when implementing your strategic goals. To remain in our bridge-building metaphor, you need to know whether the bridge will be used by pedestrian traffic (who will walk, run, or bicycle over the bridge) or by a combination of pedestrian and vehicular traffic (cars or trucks). That's why we encourage you to think about the composition of your PM audience.

Before you get too far into understanding any competency gap in the PM staff, you must first observe and evaluate the staff itself. From our experience, this is best done by *management by walking around* (MBWA). These days that is usually *virtual* walking, of course—but the same principle applies. Your *antennae* should be up. You should be attending meetings and staying in touch with your internal organizational network with the intent to observe and evaluate.

Are you working in an organization with a mature, experienced set of project managers? Are you a more entrepreneurial organization loaded with very young and new-to-the game project managers? What is the *heritage* of the PM population? We're quite familiar with organizations in which most of the project managers were engineers or scientists for most of their career before accidentally (or perhaps intentionally) becoming project managers. That's very different from the situation in which your project managers are mostly from sales, marketing, or business fields. Or, do you have a real mix of generations—a hodgepodge of technical and business folks, a mélange of inexperienced and experienced project managers?

Understanding the nature of your PM community will be very important as you plan how to build a continuous learning environment. We'll provide clear indications as to when certain techniques and solutions work better with certain audiences. The point is that even in a specific discipline like PM, there still is great variance—in background, in technical knowledge, in PM philosophy—and that must be accounted for.

GENERATIONAL DIFFERENCES

"Projects are used as a means to achieve organizational strategic goals. It is obvious that global spending on projects is in the order of many billions of dollars annually. Therefore, it is critical that organizations engage people from different generations productively in order to complete projects on time, on budget, and in line with specifications." From *Successful Project Management Practices* by Parviz Rad and Vittal Anantatmula.

Age matters. Well, not age per se, but the generational aspect of environment, upbringing, values, and technology that characterize groups of individuals. Until a few years ago, it was common for people to work for the same company they started with after graduating from a university, for decades, perhaps even retiring from that company 40 or 50 years later. Now, it's not even certain that a degree from a university is even a prerequisite for certain career paths and it's highly unlikely that a person will work for a company for more than 5–10 years before moving on. These are *norms* that form important heuristic biases in our minds and set the tone for how we behave at work, whether consciously or subconsciously. Taken a step further, these behaviors, observable in both project team members as well as the project managers themselves, must be taken into account when we're building competencies.

When it comes to training, people of the Baby Boomer generation are used to a model in which they sit in a classroom and listen to an instructor. Depending on the lecturer and other factors, the students are somewhere along the scale from *eye-rolling tolerance* to *fascinated engagement*. People who are now in their 20s—Millennials—are much less likely to even know about this *classroom* model and are much more prone to get their information in bursts of just a few minutes, in multiple forms of media, and likely while they are doing something else. One of the authors is a professor at several large universities. In one class, he observed that students, each of whom had a desktop display, also had open and were sometimes using a laptop, phone, tablet, and MP3 player. In this same class, he also noticed a student (this really happened!) checking for text messages while at the front of the class as part of a group presentation. These young people are now in the work force and are serving as project managers, technical experts, accountants, scientists, and financial analysts on your projects.

We need to recognize that project managers reflect the populations from where they're drawn. And those populations now contain (depending on where you draw your lines) three or four different generations. These generations have different attitudes toward work, toward each other, and toward the members of the other generations; they do not learn in the same way and are not motivated by the same things.

Let's have a look at the generational differences, and let's do it by using something which we're all very familiar—the stakeholder engagement matrix—a tool that shows the interests and influence of those involved in a project. We took each of the three (somewhat overlapping) generations—Baby Boomers, Gen X, and Millennials—and analyzed how we can improve engagement with populations of project managers from each of these generations.

One more consideration to add to this analysis is that, just like any other generalization, the generational characteristics make sense only when they are actually *observed*, and not just assumed. Based on the culture in your organization, you might have project managers in their 30s behaving like Baby Boomers. This means you should consider competency

Table 3.1 Impact on PM population

	Positive Impact	Negative Impact
Influence (internal to the PM population)	Motivating factors	Deterring factors
Influence (external to the PM population)	Enabling factors	Blocking factors

development strategies appropriate to that audience, rather than to any birth-year-based label.

The first thing to understand for each generation is which internal and external factors, with either positive or negative impacts, affect their ability to contribute to the project. The combinations above yield four categories of factors (see Table 3.1) impacting each generational group:

- Factors with a positive impact:
    - Motivating (internal influence)
    - Enabling (external influence)
- Factors with a negative impact:
    - Deterring (internal influence)
    - Blocking (external influence)

We bundled motivating and enabling—the two positive forces—and deterring and blocking—the two negative forces—to make the generational tables easier to read and to be able to derive key points. Then, as one does with a stakeholder engagement matrix, we list specific actions that you can take to enhance the contribution from a project manager of the particular generation. We summarize these tables below.

Baby Boomers

Your more *seasoned* project managers will particularly struggle with social media. They'll associate it with what they see outside of work—perhaps with their own children's or grandchildren's use of Facebook, and may judge its use as something that could *never* add value at work. We have noted this attitude, overtly or as a passive-aggressive reaction, over and over in our work experience as a roadblock to innovative knowledge transfer approaches. This aversion to leveraging social media in the work place leads to a set of threats in which these Baby Boomer project managers may get left behind in using important PM community tools to both deposit and withdraw knowledge for their jobs.

Another threat: the rise of the project manager as a generalist who is not always expected to be a technical expert in the practice area may leave Baby Boomer technical project managers feeling isolated or stranded. You'll also find that Baby Boomer project managers will tend to dislike and perhaps distrust directives from so-called central or global organizations. They'll want to manage projects their *own* way and any transformations (for example, a move to an automated enterprise PM tool) will require extra care and effort. Interestingly, while this group tends to not want direction from a central PM authority, they also perceive a weak level of PM support as stifling their ability to *make a difference*—one of the Baby Boomers' key motivators.

Table 3.2 has the details, but here are a couple of general responses to these influencing factors:

- Partner younger and older project managers in coaching arrangements that can yield win-win outcomes
- Consciously engage the older project managers to assure the conveyance of tacit to explicit knowledge
- Encourage knowledge-sharing forums for storytelling as a way to preserve PM experiences and lessons learned

Generation X

This is a population that witnessed an end to the Cold War, became very self-reliant, and developed an attitude of work-life balance in which they feel that a 12–16 hour (or more) work day is not an acceptable trade-off when compared to enjoying friends and family. Thus, they will want (and expect) flexibility in work hours and work situations. It's a population that embraces technology easily and seeks *meaningfulness* in their work—that is, work that benefits future generations. They will look more favorably on assignments (projects) that have considered corporate social responsibility (CSR) aspects. This leads to a set of threats unique to this generation. They will want to feel that their work is *good work*. If they are in a culture where PM is not appreciated as a discipline, they may become disenfranchised. At their age, they may still be considered *too old* by the younger project managers in the organization, and although they embrace

Table 3.2 Engaging Baby Boomer project managers

Baby Boomers – 1945 to 1962		
Motivating and Enabling Factors	**Deterring and Blocking Factors**	**Engagement Strategies**
• Driven to make a difference, they want a chance to "be a star" • Opportunities to be a team member and perform well on a team • Attention and recognition are important • Willingness to take on responsibility • Presence of mentorship programs • Easy-to-use online PM community	• Dislike changes in the way they run their projects • Older "techies" feel stranded, isolated by torrent of new tools and inability to use them • Directives from "central" authorities may be viewed with distrust or distaste • A weak PM support structure is perceived as stifling their ability to make a difference • Lack of organization's focus on PM may discourage sharing of knowledge from older project managers	• Assure strength of an active PM community • Engage Boomers in transition plans, get them involved in rollout of new PM tools: encourage them to champion their use instead of championing the complaints • Consciously leverage older project managers to assure conveying of tacit to explicit knowledge; encourage them to tell their stories • Launch mentorship programs, let Boomers take the lead (but both mentor and mentee will benefit) • Partner younger/older project managers for win-win learning opportunities: younger ones can share their knowledge of new technologies with their more experienced colleagues

technology (and are particularly fond of cutting-edge technology) they haven't mastered it as their younger counterparts have. They're hungry for knowledge, feeling that the more they know, the better their chances of success at work.

To engage Generation X (Gen X) project managers:

- Make sure that PM is increasingly recognized as a discipline and that the PM community gets the recognition that it deserves
- Stress the *giving back* and *doing good* aspects of the organization's work and, in particular, projects focused on CSR goals, including volunteer projects in the local community

- Remember that they can serve as the *bridge* between the Baby Boomers and Millennials and that their propensity for meaningfulness means that they will enjoy contributing in this role
- Be sure to provide recognition to Gen X project managers. They may be successful at a very young age; don't let their apparent lack of experience deter this recognition
- Develop competencies with an array of learning options. They'll appreciate development opportunities coming from sources other than their boss or the classroom

Refer to Table 3.3 for more details.

Millennials

This generation was raised on a digital feed. From an article in *Entrepreneur Magazine* (see Millennial reference in Appendix 1), here are five traits related to Millennials in the workplace:

1. They don't believe in being shackled to tradition or location
2. They don't believe in the inherent value of face time
3. They believe in learning, not pieces of paper
4. They believe in learning from someone else's experience
5. They believe in life, not work-life balance

From our analysis and comparison, the item of interest for a PM population of Millennials is their propensity for a list of options—a variety of learning sources rather than a certain single source of learning. They prefer strong, ethical leaders. They know they are young and capable; they want to be recognized for their capabilities and not thought of as novices even though they are relatively young. They won't do things in a certain way only because they've been done that way before and they want to see the benefit of the preferred way and will want to change it if it doesn't make sense to them. It comes as no surprise that they do not like hierarchical organizations (see Table 3.4).

So how do you engage a population of Millennial project managers?

- Allow for personalization of development opportunities
- Communicate with them electronically and take advantage of multiple forms of social media

Table 3.3   Engaging Generation X project managers

Generation X – 1962 to 1980		
Motivating and Enabling Factors	**Deterring and Blocking Factors**	**Engagement Strategies**
• Adding skills to knowledge base: the more they know, the better • Strong PM support structure and culture • Availability of social media-based PM tools • Access to information • Cutting-edge systems and technology • Forward thinking organization • Flexibility in work hours: work-life balance is important • Performance evaluated on merit, not age/seniority	• Micro-management: they don't mind direction, but resent intrusive supervision • Dislike rigid work requirements • If they can't see the reason for the task, they will question it • If you can't keep them engaged, then they will seek another position • Project managers may become disenfranchised if they sense a lack of PM culture at this point in their career	• Variety and flexibility are keys to a successful learning environment • Provide learning and development opportunities as an information provider, rather than a boss-mandated training • Provide situations to try new things: ask for their input in selecting options • Use peer experiences as testimonials • Use straight talk; present facts • Use e-mail as #1 tool • Share info immediately and often • Tie your message to "results": emphasize "WIIFM" (What's In It For Me) in terms of training and skills to build their resume • They have the potential to bridge the generation gap between youngest and oldest workers: partner younger/older project managers; build a strong multi-generational culture of project managers with lively online PM community • Recognize those who have succeeded in running projects that are technical in nature, regardless of age and background • Move to increasingly recognize PM as a discipline and to allow project managers to act more entrepreneurially and independently

Table 3.4 Engagin Millennial project managers

Millennials – 1980-2000		
Motivating and Enabling Factors	Deterring and Blocking Factors	Engagement Strategies
• Training is important and new skills will ease stressful situations • Immediate results • Balancing work, life, community engagement, and self-development • Strong, ethical leaders and mentors who treat them with respect in spite of age • Friendly work environment, less hierarchical organizations • Being evaluated on the work product itself • Better to be given a list of options: variety and innovation	• Dislike any requirement to do things just because this is the way it has always been done • Repeating tasks is a poor use of their energy and time and an example of not being taken seriously • Dislike inflexible hierarchical organizations	• Offer structured, supportive learning environment • Personalize learning opportunities and involve them in choosing optimal options for their teams; a learning plan specific to them will go a long way to engage and sustain their interest • Use positive, respectful, motivational, electronic communication style • Offer opportunities to learn in networks and teams using multimedia while being entertained and excited • Encourage exploration of new avenues of learning through breaking the rules: podcasts, flexible options to learn while at the gym (multitasking), etc. • Raise the bar on learning objectives as they have high expectations on what they can achieve • Establish mentoring programs and peer-level support systems • Leverage a sustainable approach to learning opportunities: no printing, self-sustaining communities and networks, etc.

- Challenge them with extensive and comprehensive learning; they have high expectations of themselves when it comes to development
- Break traditional rules when it comes to modes of learning; they will want podcasts, webinars, and ways in which they can develop, even if that learning takes place in a gym or while running

THE PROJECT MANAGER PERSONALITY APPROACH

In addition to generational elements, we have to consider other aspects of the project managers we plan to engage. While project managers, in general, share some personality traits (the *control freak* stereotype, for example), they are likely to have a widely diverse set of temperaments and inherent qualities. As you plan how to increase their competency in PM, you will need to leverage an improved understanding of how to reach out to these diverse personalities.

The Myers-Briggs Temperaments

The Myers-Briggs Type Indicator (MBTI) is a personality testing system created by Katherine Cook Briggs and, her daughter, Isabel Briggs Myers. Using some ideas from psychologist Carl Jung, they developed a very structured set of questions based on preference. After answering the set of questions, the assessment yields results along four scales, summarized as follows:

Introverted versus Extroverted (I vs. E)—The first scale helps you choose which seems most natural to you—introversion versus extroversion. The scale is not asking, are you an introvert or an extrovert? but rather, what gives you energy? For example, do you feel renewed and energized after being with a group of people or do you gain energy from being alone?

Sensing versus Intuition (S vs. N)—This scale deals with how one takes in information. It is geared to reveal whether one absorbs information through sensing or intuition. *Sensing*—using the five senses—involves gaining information that is (or at least appears to be) more factual and solid. *Intuition* is more about an interpretation of what is sensed—perhaps expressed as *reading between the lines*. Star Wars characters exhibit this, when they often say, "I've got a bad feeling about this. . . ."

Thinking versus Feeling (T vs. F)—This scale deals with decision making (not information gathering, as mentioned before). Here the comparison is between logical analysis and judgment based on an overall gut-feeling. On the extremes of this scale would be a person who spends 20 minutes weighing the benefits of various candy treats at the checkout line of a supermarket (*thinking*), and the person who, in one motion, scoops up that 70% cacao chocolate bar because they have a craving for chocolate (*feeling*).

Judging versus Perceiving (J vs. P)—The last scale measures judging versus perceiving. On the *judging* side, there is a propensity to prefer being organized and formally scheduled. On the other side of the scale, *perceivers* like flexibility and spontaneity. They like to consider all possibilities. You definitely want a perceiver around when you do risk or stakeholder analysis.

The Myers-Briggs assessment yields 16 types. However, some of the most valuable information lies not in the specific type, but rather in four *temperaments*. It is in these distinctions that we can learn a little about the project managers in the group and how to build their competencies based on which of the four temperaments they exhibit.

Guardians (SJ) concentrate on and talk about their duties and responsibilities—what they are *in charge of*. They tend to follow the rules, and to be respectful—even protective—of others.

Idealists (NF) focus on the future; they think about what might be possible for people. They value ethics and fairness in getting to objectives.

Artisans (SP) live in the moment, valuing what is right in front of them, dealing with what they can hands-on, and they will do whatever works—whatever gives them a quick, effective payoff.

Rationals (NT) are locked into new problems and focus on problem solving. They favor the pragmatic, the efficient, the effective way to achieve their objectives, even rebelling against tradition if they know their solution will work.

A recent article in the *Project Management Journal* (see Cohen et al. in Appendix 1) says:

> "There are significantly more NT (intuitive, thinking) type project managers than their percentage in the general population. The NT project managers base their decisions on intuition and analysis. This is expected, because project managers must make decisions in the face of ambiguity and uncertainty and have to rely on intuition while lacking some of the facts."

What this means is that you will likely be dealing with more NTs in your PM community than in a generic population. In this PM population, you'll tend to have great pragmatic capabilities that won't necessarily have to be further developed to any great extent. In effect, you have a *surplus* of these capabilities which you can use to mentor those project managers who are *not* in the NT temperament. At the same time, you will likely have the opportunity (and the need) to increase the competency and capability in the other three temperaments. You should be prepared to provide learning opportunities in the areas of:

- Creativity
- Supervision (versus leadership)
- Long-term thinking
- Coaching and mentoring skills

These are characteristics that are outside the natural temperament of NTs and, thus, may be somewhat lacking in the majority of your PM population. Of course, your population is not 100% NT so the solution to this is somewhat built-in. You are likely to have some SJ, NF, and SP project managers in that same population. In addition to providing courseware in the areas listed above, you also can partner project managers of various temperaments to take advantage of the differences in temperaments.

 While any such assessment can be performed directly as part of a PM team-building exercise if you have a relatively small number of project managers in your organization, for a large population of project managers you will have to rely on your project management office (PMO), and/or on your leaders of project managers to know who is an NT project manager and who is an SJ project manager.

A PM director ran a Myers-Briggs assessment for their group of 12 project managers—using it as a team-building opportunity. It yielded excellent information about the group, it let individuals in the group learn much more about themselves, and it yielded sustainable benefits. Indeed, the results indicated many NT personalities, but also some diversity, which came in handy when assigning projects. It also persisted in the form of good-natured *ribbing* and a form of support structure within the team—allowing them to often back each other up with a little more effectiveness because each was more aware of the others' propensities to have strengths and weaknesses for a particular project challenge. As for the director, the assessment revealed opportunities to provide partnering and training opportunities aligned with their MBTI type as well as their Kiersey temperaments (see Appendix 1).

The Pellerin Color System

One of the best ways to understand the nature of a PM community is a unique system from the book, *How NASA Builds Teams,* by Dr. Charlie Pellerin. Dr. Pellerin is the former program director for the Hubble Telescope. He learned from his experience with the Hubble's initial failure, and has made it possible for all of us to leverage on his lessons learned.

Within weeks of the launch of the Hubble, the images it sent back were blurry, indicating a serious problem with its optical system. Hubble failed to achieve a final sharp focus and the best image quality obtained was drastically lower than expected. It was an embarrassing error for NASA. The primary mirror of the world's most expensive telescope was ground to the wrong shape, and was sending back images that, in effect, made it look like the Hubble needed glasses.

When Dr. Pellerin analyzed the flaw, he determined that although the defect in the mirror could be explained with a detailed technical rationale, the issue's root cause really came down to a failure in the communication that occurred when project work had to be performed by team members working in differing personal operating dimensions. In other words, the *soft* PM skills around communication must be attuned to both the person sending the message and the person receiving it. The communication process must take into account, in particular, the way in which different types of personalities work together (or sometimes do not). Dr. Pellerin has devoted the rest of his career to teaching others how to avoid this problem.

Refer to Appendix 1 for an interview with Dr. Pellerin. Before we go any further, and in the interest of happy endings, we should remind you that Dr. Pellerin was allowed to redeem himself by launching a repair mission that (as you know from the ongoing stunning images from Hubble) was a huge and sustainable success.

Dr. Pellerin's work to improve PM via his increased understanding of how teams really work led him to create a system to understand and improve how people issues affect projects. It's called the 4-D system, with 'D' standing for *dimension*. Two scales—one from *intuited* to *sensed* (the information axis) and one from *emotional* to *logical* (the deciding axis)—yield four areas (see Figure 3.1). The upper-left dimension (emotional, intuited) is coded green and is called *cultivating*. Team members in this dimension have a caring, sharing attitude as their general style. The upper-right dimension (logical, intuited) is given the color blue and is called *visioning*. Team members in this dimension are focused on striving to achieve the best, smartest solutions to problems. Those in the lower-left (emotional-sensed) who crave integrity and relationship-building, are tagged with the color yellow, and are called *including*. Individuals who are in the lower-right (logical, sensed) are good at giving direction and focusing the team on result. They are coded with the color orange and are *directing*.

> Experience-based note: we have seen this model applied to team members, to the project managers themselves, and/or to other stakeholders. As project managers, we have seen all of these *colors* used from time to time, and as you'll read in the upcoming text, we have observed downright dangerous situations in which the project manager was *stuck* in one of the corners. It's good to self-discover and find out where your own tendencies are, but be ready to shift around this grid, as necessary, on real projects—leading real people through their real tasks and contributions, all in the context of the very real and changeable project environment. If you find this tool interesting, we highly recommend that you refer to Appendix 3, which shows you how to use this valuable leadership development tool.

We can take this theoretical model a step further to yield specific desirable behaviors that will make for a more successful approach to developing project leaders. Remember, we would like to understand motivation, but we cannot observe it. We can, however, observe behavior. The assessment for the 4-D system looks for the pairs of behaviors you see in Figure 3.2. Here you can find that each dimension of the 4-D system demonstrates two unique behaviors. Let's look at each of the four dimensions, their observable behaviors, and also some guidance for each.

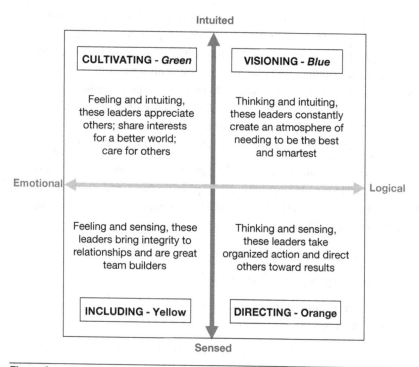

Figure 3.1 The four colors of the 4-D system

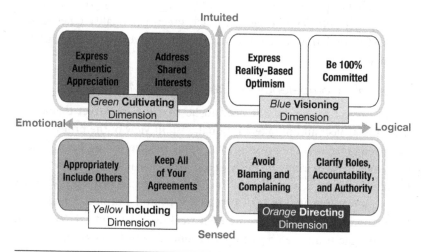

Figure 3.2 Applying the 4-D system to teams

Following our description of individual project manager behaviors and what to do about improving competency in each case, we provide some advice on how to improve PM competencies in larger PM communities exhibiting these behaviors. Our intent is to make some recommendations whether you need to use the recommended approaches directly for a few individuals on your team, or for a larger community of project managers in your organization.

Once again, we caution about taking an absolute approach to any labeling or categorization. We are striving to provide tools and methods to help you select the most effective approaches to improve competency, and do not intend to put your project managers into *boxes*.

The Cultivators (Green)

The *cultivating* (green) dimension behaviors are:

- Express authentic appreciation
- Address shared interests

Where do the cultivators perform most effectively? According to Dr. Pellerin, *the cultivating personality performs best in jobs where caring for people matters most. They frequently provide training and coaching, and are excellent team leaders when they are four-dimensional (that is, they have elements of the other colors as well). If they are only green, they cannot organize sufficiently to lead.* In fact, green personality types should be careful of victim behavior, being hypersensitive, judgmental, and/or unrealistic.

Increasing Competency for Green Project Managers

Green project managers will need to be coached to extract themselves from the project and to take a rational, *distant* view of the project. They will need to be aware of possibly identifying themselves too strongly with the project. Partnering an overly green project manager with an orange technical deputy is a good solution. The real key is helping the overly green project manager to take a step back from the project periodically. We recommend scheduling time each week with a technical deputy (or other orange team member) to get grounded with the logical, focused, unemotional insight they provide on the project—not unlike Mr. Spock to Captain Kirk in the old Star Trek TV series.

Increasing Competency for a Green PM Population

While it is a good trait for your PM population to want to focus on the team and on building an enjoyable, safe, energizing team environment, if the focus is limited to these items only, the people on the teams may be temporarily satiated, but you'll quickly find that this is not sustainable. Projects will start to fail. The other dimensions need to be there as well: blue's connectedness to the organization's strategy, orange's clear assignment of accountability and focus on the outcome, and yellow's propensity to efficiently keep agreements are needed so that this mutually respected, energized, collaborative team actually accomplishes project work.

Competency development tips for this population:

- Teach business strategy and, in particular, coaching regarding the organization's particular strategic goals
- Reaffirm the importance of the project manager role in connecting strategy to operations via the projects, programs, and portfolios (for example, training which conveys the Stanford Execution Framework viewpoint)
- Increase competency in tools that enhance clear delegation, including RAM (responsibility assignment matrix)/RACI (responsible, accountable, consulted, and informed) tools
- Develop the capability of assertiveness so that a request from a project manager is taken seriously.

Included here would be: increasing personal power, building and using a support network, and coalition-building.

The Visionaries (Blue)

The *visioning* (blue) dimension behaviors are:

- Express reality-based optimism
- 100% commitment

The visioning personality type performs best in jobs where *concept mastery and creativity matter most*. Think Steve Jobs. As you can imagine, there are some strong cautions here if you are fully blue. Strong blues can be argumentative, may be highly critical of others, and may be considered know-it-alls or *prima donnas*.

Increasing Competency for Blue Project Managers

The blue project manager knows a lot about the project, and he or she *knows* that they know a lot about the project and or its technical details. This can be an irritant to project team members, especially other blue members. Coach this project manager to frequently take the temperature of the team to assure that their leadership style is not causing unnecessary conflict. If needed, explain that the information about this team attitude is just *one more thing* for them to know. Now you are speaking to them in their own language—and that new team attitude information becomes a new piece of knowledge that the blue project manager will want to collect. It's a win-win strategy! In fact, for strong blue project managers, we suggest scheduled MBWA sessions, perhaps facilitated by a colleague in the yellow area. Although these check-ins should, of course, have authentic concern for the team, it turns out that simply the *appearance* of a blue project manager being around for the purpose of listening to and supporting the PM team has a very positive effect. Table 3.5 has some examples of how you can deal with these project managers.

Table 3.5   Dealing with a 'visioning' project manager mindset

Overly Blue Mindset	How to Resolve—Establishing Early Ground Rules
Excessive focus on performance at the expense of cost and schedule attributes	Early, conscious team agreement on the order of priorities for the constraints; if performance is the top constraint and schedule and budget targets can be missed, make this a clear decision that is bought into by the core team.
Too much casual and pairwise communication	Establish a minimum protocol of information exchange that provides an increased structure for sharing information (perhaps a SharePoint or similar site) without an overbearing communications process. State up-front that there is a broader "need-to-know" principle for this project.

Increasing Competency for a Blue PM Population

It's actually unusual in our experience to find project managers that are *too good* at visioning—at being too connected to an organization's strategy. However, if you have a population that does fit this description, you need to be sure that the other dimensions are accentuated as well. The green dimension will make sure that your focus on a long-term and highly innovative system doesn't break the team's ability to collaborate as a team. The blue population's innovative and optimistic viewpoint needs to be offset by orange's clear assignment of accountability and realistic focus on achievable expectations. And, you will benefit from yellow's focus on efficiency and the project ground rules that everyone agreed to at the start.

Competency development tips for this population:

- Understand the Tuckman model (forming, norming, storming, and performing)
- Teach contract management skills to assist in a deep understanding of commitments and agreements
- Have a balance between constraints—including the need to consciously assign priority between scope, time, and cost
- Teach knowledge and skills in the area of earned value; a focus on cost and schedule variance (and of course, attention to tracking it) will enhance the attention on the project's efficiency so that features and functionality do not become the only focus area

The Includers (Yellow)

The *including* (yellow) behaviors are:

- Appropriately include others
- Keep all your agreements

The including dimension in a project manager drives performance and results most effectively in jobs where relationships and teamwork have ultimate priority. For large, complex teams, where inspiration and inclusiveness is key, project managers with a strong *yellow* behavior are the ones who will lead effectively—of course, as long as they are not completely absent of the other colors! In fact, they need to be cautious of being conflict-averse, overly compliant, constantly needing approval, or in some cases, withholding what could be a very valid opinion for fear of disrupting the karma of the team.

Increasing Competency for Yellow Project Managers

Although all four dimensions are observable in the practice of solid PM discipline, some dimensions are more naturally enabling than others. Yellow project managers face probably the biggest challenge in terms of a natural propensity to excel at PM, which is only to say that they have to work outside of their comfort zone more than the other types. Projects are naturally seething with conflict and a strong yellow project manager will tend to shy away from conflict—wanting to be compliant and to preserve relationships.

Some examples are:

- A sponsor aggressively demands three new unplanned-for features
- Team members *A* and *B* are having a hugely counterproductive and ongoing argument, which has polarized the project team into two camps
- A team member has consistently failed to deliver their project component, neglecting to even inform the project manager of the failures in advance
- A supplier indicates that the safety feature on their project—one that prevents injuries to end customers—is *a little flaky*

In none of the above situations should the project manager say, in a soft calming voice, "Oh, it's alright, no worries." The project manager must accept conflict—even relish it—and push back. This is a very un-yellow thing to do. For the strong yellow project manager, we recommend that you partner them with a blue and/or orange colleague. The yellow project manager needs to be empowered by the facts, and he or she must build up their ability (and willingness) to *push back* firmly when there is a project issue such as those mentioned. The project manager also must be prepared to use the authority vested in him or her by the project charter and the sponsor. The project manager is indeed, after all, acting as an authorized agent of senior leadership or an important client, and needs to act accordingly—being assertive and willing to deal with conflict as needed.

Increasing Competency for a Yellow PM Population

The issues that apply to the individual yellow project manager would also apply to this population. They need the direction from orange's focus on the outcome, on clear achievable objectives, and on clear accountability and assignment of team roles. PM populations that are *too yellow* will have another overarching problem—sheer numbers. Their project teams may get unwieldy because, with their focus on inclusiveness, they'll tend to build project teams that are simply too big (in that attempt to include *everybody*) and hard to manage. So one tip: provide coaching to your yellow project managers—while it's good to build an all-inclusive team, if that team is too large, you really don't have a team any more, you have a conglomeration and you have defeated your (well-intentioned) propensity to be inclusive.

Competency development tips for this population:

- Teach conflict management skills—perhaps featuring training in the Thomas-Killmann Conflict Mode Instrument (see Appendix 1)
- Improve their capability to be assertive

The Director (Orange)

The *directing* (orange) behaviors are:

- Avoid blaming and complaining
- Clarify roles, accountability, and authority

The directing dimension is outstanding at tasks that require planning, organizing, directing, and controlling. Sound familiar? It should. These almost sound like *PMBOK® Guide* process groups (and a couple of them literally are). Thereafter, we can see that the orange dimension is a natural fit for the project manager. But be careful! You don't want your project managers to go too far in the orange corner, which could lead to an attitude represented by this quote attributed to British film producer Michael Winner:

"A team effort is a lot of people doing what I say."

In fact, the behaviors observable in a strong orange project manager are: inflexibility, closed-mindedness, micro-managing, and being insensitive to the team's needs.

Increasing Competency for Orange Project Managers

An orange project manager may run a highly successful project but they burn out team members (physically and mentally); and may give rise to a situation in which nobody ever wants to work on this project manager's projects ever again, or may leave the organization altogether. We have seen this happen with orange project managers more times than we care to mention. In other words, orange project managers may have PM success, but not long-term organizational project success. Organizational project success means that the project provides ongoing benefits realization for the organization. A strong orange project manager will have some short-term success but may yield a net-negative for the organization. A strong orange project manager should be coached to tone down overly directive behavior and to be much more aware of the needs of individual project team members. To do this, partner the strong orange project manager in your team with a green or yellow colleague to ensure a better connection to the team. Look at Table 3.6 for more ideas on how to help directing project managers.

Increasing Competency for an Orange PM Population

PM populations with strong orange tendencies need to be reminded as a group that there is a long-term problem with an extreme focus on project

Table 3.6 Dealing with a 'directing' PM project manager mindset

Overly Orange Mindset	How to Resolve—Establishing Early Ground Rules
Excessive focus on cost and schedule at the expense of performance	Early, conscious team agreement on the order of priorities for the constraints; if schedule is the top constraint and performance and budget targets can be missed, make this a clear decision that is bought into by the core team.
Documentation process overkill	Establish these processes, but establish a check on a periodic basis to see whether information is actually being squelched by excessive rigor on project communications.

outcomes at the expense of their teams. They need to be made aware of successes from project managers that keep their eyes on the prize, but *also* build good, solid teams (as yellow and green PM populations would). Ironically, if they are so focused on outcomes that their team members don't feel appreciated and don't trust each other, they may have some great initial outcomes, but will find their project teams get less and less successful over time. In other words, they are not able to sustain success, which is indeed a poor outcome.

Competency development tips for this population:

- Teach emotional intelligence and other team-building skills to target one of the key aspects of project success that is usually neglected: care for the project teams
- Focus on deliverables tracking—increase skills around monitoring and controlling all deliverables, even intermediate ones
- Build communications skills—focus on rigor and consistency in reporting project progress

4

Options

By now you have an idea of what area you want to improve in your project management (PM) community, and on whom, in your community, you want to focus. Based on the culture in your organization, some competency development options will be more effective than others. If, for example, the organization has an internal environment that fosters peer-to-peer knowledge transfer, then formal training effectiveness will be somewhat limited. For those organizations in which information and authority typically flow using formal channels, a more structured approach, even in mentoring efforts, would be a better fit.

You will also have to consider carefully the best ways in which competency development for your project managers can dovetail with the environment in which they operate. You would then be setting the *mood music*, as described in an excellent article by Mel Bost (see Chapter 8), for an organizational habit of competency improvement. When opportunities for continuous learning are an integral part of the day-to-day operations in the community, they become sustainable and part of the corporate/organizational culture.

FORMAL TRAINING

As one of the first options to come to mind when planning for competency development in any field, formal training courses may seem the obvious choice in many circumstances.

When a young mother decided to get back to work after her son had grown into a happy preschool toddler, she realized she needed to learn how to work with laptops and, among other things, spreadsheet programs. During her pre-baby career as a lead engineer, she had used Unix-based systems and customized tools built by her organization, all of which were no longer available. Believing she could master a simple spreadsheet program with some clever moves, she opened the program on her personal laptop to prepare for her first day on the job. After several frustrating attempts at *self-learning* and *trial and error*, she decided that it would be faster, more rewarding, and definitely more effective to set aside her pride (in a manner of speaking) and take a course. It was then love at first sight. No longer wrapped in mystery, the spreadsheet program became a faithful and well-loved tool to the point of assisting her in developing a patented approach to manage equipment configuration. Sometimes, a straightforward, packaged course is truly the simplest way to learn a new skill.

Depending on the situation, you might need to diversify your tactical approach to training the PM community: even the best course might fail to reach your audience if it does not have enough context and/or meaning in the environment where the project managers operate.

A global project management office (PMO) was launching a single PM platform in a large corporation. The platform was based on a standard and feature-rich PM tool, adapted to fit the corporate processes from order management to customer acceptance. The initial attempts at a formal training course were an abysmal failure: the professional instructor, trained in the use of the standard tool, had been unable to respond effectively to the many *what if* questions from the students related to specific customizations of the standard tool and to related internal corporate processes. Moreover, due to the fact that the course content (and related screen shots) had been prepared while the tool was still under development, the training material was not fully effective. No amount of *parking lot* questions and answers could backfill the wide gaps in understanding that were left in the audience after this initial delivery of (very expensive) classroom training. In the end, the PMO decided to combine an internal tool expert with a process specialist to offer a *structured knowledge transfer* learning opportunity, with hands-on learning for the students, so that the participants could kick-start their use of the new platform. The PMO also defined region-specific case studies with meaningful examples and localized situational scenarios to help project managers relate to their practice exercises. Needless to say, the outcomes were much better this time around.

When does it make sense to use formal training? When should other options be considered?

The answers depend heavily on the level of customization required for the content to be meaningful to your PM community. Even training for a commonly taught subject—let's say risk management—might have to be tailored to your specific organizational processes to become useful in day-to-day project activities. You can significantly boost the effectiveness of formal training by ensuring your professional instructors add a minimum level of context elements, such as links to the templates for risk management plans and risk registers, or pointers to the escalation process and related contacts. Table 4.1 illustrates some criteria to help you assess whether formal training is generally a good fit.

You will also need to assess the *competency levels* you want to achieve for your target audience. Does the project manager need to master some new skills, or can basic knowledge be sufficient? Once again, you should consider both the short- and long-term impact of any learning opportunity.

One more consideration is related to the type of hands-on training you want to offer to the students. If you expect a project manager to learn a new tool for risk management, for example, you will want them to have plenty of opportunities for practice before they start using it for their projects unless you can live with the inevitable mishaps of the learning phase. If you segregate student data, and thus prevent polluting actual data in

Table 4.1 Criteria for using formal training

Area	Criteria	Formal	Other
Content	Solid, well established, predictable	ILT, CBT	
	Still in pilot phase, or not yet finalized	ILT	
	Corporate standards, compliance	CBT	
	Variable based on audience, e.g., regions, products, etc.		Tailored
Delivery	Lecture	ILT, CBT	
	Prerequisite training, basics	CBT	
	Hands-on practice	ILT	
	Specialized and/or expert consultation		Tailored

ILT = Instructor-led training, classroom or virtual
CBT = Cloud-based training, self-paced. Includes on-demand, mobile-accessible, web-based training, and off-line courses delivered via a dedicated platform

your risk management tool, then the project managers can *learn by doing* after a course, even a computer-based one. In some cases, once a new tool goes *live*, it is difficult to segregate student data from operational data. In such cases, you should consider a *dedicated training environment*, an instance of the new tool to be used solely for instructional and student practice purposes. The expense of setting up and maintaining this environment would be offset by the benefits of hands-on learning in a safe platform with no impact on operational data.

Instructor Led-Training—Classroom or Virtual Participation

Active participation in instructor-led training, and plenty of *interaction* with an *experienced* instructor and with other students, is often a good way to learn and retain information. The key words (in *italics*) in the previous sentence express some of the assumptions we all make when thinking about instructor-led training.

First assumption—The students are *actively participating* in the session. This means they are not reading e-mails or texting while the instructor is speaking or during class exercises. It also means the students are listening and making connections between what the instructor is talking about and their job. How often does that really happen? These days, students routinely juggle laptops, tablets, phones, and MP3 players, all while allegedly *listening* to lectures. Consider a virtual classroom environment, even with the latest technology that helps the instructor detect the student's *presence* in the virtual classroom: what do you think is the level of active participation of each student?

Second assumption—Students are *interacting with the instructor and other students* as they learn. This means they are fully engaged, to the point of taking action (responding to questions, working on class exercises, etc.) and collaborating with the instructor and the other students to improve their learning experience, and that of their peers. They are connecting what they hear and see in the class to their daily activities, thus making sure that what they learn improves how they work. They are also leveraging on other students' experiences to learn from each other, which can only be obtained if both the first and the second assumption are true.

Third assumption—The *instructor is experienced.* This means not only that the subject is fully understood and that the instructor has recently applied the knowledge (as a practitioner) to the point of being able to teach it, but also that the instructor understands *how* to teach, including a sense of the students' attentiveness. Ask any fourth grade teacher how much arithmetic knowledge is used in their class, versus understanding when to take a break, when to lecture, or when to engage in an exercise. The experienced instructor knows how long the attention span of a number of adults can be stretched and when to take a break, initiate a discussion, or start a class exercise.

The degree to which all of these assumptions are true will govern the effectiveness of instructor-led training, more so than in other self-paced options. When students are unlikely to be able to devote uninterrupted time and attention to the class, they would be better served by taking the training at a different time, and possibly in a self-paced manner.

A very desirable *side effect* of classroom training is the potential for networking that is triggered when individuals from different parts of the organization find themselves in close contact for the duration of a class. Exchanging experiences, getting to know the realities of other departments and how they connect to their own, and *venting* opportunities can all contribute to creating a stronger community among the participants, and can potentially trigger bursts of unexpected, transversal collaboration across departments. Depending on the subject matter, it is often a good idea to shift one's thinking from *side-effect* to *planned-effect* as part of the design of knowledge transfer. In other words, anticipate and plan for significant learning *between* students. One way to encourage this is to start the session off by letting participants introduce each other, intentionally including a piece on how long they've been a project manager. Keep a running tab of the number of years of experience. You can then thank everyone for their introductions and mention that you noticed that there were three centuries of experience right here in this room—and remind people that they themselves are a huge resource not only to each other, but to you personally, as an instructor, and for future iterations of this course!

Depending on the situation, these classroom events can be enriched by inviting a local leader to join the class for a quick greeting and inspirational talk. For project managers who are often on the front line of corporate projects managing customer relationships and critical deliveries, these opportunities can provide much needed exposure to their leadership and positive reinforcement of how much the organization values their commitment to professional development.

In conclusion, both classroom and virtual options are expensive to the organization, not just for the cost of the trainer, the content, and related administrative components (enrollment, tracking, logistics, travel, etc.), but also for the time of each individual student. The benefits of formal training include structured, predictable content, delivered by a professional instructor, and remarkable opportunities for networking, dialogue, and personal growth.

Cloud-based Training

Self-paced courses are very popular in many contexts. They have well-proven, structured content; are reasonably priced compared to instructor-led training; and because they are self-paced, the student can take the course when they are more likely to have the time to focus on it rather than attempting to multitask during an instructor-led class.

In our experience, the most effective approach to a self-paced course is to provide context by requiring completion of prerequisite training prior to starting the course (we call this *pre-work*)—or to include at the beginning of the course a demonstration of the basic skills around topics that will be explored in more detail later in the course. With time at a premium, a busy project manager has few opportunities to learn in a more structured way, and has difficulty keeping up with the latest versions of common tools, processes, and techniques. Having the option available of taking some courses on a long train commute to site or a flight to a customer location can make the difference between feeling isolated, *out of shape*, and out of touch, and of being up to speed with the latest version of a tool or process.

The two most common approaches to these learning experiences are:

- Web-based: streaming from a learning site (in the *cloud*) to which students are granted access; and
- Computer-based: students install an application that allows them to *play* the course on their computer, laptop, or mobile device, and then can download from the *cloud* one or more courses available from the learning provider.

While the first option is better suited for students planning to take the courses from the office, or from a location with a high-speed internet connection, the second type is a better choice if the students are on the go and can't rely on a stable, high-speed connection. For our purposes, we will use the terms cloud-based, web-based, computer-based, or self-paced interchangeably, unless noted otherwise.

In some cases, if the organization subscribes to online e-learning services, project managers can even follow a comprehensive curriculum to improve on several new technologies, or to learn about related professional topics, such as business analysis and financial acumen, that are becoming more and more relevant in PM. Cost to the organization is limited compared to instructor-led courses, and the project manager can decide when it makes sense for them to take the courses: during project downtime, while no firefighting is required to manage a crisis, or while the customer is focusing on nonproject-related activities. The project managers perceive availability of these opportunities as a positive, empowering signal from the organization, which demonstrates trust (*we know you will choose the courses you need to get better at your job*) and empowerment (*you determine the areas in which you want to develop yourself and have the means to pursue them*). Specific topics related to organizational processes, templates, and so on, can also be conveyed using cloud-based courses to maintain a dynamic connection to the organization, even when the project managers have to stay away from the office.

A common complaint about prepackaged courses is the lack of opportunity for the students to ask questions. To help address this concern, you can set up a *frequently asked questions* (FAQ) file associated to each critical web-based or computer-based course you expect them to take to assist students with the most common questions. You can gather these questions from pilot offerings of the course, followed by either a mailbox for students to address questions, or a live *questions and answers* (Q&A) session. These FAQ files can address a large number of questions, but typically are insufficient for students to gain confidence on the topic. That's why we recommend these courses to be supported by live Q&A sessions, or to be used as prerequisite training, followed by opportunities to dialogue with an expert or an instructor with experience in your organization's practices.

Let's say you want to roll out a new process for managing projects, with checklists, gates, artifacts, and templates. Instructor-led training for all project managers would be the best option, but it would just cost too much for all your project managers to be trained by an instructor, travel to the training sites, and take time away from their day-to-day jobs. As the new process needs to be used in the organization very soon, you can't afford to delay training to a time that is convenient for all your project managers or until you have the budget for instructor-led courses. You can get an initial group of project managers to serve as a friendly audience to a course that has been designed to train the PM community on this new process. They can provide feedback to help you improve content and delivery of a self-paced course—and provide material for FAQ files as well. In a situation similar to the one described here, we have combined a voluntary registration system for project managers to enroll in self-paced training, a dedicated mailbox shared by a group of experts to use for clarifications or quick questions, and weekly Q&A calls that are regularly scheduled and available to all students who want to ask more complex questions. The experts who managed the calls would take turns facilitating each call (on a round-robin type of roster). Most of the time they would just bring up the conference bridge and work on other tasks until one or more project managers joined the bridge to ask for clarifications. Project managers felt comfortable that there would be a way to address their concerns should they get stuck on a difficult concept, and the organization benefited from professionally developed, self-paced courseware from a well-known learning vendor—simple, economical, and effective.

KNOWLEDGE TRANSFER

As in many aspects of planning, one size does not always fit all situations. Sometimes, formal training is only the starting point of a *series* of learning opportunities for your target audience.

You will see illustrated in Table 4.2 some situations in which prepackaged training, with standard content, can be enhanced by additional activities that will help solidify and improve the learning experience.

If you plan to establish a continuous learning environment, it is essential to foster ongoing knowledge transfer in your organization.

Table 4.2   Enhance formal training

When Topic Is . . .	. . . For Example	Complement Formal Training With . . .
Technical	A tool	Hands-on practice with a peer
	A process	A set of sample artifacts from the process
	A product overview	A Q&A session with a product manager
Leadership	Conflict resolution	A roundtable with a senior project manager
	Effective communication	An industry event with local PMI (Project Management Institute) chapter

In our experience, people are more likely to learn from someone whom they trust and consider an expert in that field. Sometimes, instructors who are external to the organization are not fully credible because *we don't really do things this way around here*—no matter what stellar credentials these instructors might have. This is especially true for those topics that have a profound impact in the way project managers operate every day.

In cases such as these, knowledge transfer events—from a one-day workshop to a week-long training session led by internal, experienced, respected colleagues—are the key to reaching your audience.

This approach offers advantages from both the student's perspective, by delivering training in a credible environment, and the trainer's perspective, by acknowledging their expertise in that field. Often, for reasons tied to cost-cutting measures, there is not enough recognition for those with experience and willingness to share what they have learned. By valuing and showcasing people with knowledge, the organization is sending a very powerful message to the students: our culture is based on respecting, valuing, and rewarding expertise. In the reverse, when the organization laments the need for training and related expense, it associates a strong negative connotation to learning; even when faced with lack of knowledge in a topic, project managers will be reluctant to request training in that area.

Fostering and promoting knowledge transfer is a simple yet effective way to either reinforce or trigger changes in your organizational culture so that learning is woven into the fabric of your project teams and your PM community.

Table 4.3 shows some examples of learning opportunities that can be set up for your PM community at relatively low cost—leveraging internal

Table 4.3 Set up continuous learning opportunities

Target Project Managers	Frequency	Topic	Opportunity
Product line or solution specific	Weekly—15 minute call	Consult on project issues	Expert or senior project manager touchpoint
	Monthly—1-hour call	Share lessons learned from similar projects	Roundtables with peers and expert
	Ad hoc—e-mail	Learning requirements, new requests, and updates	PMO or project manager training team
All project managers	Quarterly	Soft skills, leadership	Lunch and learn
	Quarterly	Business readout	Market touchpoint
	Yearly	Industry trends, organization's success stories	PM symposium

resources such as e-mail, conference bridges, desktop sharing applications, and experienced project managers.

We have found the use of webcasts (recorded presentations using slides and voice-over or video recordings of live events) particularly helpful in engaging project managers. Even those with the busiest schedule were able to catch up on a course or peer presentation that they could not join in real time. Although it takes a significant amount of time to prepare, record, and distribute these courses, there is also an inherent value attained for those who assemble and *perform* these programs. They perceive themselves as active contributors to the PM community and acknowledged experts in their field, while the organization clearly demonstrates how their expertise is valued.

Project Manager to Project Manager Sessions (Converting Tacit to Explicit Knowledge)

Here are some examples and ideas on how to set up knowledge transfer successfully.

A group of project managers who had known each other for some time and were operating in different organizations shared a sense of frustration about the fact that their hard-earned Project Management Professional (PMP)® credentials could not be easily maintained, as they were all too busy to sign up for all the needed publicly available courses or conferences. In some cases, they just felt that they were being inundated with dull, routine training options for professional development units (PDUs) by their constantly restructuring PMO. They decided to take matters into their own hands, and after a brief consultation with respective managers, they set up a volunteer-based project manager team who met once a month, during their lunch break, to plan PDU-generating activities for the company's PM community. They started out by planning *roundtables* on common pain points: risk management, schedule management, and stakeholder management. They asked some of the more experienced project managers to present at the roundtables while one of the volunteers would facilitate logistics, take questions, and overall coordinate the roundtable. The initiative had such success that requests for topics started to pour in from the PM community, first on generic PM knowledge areas that were applicable to both development and delivery project managers, then later to very specific technologies—even participation in industry events and readouts from conferences became topics for these roundtables. The line managers started to add these events to the project managers' development plans, and those project managers presenting at the roundtables had management recognition for their efforts. Eventually, the volunteer-based program became part of the company's training strategy for the PM community—strengthening the corporate culture around ongoing PM competency development.

Roundtables are just one example of project manager to project manager sessions. We have found them more effective when there is a new process or technology, requiring a high-level introduction to the PM community, and in the situation in which a successful project should be showcased—maybe in preparation (as a dry run with a friendly audience) for a more formal presentation to senior management.

One more advantage of roundtables is that they can be set up both in person, for those PM communities that are co-located, or via conference calls. This last method has proven to be economical for organizations that are geographically dispersed, and also an enabler for those project managers who were not comfortable presenting to a face-to-face audience or asking questions in public. Table 4.4 has a checklist you can use to set up your own roundtables.

Other examples include engaging a senior PM for specific types of projects, during which a project manager who is new to a technology or to some aspects of a project can benefit from a quick consultation with a project manager who has worked on those projects in the past. This is

Table 4.4　Checklist for roundtable events

Item	Description	Who owns it?	When is it needed?
1	Set up standard logistics (bridge, sign up, recording)	PM facilitators' team (PMFT)	4 weeks before event
2	Decide on topic for the roundtable	Initially the PMFT (push), later the participants (pull)	4 weeks before event
3	Find the right speaker	PMFT	3 weeks before event
4	Send out notice and logistics	Event facilitator	3 weeks before event
5	Promote event	PMFT	3 weeks before event
6	Dry run with speaker	Event facilitator	1 week before event
7	Send reminder to project managers	Event facilitator	4 days before event
8	Hold roundtable	Event facilitator	Event day
9	Record event, collect questions via e-mail/IM, keep time, moderate Q&A, convey e-mail/IM questions	Event facilitator	Event day
10	Send thank you note to speaker (cc: manager)	PMFT	Day after event
11	Collect event artifacts (slides, Q&A file, recording, etc.) on PMFT website	Event facilitator	Week after the event
12	Send link to event artifacts to project managers, poll for new topic	PMFT	1 week after event

what we call *converting tacit knowledge into explicit knowledge*. The senior project manager knows how to deal with that specific type of project, having managed it in the (possibly very recent) past. Even when using lessons-learned databases, not all of that tacit knowledge can be collected efficiently. A touchpoint to answer questions or give pointers translates this wealth of experience into explicit, shared knowledge. Having a 15–20 minute window on a weekly basis blocked in both calendars, even at the end of the day or at any other time that is convenient to both project managers, can provide a welcome opportunity to ask those questions that a project manager would be hard-pressed to ask others in the project team.

However, for this approach to work, there needs to be an implicit trust and sense of *safe space* between the project manager and the expert. If the project manager does not know the senior project manager or does not feel comfortable sharing what can be perceived as a weakness, then there is no point in proposing this option.

So—how do you *build* trust in the PM community? This is a sensitive topic as job security is a major imperative in most employees' minds these days. If a project manager is perceived as an expert in one field, and thus consulted by a peer on a type of project they have worked on earlier, then she/he might not feel protective when interacting with an expert on a new type of project. In other words, when consulting one's peers is part of the organizational norm, and it is done routinely as a part of every project manager's job, then it is unlikely to trigger defensive reactions. Thus, we are back to the importance of *establishing* a culture of continuous learning in the organization.

PM Symposium

Another format for knowledge transfer is the use of a major event, such as a PM symposium, in which guest speakers, both internal to the organization and/or external, address a focused set of topics aligned with a theme that has been chosen for that event. The symposium can be a face-to-face organizational or corporate event; once again reinforcing the appreciation of the importance of a continuous learning culture that the organization recognizes for both the profession of PM and the continuous development of their project managers. It could also be organized as a completely virtual experience, in which recorded interviews or presentations are shared as webcasts on a dedicated webpage for self-paced perusal from the PM community. Either way, it offers a tremendous opportunity to expand the knowledge base in the PM community:

- Showcase successful projects that have been completed without a need for escalation, firefighting, or crisis management. Management often pays more attention to projects that have required extensive *rescue* operations and escalation. Sure, the *squeaky wheel gets the grease*, but that should not preclude public appreciation and recognition for those projects that have been well managed and conducted with professionalism. What has the project manager done differently in *these* projects to effectively manage risks and issues? How were the organizational processes leveraged or improved by the project manager? Can we catch *lightning in a bottle* and duplicate this practice elsewhere?

- Invite external speakers, for example, from your local PMI chapter or from a vendor, to share their experience and knowledge on a particular topic related to the symposium theme. Sometimes, these could be very powerful insights from the industry to ground the PM community in best practices and new techniques developed outside of the organization.
- Invite PMO leaders or organizational executives to share their vision and plans for the future of the PM community in the organization. It can be energizing to hear leadership endorsement of the project managers, their best practices, and their tools—and how they fit into the future of the organization.

Especially when organized as a yearly event, a symposium can frame the evolution of the PM community into higher levels of maturity. While a young community might want to focus on the basics of PM, a more established population might benefit from advanced tools and techniques of, say, a specific knowledge area.

When a PM symposium is tied to an industry event, such as International Project Management Day, it also serves as an additional connection between the project managers in your organization and a wider community, with all the benefits of a much larger network of professionals.

 If your organization does not have critical mass for such an event, consider joining forces with other communities to which you might connect via local chapters of PMI or the International Project Management Association (IPMA)—the diversity in topics and perspectives can benefit all involved.

Lessons Learned

This is an aspect of competency development that, in theory, finds everybody aligned. Certainly we need to make use of the painful lessons we have learned while delivering projects. There is no doubt that, having found a very effective way to manage some aspects of project planning or execution, we would want to ensure that all project managers take advantage of it. Shouldn't we collect all of these precious (and hard-earned) lessons in a database so that all project managers can access them and benefit from this wealth of information? In reality, many factors intervene in making this one of the most difficult areas in which organizations struggle. Following are some typical comments we have heard, over and over, and across many organizations:

- *It is difficult to find, among all these entries, something that is applicable to my project.*
- *It might have worked for them, but we are different.*
- *My customer would never agree to that solution.*

Sound familiar? If it is any consolation, you are not alone: this is one of the most difficult areas to implement successfully in a PM community, despite being, obviously, extremely important—and supported by all professional associations and methodologies.

Well, the good news is that there are many ways to make sure that your organization benefits from what you learn during project delivery. First of all, your *internal PM processes* can be improved to leverage what has proven to be disastrous, by ensuring it does not happen again, or beneficial, by making it easier to replicate. In support of these processes, the *templates and checklists* can also reflect what has been learned during project planning, execution, and control. So, without having to refer to a database, your project managers will be using lessons learned from past projects.

One of the techniques successfully used to leverage knowledge for specific types of projects is the development of *handbooks*. These are collections of reusable wisdom that are applicable to certain types of projects. For example, for information technology (IT) projects that impact a large user group, there might be proven communication methods that have been effective in the past, and should be reused in the future on similar projects. Or user training approaches that work better for projects deploying a particular technology. When the organization sponsoring a type of project also sponsors the development of a dedicated handbook for managing these projects, they can also provide support, in terms of resources and expertise, to ensure the handbooks contain all the most recent lessons collected during project closure.

Table 4.5 Lessons learned databases

Database attribute	What doesn't work	What works
Launching	PMO launches the initiative as part of organizational process	Senior management sponsors and requires using the database as part of project closure
Format	Flat "story" file	Tags, labels, anything that can facilitate searches
Interface	10+ fields to fill up before getting to the actual entry	Reduced number of fields (no more than 5–8) to capture key elements used for search and retrieval
Ongoing	Assuming that what has started will continue on its own	Continuing to monitor and acknowledge ("lesson learned of the month" for example) entry of lessons learned, check if there is a decline in number of entries
Use	Lessons learned in database is just an item in the project closure checklist	Lessons learned are an item in the project launch checklist as well as in the project closure checklist, and senior management comments on their uses on all-hands calls

Naturally, a real *database*—indexed by topic, tags, key words, and so on—is a way to ensure lessons learned are accessible to the vast majority of project managers. Some of our own learnings with regard to these databases are listed in Table 4.5. You can implement a useful database as long as it is introduced as an element of your PM process and it gets the recognition and acknowledgment it requires to become part of the organizational culture.

Podcasts, Blogs, and Social Media for Business

From radio stations to newspapers and individuals, podcasts, blogs, and social media have become a common method to reach out to increasingly diverse audiences. Anyone with an opinion and a laptop can share their thoughts and be heard. So why not use this to improve knowledge sharing within your PM community? Project managers need to communicate more than anyone else in the project team. By encouraging the use of the latest communications techniques, you are already helping and inspiring those project managers who are not yet fully versed in these powerful tools.

We have seen many large corporations introduce social media in the professional environment in which their employees operate. Corporate versions of Jive, Yammer, or other platforms that are deployed as part of the corporate intranet allow employees to collaborate and share both professional and personal interests.

We have successfully used dedicated *PM-focused groups*, set up in the corporate social media platform, to communicate and share experiences with other project managers in the organization. Key contributors to the group can be PMO leaders, competency development managers, or simply any project manager in the community. Senior project managers can use this forum as a way to support other project managers or blog about their experience. The PMO can share trends, new course availability, handbooks, new techniques and tools, and even advertise events such as roundtables and internal seminars. Project managers can ask around for expertise or artifacts in certain areas and identify experts for consultations. Celebrations at project closure can be shared with the whole community by posting (professionally appropriate) pictures in the group page. In addition to knowledge sharing, a social media group can be used for online surveys, podcasts, blogs, and interviews to *project-of-the-month* project managers. Even debriefing from participation in industry events or vendor classes can be broadcast online so the organization's investment in sponsoring them can have a larger return.

As a side note, it is essential to moderate content that is posted for the group, as well as comments and questions, to ensure that at all times, the social group maintains a professional image for the benefit of all the project managers, and that basic principles of data privacy are respected at all times.

No social media in your organization? No problem: a *PM community webpage or SharePoint site* can be set up by the PMO, for example, and dedicated to the advancement and improvement of the PM community; and will work just as well. Commonly available features for the webpage—such as announcements, event calendars, questions, and documents—can be used to share trends, events, and even request support/mentorship from other project managers.

A mailbox managed by the PMO or competency development manager can collect materials for the webpage or, if available on the page, project managers can directly post requests, artifacts, and announcements. Once again, moderators are recommended to stimulate interaction, and of course, to ensure the tone remains constructive and professional.

So, do you just set up a nice group on your corporate social media platform or procure a professionally designed webpage where your project managers start happily contributing for the benefit of all? You might try that, but we have seen similar *sunny-day scenarios* fail for lack of interest, time, and willingness to be engaged. Why would a project manager expose their lack of knowledge by publicly asking (horror!) questions on how to do their job? Why would they even want to spend three clicks to check out a new webcast on scheduling? The only scenarios in which we have obtained real engagement in the community have been those in which the project managers—who were directly invited by the group/page moderator to join the group—had previously established a relationship with at least some of the other participants. When project managers did not know who else was contributing to the group, they did not join into the conversations or truly take advantage of the opportunities it offered.

For smaller organizations, a simple newsletter, sent periodically to the PM community via e-mail, can convey the same information. As long as there is a way to share news, learning opportunities, successes, and requests for support, the objective of this method is obtained.

The project managers know they are part of a community where participants learn from each other, rely on each other for support, share their accomplishments, and celebrate success.

Mentoring Programs

This is another way to transfer knowledge that makes perfect sense—in theory. Naturally, one would think that any professional would treasure the opportunity to have a mentor, a more experienced person, either inside or, better yet, outside of the organization, who could be a sounding board and provide pointers or insights to improve their professional life. Even more so in the case of a project manager with the need to exercise authority with the project team without any real power. Advice and support from a more experienced project manager would make perfect sense. In the reverse, what better way to showcase one's expertise than to share it with a mentee who could benefit from your years of hard-earned knowledge. Alas, reality has proven over and over that establishing and sustaining a formal mentoring program has a low likelihood of success. Regardless of the size and geographical diversity of the organization, mentoring programs require clarity of vision, focused goals, and leadership support. There is plenty of literature on how to set up such programs, but much less on why and how they fail. This is in part due to the fact that organizations do not like to advertise their failed attempts at truly effective mentoring programs, but also because it really is unlikely that expectations around a mentoring relationship can be institutionalized successfully on a large scale and for a sustainable period of time. Most of us think of a *mentor* as an avuncular figure with common interests and who can see in the mentee *something of themselves* at that age or stage in their career. Realistically, this type of event either happens or does not— depending on circumstances, personalities, and serendipity, regardless of the organizational attempts at triggering it. What *can* be triggered by the organization is a focused opportunity to discuss career choices, or job roadblocks, with another professional. Both individuals have elected to participate in a program that is sponsored by the organization's leadership and to support individual growth via career counseling provided by other individuals in the organization—possibly as a part of their own professional development plan. For example, a senior project manager candidate might have to coach or mentor a junior project manager to attain senior project manager credentials.

Again, clear scope, expectations, and time frames are key elements for this program to be successful beyond the first few months of inception.

Games and Simulations

Have you ever used games or flash cards to learn particularly *dry* material for an exam? Engaging on apparent diversions, like games and invented scenarios, can help *digest* even the stuffiest topics. You could use game-based learning to introduce new PM processes and checklists, for example.

When playing tic-tac-toe reveals to the winner the name of a new process gate and related checklist, project managers might actually smile instead of lamenting the new process and building resistance to change.

ABOVE AND BEYOND

An organization was launching a new solution that used the latest technology and had to be delivered with a high level of customization to clients around the world. Reduced time-to-service and competition-driven timelines made it very difficult for the project managers to get up to speed with the development cycles, the trouble ticket resolution approach, and the lack of established relationships between the project managers and the development organizations that is often required for them to address customers' concerns in a timely manner. While training boot camps for technical knowledge transfers had been prepared and launched, the PM community was running behind, and often was not able to keep up with the technical team on key areas for project delivery.

Formal overview courses had been delivered via classroom and self-paced classes, but the project managers were still not quite comfortable with managing these projects. The PMO competency development leader (referred to from now on as *the PMO*) devised an approach that used all of the techniques described in this chapter to turn things around.

First of all, she worked with both an experienced project manager in the field and an expert in the development organization about key areas that were perceived as gaps in what the project managers needed to know and what the project managers seemed not to understand. More organizations were later engaged to understand the full extent of the disconnect between the project managers in project delivery and the teams providing the solution. Table 4.6 summarizes initial findings for this gap analysis.

While the gap analysis was proceeding, the PMO reached out to the regional units and asked that project managers for critical projects in each region be nominated for participation in a week-long, face-to-face workshop. Dates for three such workshops were set up, and the individual participants, nominated by the local organizations, were identified. The PMO requested that all candidates for the workshop complete a series of prerequisite online classes to make sure all participants had basic knowledge about the technology to be discussed.

Table 4.6   Gap analysis for competency development

Source	Perceived gap
Expert project manager	• Development does not respond to our queries in a timely manner • We have no way to expedite a feature needed by our client • Delivery of equipment is not predictable • We do not know who to contact for questions or artifacts • Support from development is difficult to obtain • Road map is not clear for the solution and the next releases
Development guru	• Project managers expect us to drop anything we are doing to answer them • We work mostly in a time zone incompatible with the project managers • Our release management process has its own gates and timing • We get the same question ten times from different project managers
Marketing	• Project managers do not advocate our road map adequately
Supply chain	• Factories require reliable estimates of what/when equipment is needed • Third-party products need to be planned based on forecast
Individual project managers	• Specific areas of concern tied to their client • Additional areas of concern that could be generalized for all project managers

After drafting a basic agenda for the workshop, based on the gap analysis, the PMO started a series of one-on-one interviews with the participants of the first session. Each call started with a brief introduction to establish the PMO's credibility. Having worked as a project manager herself, she wanted to make sure the project managers understood that she knew what it felt like to be in front of the client with no safety net and a tight timetable to deliver. Then she would discuss the draft agenda, previously shared with the project manager, and ask for confirmation of the topics (*are these really your pain points?*) as well as any additional areas with which the project manager was concerned. Based on the outcome of the interviews, the draft agenda was expanded to include those additional topics of general interest, and a few breakaway sessions planned for those items the participants wanted to cover but would not interest other project managers. Each participant was asked to prepare one introductory slide so that other participants and the workshop speakers would know who worked where, and with which client.

For each topic, the PMO identified an expert speaker—from marketing to supply chain, from development to field support—who could talk about that specific area. The PMO recommended all participants book rooms in the same hotel so that people would be able to socialize on their way to and from the office. A local executive was contacted to provide a quick kickoff and clear leadership endorsement. Calendars and planets thus aligned, the first workshop was launched with a 7 a.m. to 6 p.m. agenda, lab visits, team dinner, meet-the-speakers breakfast, and specialized sessions. A half day was reserved to discuss any additional topics that would emerge during the workshop so that there would be no question left unanswered by the time the participants left.

All critical areas were covered—the project managers had been able to see the *big* picture; had networked with the individuals and managers who could provide critical support; had a clear understanding of the release life cycle, escalation path, and road map; and could finally manage their projects with clarity. Conversely, development and other organizations had heard firsthand the issues faced onsite, along with the questions from the customers. They were able to agree on single point of contact individuals who could quickly address site concerns—and yes, even join on the last day of the workshop a dedicated online community for project manager support in this technology. The group was formed by individuals (project managers and speakers) who had shared long days, questions, answers, dinners, and car rides—and could now see some light, midway through the tunnel. They had built trust and could share, ask, and contribute; it was a natural extension of what had been built during the workshop. A similar pattern was followed for the two subsequent workshops, and the resulting online group grew to become a very effective tool for knowledge sharing. A project manager would ask at the end of their day if anyone could help provide a response to their client on a certain topic, and by the time he started work in the morning, a colleague from the other side of the world had shared an artifact that had helped her answer a similar request from her client.

This was a relatively expensive exercise with project managers traveling to the workshop location and spending a whole week away from their projects, the preparation time from the PMO, and the speakers' time. The benefits, however, far outweighed the cost to the organization: efficiency in delivery, confidence in managing the projects, better risk management, and faster response to the clients.

Many of the techniques described in this chapter were used to reach this result. Leveraging on the advantages and strengths of both formal training, peer-to-peer knowledge sharing, expert consultation, and on-line collaboration, a difficult situation for the PM community was transformed into an opportunity to showcase cross-organizational teamwork.

Industry Engagement

How many of your project managers are part of a professional organization, such as PMI or IPMA, which fosters and promotes the PM profession? What percentage of them holds a professional credential as a project manager?

Exposure to industry standards is very beneficial to the project managers in any organization so that they can see beyond the immediate day-to-day horizon. Whether as a part of a local chapter, or by volunteering their PM skills to the local food pantry, by taking a professional accreditation exam or by listening to a PM podcast, project managers can and should give back to the industry using their talents and knowledge. In turn, they do acquire a higher appreciation and knowledge of the profession, which can be used on the job.

Joining LinkedIn interest groups, for example, could support and expand the project manager's engagement in industry best practices, as well as provide ideas on how to manage day-to-day scenarios.

Community Outreach

An organization had limited funding available to contribute to community initiatives so the PMO proposed to ask for any volunteer project managers who would help plan and build a playground. Over the course of a few weekends, volunteer project managers were able to sit down with a representative from the township, identify a likely spot, get permissions, and plan the playground. They leveraged a nonprofit organization with a proven record of successful playground construction to get some key principles and construction guidelines, and also held fund-raisers at the office for materials. It was a fun activity that built team spirit in project managers who were otherwise engaged in different areas of the organization. Each project manager felt energized and proud to use their skills for the benefit of their community.

Other examples that come to mind are of project managers who teach in local colleges, often running between meetings and grading student papers, to show how PM can increase young adults' chances to get a job.

So, what does the organization gain from community outreach? The answer is a more balanced PM community, whose individuals can go beyond the confines of their job and increase the overall contribution of the entire organization to the community in which it operates.

Planning Your Bridges

We have discussed goals, strategies, and tactical options for your specific project management (PM) community. You might have noticed how much time we are spending on getting ready to plan the activities that will achieve your goals. Without proper reflection, careful decisions, and consideration—or in other words without adequate *readiness*—we have found out (the hard way) that the best laid competency development plans often go astray. This is due to the fact that we are planning a series of cultural changes in the way both the project managers and the organization manage competency development, and such changes require a deep understanding of organization, the project managers, and your current culture.

In a continuous learning environment, the project managers work in a culture that recognizes and promotes improvement in their professional skills, attitudes, and knowledge, and they drive their own competency development on an ongoing basis.

And what enables us to deliver procedural, organizational, and operational change, if not a *project*?

READINESS

It is widely acknowledged that well-managed projects have extensive planning phases. The better, more comprehensive the plan, the smoother the execution of the project (at least until one of Murphy's many laws or corollaries intervenes). Planning is the time for estimating, for consulting the experts, and for listening to lessons learned by those who have traveled similar roads before us. Any changes in fundamental starting assumptions, scope, project team composition, and other key elements of the project are best identified as early as possible to contain impact on the project costs and schedule.

Extensive readiness activities, such as the ones described in Chapters 1 through 4, are needed to ensure that planning is effective. Just as knowing the *lay of the land* is a necessary step in planning where to best build physical bridges to take vehicles across a river, the same level of forethought is needed to plan your competency bridge to get to the required competency levels and beyond. And we are using the plural—bridges—because you might have to plan on multiple stages to achieve your vision.

In Table 5.1, you can see a list of high-level planning elements developed during the readiness period; they provide the foundation to actual planning. We have included sample data to illustrate what we mean by each planning element. A template for you to use can be found in the Web Added Value (WAV)™ section of the J. Ross Publishing website at https://www.jrosspub.com/wav/.

Identifying your high-level phases, goals, and time frames helps in building an overall plan. With phases and short-term measurable goals, you can focus activities on achieving visible gains, which will show progress to senior management and build credibility in your PM community while pursuing your long-term goals of continuous competency development.

The amount of *change intelligence* (refer to Barbara Trautlein's Change Quotient in Appendix 1) in the organization needs to be accounted for in your plans: the extent of the cultural changes you need and how long the time frame is to implement them; how adaptable your project managers are; and even more important, how agile and ready to deliver change your senior management is.

You and your leadership team are the only ones who can determine which *measurable, time-bound, achievable* goals will allow you to reach your end vision. This is where lean quality improvement techniques can help optimize how to break down your initial problem statement (projects are delivered late, for example) into organized, structured process flows (achieve basic competency in 70% of the project managers with a supporting project management office [PMO], for example). The financial business impact for each phase can be considerable and should be quantified to justify continued sponsorship.

Table 5.1   Planning elements: high-level view

Planning Element	Example
Vision	Competency in basic PM for all IT (information technology) projects
Target audience	Gen X
Technical heritage	High: most project managers have technical competencies
Level of PM maturity	Low: projects leverage resources from multiple departments
Phase approach	Hybrid: each phase is a project with a defined scope, managed leveraging agile methodology
Measurable goal Phase 1	Establish PM support infrastructure: 70% of project managers know where/how to contact PMO
Duration Phase 1	Six months
Strategic approach Phase 1	Set up PMO and PM community
Tactical options	Focused Program Office PM blog Online coaching support Virtual roundtables
Measurable goal Phase 2	70% of project managers have industry credentials
Duration Phase 2	18 months
Strategic approach Phase 2	Build a project manager career path in the organization that leverages Project Management Professional (PMP)® and/or PRINCE2 credentials
Tactical options	Project manager job categories defined with human resources (HR), including perks PMP/PRINCE2 courses available Virtual PMP/PRINCE2 study groups PM symposium PMP/PRINCE2 recognition from chief information officer during town hall meetings

SPONSORS

You do need executive sponsorship—a senior manager who is willing to invest in building these bridges and who will support the effort to establish the necessary organizational culture—a champion to ensure this is not an expensive exercise with minimal lasting effects on the competency of your project managers.

It is not possible to proceed with any serious planning unless senior management is fully behind you. Just like investors are needed when building a new enterprise, you will need a senior manager to send a consistent and persistent message of urgency, importance, and priority associated with improving project managers' competency. You will need a senior manager to grant you authority and enable you to move on with your plan. In other words, to provide the *executive capital* for your venture.

Why? Because this is an effort that requires commitment, continuous engagement, and willingness to go beyond the *established* operational models and *business as usual* approach that afflict most organizations and prevent them from achieving the results they need to move beyond the (often inadequate) status quo.

Let's say it's the end of the quarter and all project managers are working hard to ensure that revenue is actually invoiced or target deliverables completed before the next quarter starts. It is perfectly acceptable to agree with the competency development team that training activities should not be planned during this critical period. However, on the tenth day of the new quarter, the project managers should be able to access a webinar on how to use the latest techniques to improve, for example, project risk management. Competing demands between business objectives and fostering continuous learning must be balanced to avoid stifling the organizational ability to grow its overall competence. Unless such efforts are publicly acknowledged and given recurring positive significance and import by leadership, no project manager will want to walk the extra learning mile, leap into a new tool, or invest in their own professional skills.

An executive sponsor *will* make the difference between success and failure. There is no way a competency improvement plan will deliver results if you do not have a senior enough sponsor. When a CEO or other C-level executive is the keynote speaker at your PM symposium, he or she is sending a very clear message: I think PM competency is important today and *every day* for our organization.

When experienced project managers who are sharing their knowledge and experience with other project managers are acknowledged—even praised—during a town hall meeting, all project managers will *know* how much more sharing is valued as opposed to knowledge retention. When professional credentials are recognized as an integral part of organizational advancement, then a project manager will be even more motivated to engage in their own professional development.

A project manager started to blog about her lessons learned. She published several white papers on the techniques that she discovered were actually helping her improve the quality of her projects. She did so in her spare time with the intent to give back to the profession by sharing what actually worked (or did not) for the type of projects she was managing with the PM community at large.

When her senior management blocked her participation to a major international event whose organizers had requested her contribution, she *learned* that her personal commitment to improving knowledge and competency, including paying for her own airfare and other travel expenses, was not aligned with the company's priorities. She started looking for a new job and moved out of the organization within a few months.

Who do you think missed an opportunity in this case? Hint: it was not the protagonist, participative project manager!

PHASES

We project managers know that one can achieve what seems impossibly complex by breaking it down into smaller, more manageable elements. Like a green gardener, decomposition is seemingly one of our favorite things. Using the outcome of readiness efforts, you now have a set of charters, one for each phase, with clear deliverables.

Based on what you are planning to achieve in each phase, and on what strategic/tactical approaches are best suited for your PM community, you can now focus on preparing a work breakdown structure for each of your *bridges* (or projects)—timeline and ownership, dependencies, resource planning, and risks. All the fundamental building blocks of sound PM come together to help us as we plan each phase.

Table 5.2 provides an illustration of a high-level plan for a single phase. Keep each phase contained and build a buffer in between phases so that you can verify and control the previous phase outcome before starting the next one. Chapter 7 will provide a good idea on how to identify and monitor your indicators of successful deployment. While we found it helpful to have a clear charter for each phase as part of our overall plan, we have also determined that it is better to start detailed planning for a subsequent phase when the previous phase is wrapping up. This approach allows you to leverage lessons learned, incorporate deliverables de-scoped from the earlier phase, and use the feedback obtained by the techniques

Table 5.2   Phase planning: an example

Goal Phase 1 (Six Months)	Establish Project Manager Support Infrastructure: 70% of Project Managers Know Where/How to Contact PMO	
Phase Element (How Long)	**Description**	**Who owns it?**
Focused PMO (Two months)	Consolidate current PM support functions in a single PMO—nominate PMO Director	COO (chief operating officer) Deputy
	Prepare and validate mission statement and clear objectives	PMO Director
	Select personnel with required skills: PMP, field experience, social media attitude	PMO Director
	Launch PM blog during high-visibility organizational event (e.g., town hall)	COO Deputy
PM blog or newsletter (agile approach)	Plan PM blog content and frequency of posts based on lessons learned and/or best practices from latest project deliveries	PMO Blog Leader
	Establish (propose, review, get approval) PM blog format, quick pilot with friendly users	PMO Bloggers
	Launch PM blog during same high-visibility organizational event as PMO launch	COO Deputy
Online coaching support (agile approach)	Establish project manager coaching team and website, including instant messaging capabilities; run a quick pilot with friendly users	PMO SME (subject matter expert) Leader
	Launch project manager coaching program during same high-visibility organizational event as PMO launch	COO Deputy
Virtual round-tables (agile approach)	Establish (propose, review, get approval) project manager roundtables format and content plan, leveraging blog material; run a quick pilot with friendly users	PMO Competency Development Leader
	Launch project manager roundtables during same high-visibility organizational event as PMO launch	COO Deputy

illustrated in Chapter 8. Figure 5.1 shows an example of how you can stagger your phases.

Once you have a high-level plan for each phase with a related charter and measurable targets, you can identify owners, or project managers. From this point onward, a phase is *just* a project to be delivered within the time frame established in the charter. Robust PM tools and techniques, appropriate to the scope of the project, should be used to deliver the agreed upon *measurable targets*.

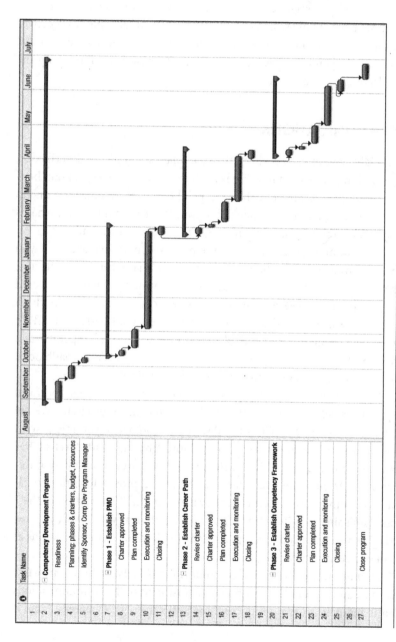

Figure 5.1   Example of a high-level schedule for a competency development program

Based on the organization, its culture, and its composition (your target audience) you might decide to use an agile approach instead of a waterfall sequence of phases. When the overall quantifiable phase objectives are met and you can verify they are actually part of the organizational culture, then you can proceed with the next phase and move along the path leading to your vision.

COMMUNICATIONS

You might have already realized that the *collection of phases* described so far is nothing more (and nothing less) than a program. The program benefit is an improved project delivery capability for the organization due to an overall increase in competency for your PM community. And what is more important for a program manager than communication?

The communications plan for the program must leverage what you have determined during the readiness phase so that it can be an effective *instrument of cultural change.* Make the most of what you have discovered during *readiness* by identifying the most effective methods to reach all of your audience: from the sponsor to the project managers, from HR to senior management. They will all need to know what is happening and why; they'll need to be kept up to date on achievements and roadblocks, and what is expected of them as this program evolves.

Table 5.3 shows an example of the type of analysis you can perform to prepare a solid communications plan for the entire program. We are showing an age-based split of the PM population, while you might want to approach this analysis based on technical background, level of PM maturity, or organizational role. In any case, it is worth performing this analysis as its outcome will determine the best approach to communication. As in other cases, a template is available in the WAV section of the J. Ross Publishing website at https://www.jrosspub.com/wav/. With a mixed audience, you will need to adopt as many methods of communications as needed to reach every group.

Finding an effective mix of communications tools might require a few attempts, and a periodic revision and adjustment of the communications plan is required to ensure its continued effectiveness. Chapters 7 and 8

Table 5.3   Communications plan—example of age-group based audience analysis

Audience	Listening Aptitude	What communication style is likely to work?
Baby Boomers	Receptive to formal/ informal communication from senior management	In person using an open, direct style Present options (flexibility) Answer questions thoroughly and expect to be pressed for details Avoid manipulative/controlling language Like the personal touch from managers Get consensus; include them or they may get offended Establish a friendly rapport Emphasize company's vision and mission and how they can fit in
Gen X	Expecting evidence that there really is a competency development gap	Blunt/Direct and immediate style; present facts Use e-mail as #1 tool Learn their language and speak it Share info immediately and often Tie your message to "results" Emphasize "WIIFM" (What's In It For Me) in terms of training and skills to build their resume
Millennials	Peers play a key role in spreading information and ensuring its credibility. Blogs, social media, and online collaboration are enablers and used daily to share, learn, and plan	Use positive, respectful, motivational, electronic communication style Communicate in person if the message is very important Use e-mail and voice mail as #1 tools Use action verbs Be positive Options, options, options! Prefer to learn in networks; teams use multimedia while being entertained and excited

talk about this and other sorts of adjustments you will need for this to be a continuously improving program. So make sure your plans include regular pulse checks, scheduled revisions, and approach updates. Some of the options discussed in Chapter 4 can be effective ways to launch, report on progress, and celebrate the accomplishments of each project.

An organization had a target increase of industry-recognized certifications for their PM community to improve their overall project success rate. The PMO, among other pertinent activities, planned a yearly PM symposium on International PM Day, the first Thursday in November (refer to Saladis in Appendix 1), which was advertised in the company's newsletter and was open to all project managers, even those in other organizations. The symposium had a dual purpose: to celebrate both the PM community across all organizations, thus recognizing the importance of PM for the entire company's success, and to inspire project managers to continue investing in their own development by learning something new about project management from industry speakers and/or by presenting at the symposium themselves.

The keynote speakers were selected each year from within the company's senior management so that they would promote and support the objectives for that year. The first year they launched a new professional accreditation path in the organization that would require industry credentials to advance the careers of those project managers who achieved specific PM goals. While the focus was on career development opportunities, the organization also made it clear that solid, industry-recognized PM skills played a key role in organizational advancement.

There were internal speakers from HR, illustrating the new career development path, and from the PM community, describing the way in which their projects had been delivered successfully or closed early when they did not comply with the expected guidelines.

The external speakers—highly regarded professionals who donated their time and knowledge—brought into the symposium a taste of what PM is *out there*, beyond the boundaries of the organization with a focus on the theme of that year: the advancement of project managers' careers tied to improved standardization of best practices, tools, and techniques.

The event became a strong element in the communications plan—targeting project managers, senior management, and supporting organizations. It was a way for the PMO to share, in the following years, the growing number of industry certifications and career advancement achievements in the organization, as well as the financial impact that the PM community delivered as improved success in project delivery.

The International PM Day Symposium is still a yearly occurrence in this organization even after the goals of that competency development phase were achieved. It has evolved into a knowledge sharing forum, a public speaking opportunity for project managers in a friendly environment, a window into the state of the art beyond the organizational boundaries, and a way to keep up with and increase professional development units (PDUs) (which, in turn, helps the organization's PM professionals retain their certification). The symposium has become an ongoing element in the organizational culture. Table 5.4 shows a planning outline and Table 5.5 shows a sample agenda, with fictitious names, of course, of an International PM Day Symposium. Templates for both can be found in the WAV section.

Table 5.4 Planning outline example for a PM symposium

Symposium Planning Element	What does it mean?	Sample content
Style	How do you want the Symposium to be available to your audience?	• Live in person • Live online webcast • Pre-recorded webcast
Keynote	Who should be launching the Symposium?	• PMO Leader • Head of PM organization • Head of HR • CEO
Keynote topic	What is the strongest message you want to share with the audience?	• Project managers are key to company's success • Launch new accreditation program for project managers • Celebrate project managers who have industry credentials
Theme	What do you want to convey in this event?	• Project managers who have industry credentials are key to the organization's success
Title	What catch phrase do you want to use to advertise the Symposium and convey the theme?	Our projects deliver success!
Team	Who will make this happen? And what role will they play? Who will be Master of Ceremony, i.e., conduct the event?	• MC & scheduler: Mary H. • Internal speakers' coordinator: Jim K. • External speakers' coordinator: Hiroko T. • Keynote interface: Mary H. • Advertisement: Tinnelle C. • Logistics: Tinnelle C.
Timeline	What needs to happen? And when?	• Planning outline completed: June 1 • Sponsor sign off for title and theme: July 1 • Speakers lineup complete: Aug 1 • Keynote confirmed: Aug 1 • Advertisement plan ready: Aug 1 • Launch: Townhall, Aug 20 • Start Ads in newsletter: Sept 1 • Logistics lineup completed: Sept 15 • Keynote checkpoint: Oct 1 • Dry run with speakers completed: Oct 15 • Logistics dry run: Oct 20 • Keynote dry run completed: Oct 25 • Dress rehearsal: Nov 2 • Symposium: Nov 3

Table 5.5 Sample agenda for a PM symposium

Time	Topic	Speaker
9:00	Welcome	Master of Ceremony: Mary H.
9:10	Keynote: Impact of PMs in our Success	CEO
9:55	Introduction to Internal Speaker 1	Internal speakers' coordinator: Jim K.
10:00	How We Recovered a Failing Project: Lessons Learned	Kathleen S., PMP
10:40	Q&A (questions and answers) for Speaker 1 via Instant Messenger or e-mail	Internal speakers' coordinator: Jim K.
10:55	Introduction to External Speaker 1	Internal speakers' coordinator: Jianlin
11:00	Stakeholders Management: Internal and External Project Customers	Aditya F., Founder and COE of ABC Consultants
10:40	Q&A for Speaker 1 via Instant Messenger or e-mail	Internal Speakers' coordinator: Jianlin
. . .		

When this program started, it was a considerable effort to coordinate a large video-based conference call, however, with new tools such as *Skype for Business* and *WebEx*, and their built-in recording capabilities, the entire program changed. First of all, with a global company, having this scheduled at a particular time is problematic, not only due to time zone differences, but because the first Thursday of every November is often a national and/or religious holiday in several countries. Second, vendors and PMI chapters are also having International PM Day celebrations which potentially conflict with the organization's observance. On top of all of this, even if those were not problems, it's difficult to schedule any eight-hour session for a busy audience of project managers. As the new technology for online screen sharing and self-recording became available, the organization realized that the sessions could be made available at any time via replay. The *day* was still recognized, but the content became flexible, the scheduling of speakers became easily accomplished, and now the session is run as a 24×7×365 opportunity to download and play the topic of choice in a voice-over-slides format that is friendly and accessible. In fact, as we mentioned in Chapter 3, this becomes (especially for Millennials) a familiar and easy-to-use format, not unlike YouTube. This organization progressively elaborated their program based on lessons learned—you

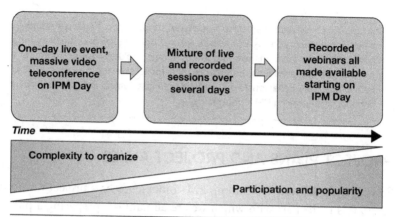

Figure 5.2   Improvement of an International PM Day event

can take advantage of that decade of lessons learned just by heeding the example. See Figure 5.2 to note the continuous improvement as this initiative moved through an entire decade. Two other notable comments:

1. The organization collected significant data from attendees via follow-up surveys, which triggered most of the changes that they made to the program, and

2. The organization realized that the speakers themselves were key stakeholders.

Thank you notes and certificates of appreciation were always sent out to the speakers, acknowledging their participation and allowing them, where appropriate, to include their contribution when they, in turn, were seeking PDUs or wanted to use this organization as a reference for other speaking opportunities.

Another example of effective communications comes from a different organization, in which the PMO established a PM competency group in the company's social networking platform that is used for artifacts publishing, blogging, and Q&A on PM tools and techniques. The target audience was the entire PM community, composed mostly of Millennials, who responded better to an approach closer to immediate collaboration postings and dialogue-based interactions, using the messaging capabilities of these websites. The deliverables from each phase, from templates to process diagrams, were published, updated, and commented on with the whole community in real time. Events such as roundtables and industry seminars were also advertised, and related materials could be shared when applicable. A PM *ask-the-expert* opportunity and other informal knowledge sharing options were added over time, including a monitored community board for questions, comments, and roundtable topic requests. All of these efforts were consciously put in place to help establish the groundwork for continuously improving PM competency.

PROJECT PLANS AND PROJECT ALLIES

Staying with the idea of building PM competency as a project or a program, this is the part with which we are all familiar: preparing a project plan for each phase, including risk management, resource management, schedule, and communications.

Approvals for the plans, along with regular reviews, appropriate tracking, and necessary reporting, especially for your target audience and sponsors, are all steps that the competency development program manager has to oversee to ensure consistency and harmonization. Changes to the scope of each phase must be managed via change review boards and recorded so that deliverables can, if needed, be moved to a different phase, or eliminated altogether from the overall plan—if, for example, they are out of scope, contain too many threats, or are considered *undoable*. Management plans for risks, issues, decisions, and action items must be set up according to organizational processes.

As you go through planning, you will likely identify those leaders or individual contributors in your target audience who are more receptive to the continuous learning environment initiatives; the individuals or departments who ask the most questions, have suggestions, and follow up on the organizational social media; and even those who seem overly critical. Remember that criticism is actually a way of showing passion about the subject. You should build a network with these individuals. These are your allies—your change agents.

We have found that understanding how to leverage the change agents in the organization can make a tremendous difference. These change agents can find ways to reach the remaining project managers more effectively than anyone in a PMO or competency development role because they are known and recognized among their peers. They are not *outsiders*, who, however nicely, are trying to tell them how to do their job, they are an integral part of the community that you are trying to reach. The change agents can help you identify, ahead of time, pitfalls and gaps in your plans—and possibly roadblocks—once they are engaged at the right level. Again, that element of criticism, which may be tempting to interpret as *negativism*, might be a strong ally in disguise.

PILOTS

If you can engage the project managers who are most receptive to your objectives, and set up small groups of *friendly audiences*, you can pilot some of the phases and/or initiatives with them or their departments. Adding a pilot to your schedule means additional time and effort, no doubt. It also means that you can improve the effectiveness of your initiatives and project deliverables by learning with a smaller group what is likely to happen when you launch these initiatives to a wider audience. Mistakes are less costly overall—both financially and psychologically—and you are reducing the threat of widespread failure by proposing your initiatives to a more forgiving audience. You will have a chance to try out on a friendly audience some elements of your projects, and thus gather useful information prior to deployment in the whole organization. A pilot can highlight what works on paper, but would not be effective in the PM community.

Another aspect to consider is that a pilot allows change agents to be engaged more quickly, to get involved sooner than others in something that obviously catches their attention, and resonates with their approach to competency development. You're activating your change agents earlier in the scheme of things and building momentum. You do not want to lose this momentum with your allies.

For example, if you are planning to launch a PM training program with a vendor, students for the first class should be selected from a *friendly* project managers group—those project managers who understand and support what you are trying to accomplish. They will likely be more cooperative in providing feedback, and in helping the vendor understand how to improve the class and reach your audience because, like you, they want the class to be useful. The change agents will also appreciate your acknowledgment of their contribution and the importance of their support

for the whole plan. Where do you find these people? You'll be surprised—
many will come to you once they understand that you are a proponent of
advancing PM in the organization. Also, watch the *feed* of the organizational social media; some people will be the *frequent commenters*. Not all
of these people are necessarily change agents or even allies, but this is a
tremendous resource pool from which you may be able to draw.

6

Time to Deliver!

Once plans are completed and approved, we *finally* get to execution. Competency development initiatives have been kicked off, the project teams are in place, and we can get to the *doing* part. What competency development initiatives are you implementing? You may not know as you read this chapter. However, whatever collection of initiatives you put in place, there will be common elements—connective tissue—that we can discuss here to help assure good governance and a smooth program execution. What are the tools and techniques you can use to deliver your project management (PM) competency program? What are the challenges? What can go wrong at this point, and what can help you deliver on each phase of the program?

Obviously, there are many different types of competency development plans, communities, and organizations so we will address generic elements of delivery, while continuing to offer examples from the organizations and professionals that we consulted as we researched the field when we were preparing to write this book. Some of these examples are anonymous, offered to us in response to our informal survey mentioned in Chapter 1; most have been shared with their explicit permission by trusted and widely respected professionals who have agreed to help us and our readers by providing their insights and experiences.

During the execution of PM competency development projects, some key elements are often recurring. One of the common themes is around the challenges from a wide variety of stakeholders, as well as the many opportunities for learning that are present both within and from outside of your organization. Another is the set of control mechanisms you should put in place to manage the execution of individual projects or initiatives—the assessments. No matter how, why, or when, you will need to be able to ascertain status and degree of competency in your PM community: for baselining purposes, for progress tracking (as described in Chapter 1 and as you will see in Chapter 7), and for certifications. Learning will have to become part of your PM community culture regardless of who delivers the training and what delivery options you choose.

We will explore these issues in this chapter, in no particular order of importance or temporal sequence. Use the information in these pages as needed, while adding your own ideas and approaches that you believe will work for your PM community.

GOVERNANCE: YOUR KEY TO CONTROLLING OUTCOMES

As you need to do when managing any program of work, establishing a flexible, effective, governance infrastructure is one of the elements that will directly impact the delivery of your bridge. Notice the attributes we are assigning to the competency development program's governance.

Flexibility is often overlooked when we plan and more important, when we deliver a program. Have you ever started out thinking: *this is how we will do it—it is the best way, and so we will do it this way*. No matter how solid and how proven your governance approach, no two programs are the same. Without a built-in flexibility factor, the first minor tremor in the organizational fabric will pose a threat to the stability of the program and can potentially compromise delivery of the program benefit. So, make sure your governance is based on flexible foundations: it needs to be able to adapt to changes—in the organization, in the people who make decisions, and in those who run the individual projects. A rigid, solid system will not allow a response time that is fast enough to keep up with changing organizational structures, new technologies, project management office (PMO) priorities, and management styles. Any program that affects people in the organization needs a higher level of adaptability than other technical deployments. A flexible approach to governance has an overall structure around decision making, progress assessments, and escalations; and allows for fast-track management of urgent situations and high-priority issues. Empowerment and delegation are used constantly to push decision making as close as possible to delivery teams.

Effectiveness—now that's a slippery word: a project manager's *effective* approach to communications, for example, can easily translate into a lack of critical information for stakeholders; what can be perceived as effective by the project manager might result in an incomprehensible set of dates to a senior manager. Effectiveness, like beauty, does lie in the eye of the beholder. At the outset, we recommend that you make sure expectations are clear for all involved, and that all stakeholders are aligned on the *minimum common denominator* for all governance elements. What information is *really* needed to make a go/no-go decision? Not what you might like to know but what you absolutely need to know before approving a request. What data is really *important* when assessing progress? How many meetings do you need to manage an escalation? Last, but not least, do ask *continually* for ways to improve, simplify, and streamline procedures, measurements, reporting, and all other elements of governance.

Reporting as a Communication Technique

We have all been there: hours and hours of report preparation, formatting, template manipulation—all to obtain a set of slides that will be (or not) part of a lengthy presentation (or not). In the end, it is never clear in our experience, how much return on investment is derived from all the time spent in preparing reports. One of our guidelines is: if someone must touch a piece of information (metrics, results, action plans, etc.) more than once, then you have introduced an unnecessary delay in program communication and a maintenance threat to your program information flow. If the questions asked after a roundtable on risk management are not recorded, written down (including answers), and distributed (via newsletter, blog, frequently asked questions file, etc.), then the same questions will come up again at the next discussion on risk management. Similarly, if data on the number of internal certifications is stored in two different reporting engines (in a SharePoint list and in a PowerPoint presentation delivered monthly, for example) you *will* have data out of sync, and duplicate efforts in keeping the data up to date. While it is true that executive presentations are usually more attractive in a smart slide show, accessing data using equally effective database interfaces might save time (yours and the project manager's) and money (your organization's).

Individual Assessments: Beyond Tests

Program governance uses measurements to assess progress and make decisions. For a competency development program, the immediate association is to student assessments. Along the same lines, when thinking about assessments, one of the first things that comes to mind is a test. Of course, we all have grown up professionally in environments (schools, universities, professional associations) that seek to establish a person's level of knowledge and understanding using tests. These types of assessments are expected and useful in some situations, for example, to attain professional credentials, but, particularly in organizations that span multiple countries and cultures, they can also prove to be insufficient, at least on their own, to establish project managers' competency. Managing, recording, and retaining test records are aspects to be considered when planning formal test-based assessments as are legal implications around ensuring appropriate privacy for any personal data, such as test results. You might also want to evaluate specific knowledge around aspects related to the projects, or to the internal processes of the organization. There are other ways to perform basic assessments beyond tests.

Self-assessments, corroborated by the line manager and backed by practical evidence, can be a simple way to assess competency in your PM community. We will discuss these assessments in more detail in Chapter 7. For example, if you wanted to evaluate how well your project managers understand and use risk management tools and techniques, you could develop a self-assessment questionnaire, supported by examples of real-life project risk management for one or more past projects managed by that project manager. This *collateral* information can be risk management plans, risk registers, and evidence of their continued use during the life cycle of the project. Endorsement from a line manager or other managers (maybe from departments who contributed to the projects) can ensure impartiality and objectiveness in the evaluation.

An organization had a need for specialized project managers who could manage delivery of complex projects based on the technical aspects and challenges of these projects. They developed a database of skills, each with a range of competency, and a workflow supporting self-assessment, validation (by the line manager), a reference system (other managers), and evidence collection. They launched the database in the organization and started to monitor on a yearly basis how the competency levels were impacted by the knowledge transfer sessions and other learning programs developed by the PMO. In a few years, they were able to predict how to best formulate competency development programs for their community based on the trends and results shown by this database.

Individual Assessments: Peer Reviews and Jury Boards

When the outcome of assessments has an impact on the project manager's career, for example, a bonus or a leadership position, we recommend a more formal approach.

You can set up peer reviews, in which experienced project managers from relevant departments are called to review and endorse a project manager competency assessment based on their direct or indirect interactions with the project manager and on artifacts, deliverables, and process adherence that the project manager has demonstrated. A presentation, prepared by the candidate project manager and undersigned by his/her line manager, can be the starting point of such a review. These project managers are all part of a group of experienced project managers, likely in a position of higher responsibility in the organization so they can assess with more accuracy which areas might still need to be developed or improved to reach, for example, the *expert* level of competency.

Another possibility is a jury board of experts and senior managers in the organization who are called on a regular basis (quarterly or twice a year) to evaluate the candidate's competency *based on tangible results delivered* to the organization. These boards are more difficult to organize, logistically, so enough preparation and vetting must be done in advance, but the impact of this level of acknowledgment is considerable, and it enables some unique opportunities for best-practice sharing. We have seen many cases in which a presentation for a jury board becomes a one-hour learning *nugget*. Chapter 7 will illustrate this approach within a proposed work flow for internal certifications.

Competency Development Project Assessments: Surveys and More

From a program governance point of view, decision making, sponsorship, and escalation need to rely on data that includes more than the sum of individual achievements: they need project-level evaluation of the effectiveness of both the tactical options chosen (which translate in the initiatives or projects) and of the strategic approach you have selected for the organization. Cumulative data on individual assessments need to be complemented by information on what initiatives yield better outcomes *for your organization at this moment.* Maybe your PM community is not yet ready to self-direct roundtables, and it needs more guidance. Maybe your project managers have much more energy to blog and share than you originally estimated—or have gained a higher level of maturity more quickly than expected. In all of these scenarios, you can gain useful pointers by looking at the results of each competency development project and/or initiative. What worked? What was not well received? What needs more attention? For you to control the program, the answers to these questions need to become inputs to your decisions on the next steps in the execution of your competency development program. One way to get direct feedback on whether initiatives are delivering the expected outcomes is to use surveys. As we said in Chapter 1, a baseline is needed *before* any initiative; and subsequent surveys should be conducted—with similar questions—during the delivery of each initiative.

BUDGETING

Although not mentioned by name in the 5th Edition of the *A Guide to the Project Management Body of Knowledge (PMBOK® Guide)*, the Iron Triangle of scope, cost, and time lives on, at least in our minds. There is a constant battle of these constraints, and that battle is prevalent in these initiatives to improve PM competency. For example, many of the leadership competencies really require on-site training, bringing project managers together into encounter sessions where they can practice negotiation, conflict, presentation, and other people skills. That's expensive. With so many virtual office employees, you are talking about a lot of potential travel. Is travel even allowed? What are the other options? Can you use your own internal instructors for this? If you do decide to go to external consultants to provide the training, that's even *more* training money required—and there is a limited budget. And, what about the *opportunity cost*—the time away from money-generating projects with customers? The point is that for these initiatives, a conscious, focused budgeting activity must be planned and executed. A detailed business case must be prepared for a variety of competency development options, and defended with senior management.

Table 6.1   Using the *Pulse of the Profession*® reports to justify PM training

Title	Date	Comments
Pulse of the Profession® Overview	May 2016	Powerful graphics show justification for PM training overall
Delivering Value: Focus on Benefits During Project Execution	June 2016	Good focus on communication and stakeholder management competencies
The Strategic Impact of Projects: Identify Benefits to Drive Business Results	March 2016	Good focus on long-term thinking and benefits realization
Capturing the Value of Project Management	February 2015	Excellent justification for improving knowledge management and for building risk management skills
Capturing the Value of Project Management through Decision Making	August 2015	Good focus on the need to connect to organizational strategy

We highly recommend the Project Management Institute's *Pulse of the Profession*® reports as a way to justify the money for PM competency as money well spent. Studies comparing the results of thousands of companies are used to demonstrate the very real monetary benefits of such an expense. In Table 6.1 we provide a summary of the *Pulse* reports and how they could be used in this way. In addition, others have studied the effects of investing in PM training to build PM competency and to get results; for example, *The State of Project Management Training* from PM Solutions noted a 26% improvement, on average, in eight measures of business and PM performance because of their PM training initiatives. These performance measures, which we believe are relevant in most organizations, are: strategy execution, shareholder satisfaction, financial success, schedule/budget performance, customer satisfaction, resource allocation, strategic alignment, and project prioritization. A more recent report from this organization (*Project Manager Skills Benchmark 2015*) indicates that skills make a significant positive difference in these eight measures of PM. The organizations that had project managers with high skill levels were outperforming those with low skill levels 3.7 to 2.48 on a scale of 1 to 5 (see Figure 6.1).

Once you have attained a budget, it's critical that the budget gets allocated in a way that most effectively develops PM competency for your particular organization—and that's what this book is meant to do for you.

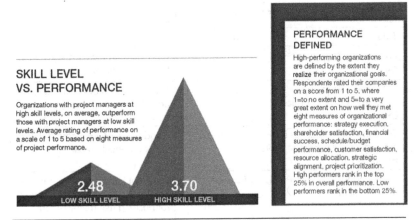

Figure 6.1   Skill level versus performance (from PM Solutions)

ORGANIZATIONAL CHANGE MANAGEMENT

Any initiative in the area of competency management is not only going to be considered a change—and therefore difficult enough in nature—it's a powerfully felt change. Why? You are changing declarations about what the project managers need to know to excel at their jobs and their projects. That's a *significant* message to the project managers. It's not often perceived as an interactive decision, even if you take steps to engage some project manager representatives in the decision-making process. They'll look at these changes even more critically than the *usual* change in processes or tools, which provide significant challenges in and of themselves. We've discussed the general topic in Chapter 5. Here we provide some tips based on our knowledge of these initiatives and also by drawing from some of the wisdom in Dr. Barbara Trautlein's book, *Change Intelligence*. We summarize the tendencies in Table 6.2, including the strengths and developmental opportunities for each of the three tendencies.

Trautlein's system identifies three different styles of leading change management:

- Heart—engaging, caring, people-oriented
- Head—strategic, futuristic, purpose-oriented
- Hands—efficient, tactical, process-oriented

Table 6.2 Trautlein's *Heart, Head, Hands* styles of change management tendencies

	Leads Change from the *Heart*	Leads Change from the *Head*	Leads Change from the *Hands*
Style	Engaging, caring, people-oriented	Strategic, futuristic, purpose-oriented	Efficient, tactical, process-oriented
Strength	Motivating and supporting coach	Inspirational and big picture visionary	Planful and systematic executer
Developmental Opportunities	May neglect to revisit overall change goals and may not devote attention to the specific tactics of the change process	May leave others behind, wanting to move sooner than people are ready for, and lack detailed planning and follow through	May lose sight of the big picture and devalue team dynamics and individuals' emotions

Most project managers are Hands people. When the authors attended Trautlein's seminar at a PMI North America Congress, she ran an exercise with a quick initial assessment, and almost all attendees in the room—who were, of course, project managers—went to the Hands corner. This means that you will naturally be tempted to lead these initiatives from the Hands perspective—and given that your PM audience is mostly a Hands audience, it will likely be a good start. This is not going to be an ideal approach, however. You have some strengths, in that your competency development initiatives will likely resonate with your audience, but you also have some blind spots and weaknesses because you might be missing vision (Head) and inspiration (Heart) for the people in your PM community. Trautlein identifies seven Change Leader styles (Coach, Champion, Visionary, Driver, Executer, Facilitator, and Adapter) from combinations of these three *Tendencies to Lead*: Head, Heart, and Hands. Among those three tendencies, identified in Table 6.2, it is the Executer that is the most extreme case of a *Hands* style. This is a strength for a project manager when leading a technical project, but not always a strength when nurturing a new people-based initiative. In Table 6.3, adapted from Trautlein's description of Executers, we provide some of the strengths and weaknesses of the Executer Style that could help ease competency development plans and initiatives into action.

Table 6.3   The PM (Executer) Style: strengths and weaknesses

The Executer (high hands—most project managers) as a change leader	
Strengths	**Weaknesses**
Most of the time, you:	*. . . . but sometimes you:*
Excel at project planning and execution	Lose sight of the big picture–the goal of the initiative
Accomplish accountabilities in a timely and efficient manner	Lack patience with people and process issues and may react to what looks like failure, but is simply hysteresis
Are dependable for requested tasks	Push for unrealistic performance standards
Deal with lots of data, information, reports	Go into data overload mode, providing too much information; unnecessarily long readouts

THE KNOWN UNKNOWNS

Uncertainty is part of every human endeavor and we can anticipate some of the challenges and opportunities that you are likely to encounter. We recommend some thoughts and efforts be invested in identifying any additional factors to be added to your program risk management.

Challenges

Where to start . . . ? Left and right, top and bottom, front and back—you can expect challenges from just about any direction because changing the way we operate is usually difficult, regardless of the change itself and of the acumen and skills in the organization. Change resistors will be there at each turn so do expect them. The information in Chapter 3 and some of the options in Chapter 5 might help you identify the best strategy to manage them.

Head-on, open resistance might be more easily recognized and dealt with: training classes can't be scheduled for lack of students; completion deadlines come and go without achieving the expected number of trained personnel; websites or newsletters, if not presented well or if improperly promoted, have scarce participation or readership.

Passive resistance is usually highlighted when an apparent compliance to your initiatives is followed by limited or no results, despite all other progress indicators, such as training completion data, being positive. Project managers go to the training classes but do not apply to take the Project Management Professional (PMP)® exam, or, if they do take it, do not pass it; internal jury boards lack experienced contributors; or desultory questions are asked during a roundtable.

Let us consider some of these circumstances and see how we can tackle them:

- *Management does not approve training expenses or allow time for project managers to take a class*—This is a situation in which your sponsor needs to step in and empower you and the project team. We have found that a clearly stated decision on adding your PM competency improvement program to the list of high priority initiatives during a senior leadership meeting makes a big difference. If the meeting organizer issues a set of notes that are suitable for wider organizational disclosure, the notes, and the decision therein, can be a very strong reference when there is resistance from other senior managers and from your peers. If the notes can't be disclosed to others, then a notice via e-mail to all in the organization, not just the project managers, will ensure that your program is perceived as a priority by senior management. Equally powerful are statements during town hall meetings or general meetings in which your sponsor, or even a more senior official, announces the kick off of the program or makes a strong supporting statement on its value to the organization. Once again, a written (thus reusable) formal statement needs to follow so that you have an effective way to manage these situations. Agreements on appropriate time frames, as well as budget constraints, must be developed so that all stakeholders who are impacted are able to perceive that their needs have been met.

Now let's look at what is coming from left and right . . .

- *Project managers do not respond to invitations to training, roundtables, events, etc.*—Call in your allies! Change agents, volunteers, people who have had some exposure and who support your plans—they can invite others to join an event or take a class. Making training a mandatory element in people's day-to-day activities does not really work: anyone can sit in a class, in person or virtual, and go through the appearance of listening, without retaining a single concept. If you have participation in the first events, only to notice dwindling numbers later on, reach out to those who were there and ask about the content, delivery, and usefulness of the initiative. Find out where they are *dropping off* and *why*. Chapter 7 will provide more ideas on how to track progress. These are the challenges that require the support of your change agents—your local champions.

- *A vendor fails to deliver training content for one of your programs*—As experienced purveyors of PM training, we have seen many varieties of vendor failures. We have seen expensive consulting organizations completely misunderstand requirements and deliver what they have *in stock* instead of what was needed. We have seen vendors understand requirements, but miss a major expectation—one example being a vendor who provided required e-book training in the form of a proprietary format that only could be downloaded and played on one particular smartphone and tablet system. Make sure you—as a customer—know the difference between expectations (often unvoiced) and requirements (technically/contractually listed), and then make sure they are aligned!

Organizational Opportunities

Some organizations are large enough to be able to rely on a department entirely dedicated to training and learning development. Even if such a department is positioned in a different organization, you should seek to leverage their expertise and knowledge as *internal consultants*, and take advantage of their specific expertise in the art and science of training. Over and over, we have experienced the difference in our planning and delivery of learning events whenever education professionals were able to assist us. Timing of the knowledge transfer sessions, dynamics in roundtable facilitation, and every single aspect of your competency development plans will benefit from the participation in, and contributions of, your internal training specialists.

Engaging motivated individuals as volunteers, with appropriate recognition, is a great way to ensure you will benefit from a variety of experience as you deliver the learning events that are part of your plan. Different departments can ask for volunteers to support you, or the individuals can offer their time in response to a specific blog post or e-mail distribution.

When you mix different levels of understanding and experience, you create options for different voices to be heard, and diverse points of view will yield overall better results.

An organization wanted to increase the number of project managers with industry accreditation, but could not afford external classes to prepare their project managers for the exam. This organization chose an approach in which the material intended to prepare candidates for the PMP exam would provide retained knowledge of the important framework and vocabulary in the *PMBOK® Guide* rather than serving only as a vehicle for preparing students to take and pass the exam. Of course, it also did have to prepare them, but the organization, which uses the *PMBOK® Guide* as a basis for its methodology, wanted the learning to *stick*. So, rather than hiring a consultancy or a *canned* solution involving *boot camp* (three-day solutions after which the material is rarely retained), they chose to negotiate a deal with a provider of the training materials and test simulator, where the organization would provide its own PMP certified instructors. These instructors lead the candidates much more slowly and deliberately through the material—over a period of several weeks—augmenting it with real-life examples based on projects delivered by the organization.

The organization built a team of about 15 instructors from all over the world, and aligned the classes with the time zones in which the instructor was located. The instructors were trained by a lead instructor to assure consistency, and this lead instructor also provided a significant amount of adjunct material, using examples from the company's own projects to make some of the points from the *PMBOK® Guide* material more relevant to them.

The instructor also acted as a coach and mentor, especially during the latter part of the course when students were taking simulated exams. The trainers were PM advocates and many of them aspired to eventually become university-level instructors so this became a true win-win situation.

The course provided 28 hours of virtual instruction (using screen-sharing software) and at least seven hours of assigned homework and practice exams, yielding the 35 minimum hours needed for the PMP exam application. All sessions were recorded to allow for replays if any student wanted to review a topic. The instructors also received up to 35 professional development units (PDUs) for their own PMP certificate renewal. The company knew the instructors liked this by virtue of the fact that when there was a second round of the class offered, almost every one of them came back and raised their hands to do it again.

All in all, about 300 candidates went through this program, which yielded a very high passing rate. This program continues because of its low expense; its ability to turn the cadre of instructors into a center of *PMBOK® Guide*, PMP, and PDU expertise; its success in getting people through the PMP exam; and because it provides the instructors with a significant award of PDUs for their own efforts, as well as hard-earned lessons as instructors (project managers are tough students).

External Opportunities

From the local chapter of your favorite PM professional association to universities offering PM evening classes; from conferences to volunteering opportunities; from magazines and blogs to user groups on professional networks—there is so much out there! For example, PMI offers a Registered Company Coordinator (RCC) program which has the objective to *develop stronger relationships with local employers who promote and value PM as a critical competency within their business . . . to improve communications, coordination, and recruitment of prospective chapter members.* Participating in the RCC program is an excellent competency development opportunity.

If you have planned a blog, you should leverage podcasts available online from specialists in the area you want to cover. There is always a breath of fresh air coming into the organization when you open your windows. Do check your sources before committing time and money. For courses and consultants, leverage your connections in the industry for advice and recommendations, or reach out and form new connections if you do not have them. A large external network of project managers across different industries—and also including academics and other PM thought leaders—is an important ingredient for those planning to use external sources of knowledge transfer. This network can help:

- Suggest sources of training, with recommendations based on experience, and
- Provide direct assistance, sometimes becoming speakers or providers themselves (as long as they have been properly vetted with others from the network and your own procurement organization).

Auditing a class offered by an external consultant is a good idea, as you can form an opinion on how effective that class can be for your specific audience. It can also alert you to the need to tailor the class content or its delivery.

If you have a medium or large organization (or at least one containing a large number of project managers) then vendors may be willing to provide you with new programs at a low cost—or possibly, no cost. One organization with whom we spoke was able to *test drive* very expensive advanced PM training sessions from a top university because the university needed to increase the number of corporate references it could advertise to others. In another example from a different organization, they were able to get a significant discount on access to PMP exam prep simulations from a fledgling company, which despite excellent credentials, needed a large company's endorsement before going public.

A Case Study

All the analysis, the readiness, the planning, the struggles, and the challenges: are they really going to yield results? We know—from what we discuss with our peers and from our own experiences—that the answer is *yes*. You *can* improve PM competency and establish an environment in which learning, formally or informally, takes place continuously in your PM community. We will show you here a real-life example—a case study of what can be achieved when you lay out the right foundation.

Our colleague Helen Bull has kindly agreed to share with our readers the outcome of a similar effort as the one we have described in the company she works for—Philips. You will find more details about this case study in Appendix 4. Observing the results of careful preparation, planning, adjustments, and lessons learned can be an inspiration to us all.

PM Excellence at Philips

The PM practice was created to ensure that all employees had access to standardized, yet tailorable assets to support them in the discipline of PM, and to continue to improve the maturity of the project managers. Projects underpin so much of the work that is undertaken in Philips, and we see that employees throughout their careers will at some point be impacted by projects, either as project managers, PMO team members, sponsors, subject matter experts, or end users (among others). It is important that we can all speak *the language of PM*—language that covers topics as wide ranging as risk management to change management. Philips has a significant number of employees globally, hence the programs that we have created are tailored for specific audiences, from introductory measures at the entry level to structured C-suite interviews and a mandatory boot-camp course to really test our experienced project managers. We have established a set of assessments for PM competency, as shown in Figure 6.2.

Our training has been tailored to ensure that this *language* can be learned by all employees, not just project managers and their teams—and because everyone is busy, it can be taken via e-learning courses through the company's own university (a.k.a. *click not brick*) whereby a significant number of virtual classroom are loaded for use by our PM community. We also hold specific classroom sessions for courses which are more apt in a face-to-face situation (think schedule management as one example).

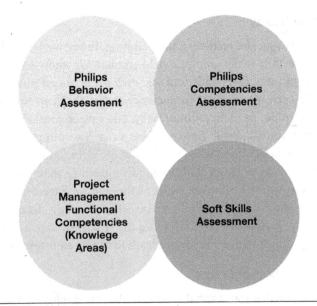

Figure 6.2   Philips PM competency assessments

PM Certification Program

PM is a portable skill set, meaning that the core of an effective project manager is excellence in hard skills and, more critically, soft skills. The Philips PM certification program targets specific audiences in the company. As shown in Figure 6.3, our model is based on a pyramid whereby as you head up through the levels, the audience becomes smaller, but also the content and criteria for successful passage becomes more intensive and scrutinized:

- *Foundation*—this entry level targets all employees to undertake a 12-hour online course introducing them to the knowledge areas of PM.

Figure 6.3 Philips Internal Certifications in PM

- *Practitioner*—this next level targets PM employees with five or more years of PM experience and those who tend to work in project environments on a regular basis. This level is a tectonic shift in mindset in what it means to be a project manager at Philips. In addition to continuous learning requirements, we put a lot of emphasis on community building: supporting all project managers and the practice through participating in our coaching program, completing peer reviews, and attending round-table events, among others.
- *Expert*—applicants here are practicing project managers with 10+ years of PM experience, confirmed by the fact that they must hold a PMP certification. Refer to Figure 6.4 for more information on the requirements for this level. We support our staff in attaining this globally recognized PM credential. Expert level certification steps up the community building and learning requirements, and candidates must have specific interviews with senior leaders to pass expert level certification.
- *Master*—at this level, applicants are expected to have executive presence and a consultative mindset. Here, soft skills are key in determining how to lead teams and communicate at all levels, especially to senior executives in the company. Prior to applying for Master level certification, applicants must have 15+ years of PM experience and must have taken dedicated coursework.

Figure 6.4   Philips Internal Certifications: PM expert level

A Bespoke Support Program

We see PM as a core capability in Philips, and we also see it as a career, not just something one *does on the side*. This means that we need to look at the skills that a project manager needs to have to operate optimally as different pillars. The first are the *portable skills*, namely those that are PM 101—for example, planning (scheduling), risk management, HR (human resources) management, etc.—basically the ten knowledge areas of the *PMBOK® Guide*. Second, the *soft skills* require the most focus, as while these are assumed in a project manager, often they are overlooked.

Hence our PM coaching program enables the coach and *the coachee* to connect. In addition, we hold events to enable project managers to come together and hone their skills; we are also looking to launch a Toastmaster Club to support project managers in something many of them find daunting—presenting to large audiences. A program we have recently created, illustrated in Figure 6.5, also looks to offer that much more to project managers—a personal network. Together with the line manager and a senior project manager, this small group is entered into a program which enables a continuous cycle of learning, support, and improvement.

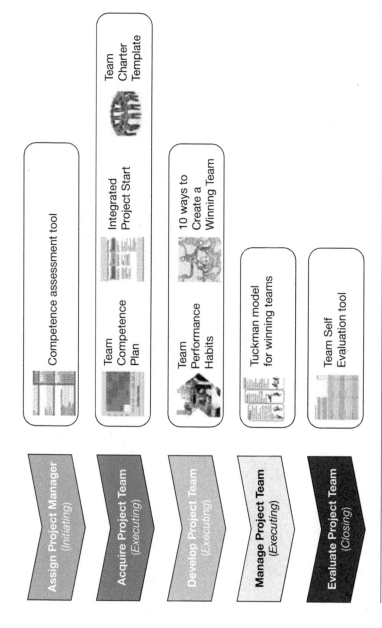

Figure 6.5   Philips PM Winning Teams model

7

Indicators of Success— How Do You Know if Your Bridge Is Built and Working?

One of the major pieces of advice we give all new project managers is: make sure you *know what success looks like*. Otherwise—and you have all seen examples of this—the project goes on indefinitely. An initiative to build a bridge, whether metaphorical or real, is a project, so the initiative of improving project management (PM) competency that is being covered in the book is no exception. When you start, you should have a vision of success in mind, as we discussed in Chapter 1. Later, you must identify measures of success—*ready to go*—as covered in Chapter 2. Then you will need a way to use the measures to make improvements as we will see in Chapter 8.

Those measures may include levels of accomplishment in the areas of internal and/or external certification, key performance indicators (KPIs) of project success, or, even better, a combination of all of these elements.

CERTIFICATION PROGRAMS

One way to get a handle on progress—one that brings with it a whole set of related benefits—is to employ certification programs to formalize PM

Table 7. 1   Benefits of PM certification programs

Attribute	Benefits of certification program(s)
Morale	Sense of individual project manager accomplishment, pride
	Sense of advancement for career path
	Acknowledgment by leadership of the importance of PM discipline
Career path	Facilitates consistency and fairness in career movement (same key milestones used by all)
Marketing advantage	Provides certainty for customers (of experience in projects, and of knowing how to get things done within their organization)
	Allows organization to formalize "PM as a service" and/or to charge more for projects, including the project manager element
Governance	Consistency of overall PM methodology and use of a common framework
	Helps assure use of same templates and tools across geographies and business lines
	Promotes use of a common language between internal organizations as well as with customers

knowledge transfer and achievements in the application of PM methodology in the organization. This can be done in a variety of ways, and is by no means a simple effort. For example, to *prove* PM capability is very different than proving understanding or the attaining of any particular single skill. You will see in the sections that follow that a combinational approach is needed—one that involves verifying *knowledge* (quizzes, knowledge check-ins, exams), verifying *experience* (resumes, formal presentations of project case work), and even peer observation of actual project work and behaviors.

This powerful combination of assessments for both knowledge and experience will help you understand the effectiveness of your competency development programs. We will look at both internal and external certification programs and discuss their benefits. As you can see from Table 7.1, the advantages of such programs are numerous.

INTERNAL CERTIFICATION

There are a series of important decisions for an organization to make with regard to establishing an internal certification program.

If such a program is to be instituted, the organization has several decisions to make:

- What is the level of formality?
- What are the prerequisites?
- What judging bodies (juries) will be needed?
  - Who staffs these judging bodies?
  - Are any external resources used?
  - How often do they meet?
- What are the boundaries (geographic or business group, for example) within which these bodies will work?
- What level of consistency is required between the geographic and business lines? Do the requirements and thresholds for certification need to be rigid and identical or may they fluctuate depending on application, region, and culture?
- How is consistency and impartiality maintained?
- How can jury reviews become *teachable moments* for both the jury members as well as the candidates?

You should be asking these questions of your own (existing or planned) internal certification program, but we have duplicated this set of questions and provided some advice from our background and experience in Table 7.2.

When establishing an internal certification program, visualize it as a system with a workflow, decision points, and critical feedback loops. Figure 7.1 illustrates the flow of information in a way that shows not only the value of the process, but the connection to some of the foundational parts of any good competency improvement program: the competency model, job profiles, learning opportunities, a career path, and a strong PM community. Critical to the success of the process is the inclusion of feedback (represented by dotted lines in Figure 7.1) to ensure that you maintain control of the program and set up ways to continuously improve it. Let's discuss the general flow of Figure 7.1 from the bottom up.

The Foundation

Supporting the entire internal certification process is a group of fundamental elements: a competency model; a set of well-defined job profiles, connected as a career path for project managers; and learning opportunities

Table 7.2   Internal certification attributes

Level of Formality	Can vary depending on level. For entry-level, a less-formal review and approval system can be used. Higher formality, rigor, and structure should be present for the higher level project managers.
Prerequisites	Things to consider: • PMP, PRINCE2, or other external certifications could be used as prerequisites for higher-level internal certificates • Establish minimum years of experience for the higher level certifications, and establish clear guidelines for people moving into these higher level positions from other organizations
Judging Bodies (Juries)	Keep in mind that the effort to serve as a juror is not trivial. It's a rewarding experience but involves the commitment of time, focus, and energy. It's best to limit the number of times per year that internal certification takes place to two or three, and they can be done on a regional basis to facilitate the process for a global organization.
Boundaries/Transparency/Impartiality	In a large multinational organization that has several business lines, it's likely that you will have certification juries split along those lines. This is fine as long as a global organization is able to audit the process for consistency and transparency.
Teachable Moments	It's critical that the process "pay off" sustainably, not just in allowing (or disallowing) the certification of an individual. Outstanding example projects will be presented. Archive these and share them, both for their *PM excellence* as well as the way in which they represent good *certification process* examples. Poor examples of applications and presentations will also exist. Hold these up as examples of what not to do, after, of course, anonymizing them.

to build skills and competencies. These supporting fundamentals, in turn, are not created in a vacuum. They are built with input from industry best practices and of course, the customer. Your customer will sometimes tell you, in not-so-subtle ways, where you are lacking in competency: it is worth your time to listen! These elements will become very important in the next chapter (see Figure 8.1).

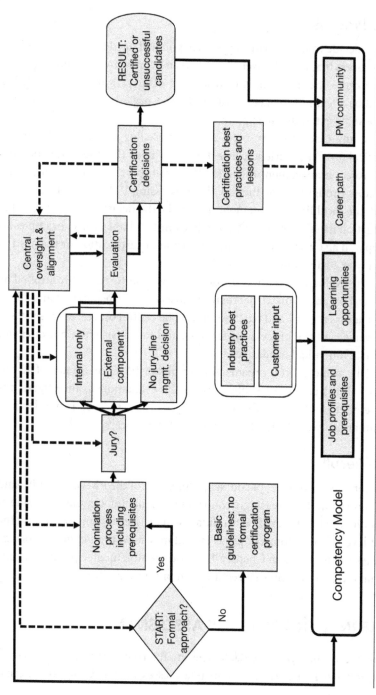

Figure 7.1   Internal Certification: Flow and Decision Diagram

The Process

If you decide to use a formal approach, you will need to select a nominating process that includes well-described and communicated prerequisites. Next comes the decision as to what type of jury, if any, will be used. It could be a team of managers within the line organization, or it could include some external participants.

In any case, the jury must consist of senior managers with recent practical project experience. By *external* we mean that they could be from the project management office (PMO), from other organizations, or facilitators brought in for their skills in assessing PM talent. If no jury is used, the local line management may make the decision. Next comes the evaluation itself, in which the candidate (and perhaps project examples) is compared against standards with a decision of certification or the need to reapply at a later time.

The evaluation (but not the decision) is monitored and controlled by a central organization so that there is consistency, transparency, and alignment across regions and business units. The central organization serves as an overseer of the process, its fairness, and its consistency, but does not evaluate individual candidates.

That same central organization (a global PMO or Center of Excellence [CoE]) also uses feedback from the evaluation to investigate improvement to all of the preceding subprocesses, such as jury selection, nomination, even the level of formality of the process.

The Result

The certified candidate, of course, is a member of the PM community, and can (and should) increasingly contribute as a mentor. On the other side of the coin, the newly certified candidate will just be starting to work on the next level of more complex projects, and may need their own mentoring.

As we discussed in Chapter 4, a good mentor/mentee program is important to help the internal certification program really work.

INTERNAL COMPETENCY ASSESSMENT

Whether or not you decide to use an internal certification program, you will need to perform competency assessments. Using an internal assessment for PM competencies has a *hidden benefit*. Let's talk a bit about the obvious benefits, and leave a sense of mystery about the hidden piece for now. By assessing individuals' competency in your project managers, you will certainly develop:

- An inventory of PM competency so that you know which project managers are capable of handling which upcoming projects;
- A means to develop individuals by joint understanding of where there are gaps; and
- A means to drive the organizational curricula and learning goals by understanding where there are generic gaps in competency.

These benefits in and of themselves are valuable, and justify the idea of a PM competency assessment. But here's the *hidden* benefit: by going through this exercise, you let the project managers know that the organization: (1) knows that there indeed is a recognized scale of PM competency and (2) cares enough about the PM staff to assess where they stand along this scale. These may seem like trivial items, but the strong yet subliminal message sent to the staff by doing a competency assessment is as follows: *we know that there is a range of PM competency and we care enough to measure you along this scale; and we also care enough to help you advance your competency—for your sake as a member of the staff, for the success rate of our projects, and, ultimately, for successful benefits realization for our customers and shareholders.* That is an outstanding message to send.

There is a possible Hawthorne Effect here as well. The Hawthorne Effect is the result of a series of social experiments in the 1920s and 1930s at Western Electric factories outside of Chicago, which were rather earth-shattering at the time. The experimenters changed the working conditions (e.g., lighting) in a factory setting and observed the results. What they found was astounding:

The employees' working conditions were changed and in all cases their productivity improved when a change was made. Indeed, their productivity even improved when the lights were dimmed again. By the time everything had been returned to the way it was before the changes had begun, productivity at the factory was at its highest level. Absenteeism had plummeted.

The experimenters concluded that it was not the changes in physical conditions that were affecting the workers' productivity. Rather, it was the fact that someone was actually concerned about their workplace, and the opportunities this gave them to discuss changes before they took place (http://www.economist.com/node/12510632).

In this case, the intent is indeed to make positive changes, but let's not overlook the positive effect of showing concern and care for the PM population.

Of course, you will need to be able to *put your money where your mouth is*, so to speak. For example, if you do identify a gap for an individual, the organization needs to be able to follow through with a commensurate *gap-filler*—a learning element of some sort: a book, a suggestion of a course, a recommendation to partner with a mentor—something that can fill the identified competency gap.

We've provided the basis for you to do such an assessment. Let's look at Table 7.3. Here you'll see three different elements:

- Attributes and behaviors
- Knowledge and consulting
- Direction and strategy

Each of these are mapped against five increasingly advanced competency levels (we call them the 5 Es):

- Entry
- Elementary
- Effective
- Extended
- Expert

This makes for a generic guide—and overview—of PM competency. You would then use this table to generate the actual assessment, which would have to reach across all of the competencies you have identified for your project managers.

The assessment could work as follows:

1. The CoE or Global PMO would develop competency-by-competency 5E assessment tables, applying the basic guidelines for *Entry* through *Expert* to the particular competencies.

2. Individuals self-assess on each competency using tables like the one in Table 7.3 as a guideline.

Table 7.3 5E competency assessment level guideline

Level	Assessment guideline
Entry	I'm familiar with the need to develop the project team and am willing to learn how to best do it.
Elementary	I use my interpersonal skills to help build the team. With coaching, I have built a project team that has had good results.
Effective	I know the importance of, and apply, ground rules, team-building activities, and the use of recognition and reward, as well as the forms of power that I can use to derive the most effective results from my team.
Extended	I understand that team performance needs to be constantly improved and use team performance assessments to continue to develop the team. My project team building techniques have been acknowledged as best practice.
Expert	People from former project teams I've led have specifically asked to work on my teams again due to the positive experience and success. I have mentored several project managers developing their project teams and I'm considered the "go-to" person for project team development in my organization.

3. The individuals' supervisor would review this assessment and plan a focused conversation around the set of assessments of all competencies, validating and reaching consensus on self-assessments.

It is important to make this at least a *180-degree* assessment—involving the line manager—but if it's possible, the assessment could also be expanded to allow peers and, if it applies, employees of the individual to provide a 360-degree view. We recommend that this assessment be revisited annually and, although not directly tied to the performance review, it can be a valuable input for the individual's performance review conversation because of the forward-looking coaching (via gap identification) that it provides.

To offer further guidance on how to create the competency-by-competency self-assessments, refer to Table 7.4 to see how you can apply the 5E levels to look at a competency and find descriptors for each of the five levels. Each level of a given competency can be built using the characteristics in the ABCD columns. Draw from the cells in the table as necessary and appropriate.

There is no need for each descriptor to have every element in every level. Also, to make this easier, each of the 5E levels are considered to

Table 7.4   5E "ABCD" attributes, behaviors, consulting capabilities, and direction

The "5E" Level	Attributes and Behaviors	Consulting Capabilities	Direction
Expert	Invents new ways to do things. Leads transitional change (e.g., new methods). *Charismatic, Engaging, Humble, Team Builder, Leader, Consultant, Change Agent*	Considered leading resource—the "go-to" person in the area. Self-motivated learner, hungry for knowledge. Often creates learning elements for others.	Organizational strategy is linked to all project work. Expert and holistic problem solver. Applies strategy in decisions, even in complex, unique, and unfamiliar environments.
Extended	Able to perform full range of project activities even in complex, unique, and unfamiliar environments. Implements new techniques. *Director, Coach, Innovator*	Considered a "go-to" person in the area. Actively seeks any missing information or training in the area.	Strategic linkage is evident in project work. Outstanding problem-solving capabilities.
Effective	Demonstrates solid performance in a stable, familiar environment. Makes suggestions for improvement. *Solid, Reliable, Dependable, Team Player*	Effectively fills the role of consultant and trainer when needed. Seeks any missing information or training.	Fully aware of linkage to organizational strategy. Good problem-solving capabilities.
Elementary	With assistance, can produce good results in the area. *Good learner, excellent at taking direction, asks insightful questions*	Occasionally fills the role of consultant, sometimes must be prodded to do so. Often needs direction and coaching to "know what they don't know."	Understands the need to link to strategy but must be reminded to make the connection. Has basic problem-solving capabilities.
Entry	Although capability may exist, the individual has not yet demonstrated expertise in this area.	The knowledge and consultancy level of the person in this area is unassessed.	Strategic and problem-solving capabilities are unassessed.

build on the prior level so that you don't have to repeat the attributes in the lower-level descriptors.

For example, if the competency is *develop project team*, you might provide the following descriptors:

- *Entry*: "Although I have participated in project teams and managed small projects, I have not yet had the opportunity to demonstrate project team development."
- *Elementary*: "I have developed my project team with help from an experienced project manager and have been able to demonstrate successful results thanks to an increasingly capable and cohesive project team."
- *Effective*: "I consistently develop project teams with good results and connect the project teams' goals and objectives with the higher-level strategies of the organization."
- *Extended*: "I have developed project teams in complex projects that are large, strategically important, unusual, and/or complex. I often coach other project managers in my area on project team development."
- *Expert*: "I'm an innovator in the area of project team development. Successful results in my projects—attributable to the strength of my project teams—have led me to become a mentor for my entire region on this topic. I have created and shared new techniques for accelerating the project team development process."

EXTERNAL/INDUSTRY CERTIFICATION AND CREDENTIALS

The PMP® Credential

Let's start with, by far, the most prolific and well-recognized industry certification in project management—the Project Management Professional (PMP). This is one of several credentials offered by the Project Management Institute (PMI) (we'll cover the others in the following sections). As of this writing, over 740,000 individuals have achieved the PMP credential. It is exceedingly important to understand several key points about what this certification is *not*:

- It is *not* a certification regarding any particular methodology.
- It is *not* only an exam-based certification. Yes, it requires passing a 200-question, four-hour, multiple-choice exam; but to even take the exam, you must submit (subject to audit) a rather lengthy application which documents your three years of experience in leading projects and 35 hours of PM training.
- It is *not* a certification for life. The credential lasts for three years and must be renewed by submitting 60 professional development units (PDUs) and a renewal fee to PMI.

Here are some things that this certification *is*:

- It is a global certification. Although headquartered in Pennsylvania, USA, this credential is increasingly pursued by project managers and required by organizations from around the world.
- The exam is based mainly on the *PMBOK® Guide* (full name, *A Guide to the Project Management Body of Knowledge*), and is focused on the framework, processes, and knowledge areas covered in this standard document published by PMI. The *PMBOK® Guide*, as of this writing, is in its 5th Edition—but the 6th Edition is expected to be released in 2017. The exam changes commensurately soon after the new editions are released.
- The exam is challenging (despite the 740,000 number). It is a timed, closed-book exam which verifies that you understand and can reflect on the specifics of the *PMBOK® Guide's* framework and vocabulary, along with the inputs, tools, techniques, and outputs of its 47 processes tucked into five process groups and also into 10 knowledge areas.

It is for both the aspects of certified and auditable experience, as well as the hurdle of the exam itself that employers often cite the PMP as a prerequisite or at least a *strongly desired* differentiator for their project manager positions.

PMI has also introduced certifications for other *angles* of project, program, and portfolio management, including those in the areas of business analysis and agile PM. Table 7.5 summarizes PMI's certifications.

Table 7.5 PMI certifications

PMI Certification	Description	Credential Holders as of July 2016
PMP®	Project Management Professional (detailed previously)	723,068
CAPM®—Certified Associate in Project Management	Non-renewable 'starter' certificate for those without the required 3 years of project leadership experience	31,597
PgMP®—Program Management Professional	For those overseeing programs (groups of related projects)	1,626
PfMP®	For those overseeing portfolios (collections of programs and projects at the strategic level)	332
PMI-RMP®—PMI Risk Management Professional	Focused on risk management aspects of PM	3,634
PMI-SP®—PMI Scheduling Professional	Focused on aspects of PM related to scheduling and controlling	1,516
PMI-PBA®—PMI Professional in Business Analysis	This is PMI's way of acknowledging the importance of the field of business analysis	804
PMI-ACP®—PMI Agile Certified Professional	Most traditional PM uses *waterfall* methods of development. Newer techniques, especially in software development, center on *agile* techniques—this certification acknowledges that approach.	11,801

IPMA Certifications

The mission of the International Project Management Association (IPMA) is to:

- Facilitate co-creation and lever the diversity of our global network into benefits for the profession, economy, society, and environment;
- Offer know-how, products, and services to the benefit of individuals, projects, and organizations across public, private, and community sectors;

Table 7.6 IPMA certifications

Long Title	Short Title	Assessment	Certification Process					Validity
			Stage 1	Stage 2	Stage 3	Stage 4	Stage 5	
Certified projects director	IPMA Level A			References [+ options]	Projects director report [+ options]			5 years
Certified senior project manager	IPMA Level B	Knowledge + experience	Application curriculum vitae, self-assessment, project list, report proposal	References [+ options]	Project report [+ options]	Interview [+ options]	Final evaluation, feedback [+ options]	5 years
Certified project manager	IPMA Level C			References, exam [+ options]	Project report [+ options]			5 years
Certified project management associate	IPMA Level D	Knowledge	Application curriculum vitae, self-assessment [+ options]	Exam [+ options]	[options]	N/A		5 years

- Maximize the synergies in our global network to help all member associations develop according to their needs; and
- Promote the recognition of PM and engage stakeholders around the world in advancing the discipline.

The IPMA offers several certificates, with 'A' being the most advanced and 'D' being an *associate*-level certification. Here is a summary of those certificate levels:

- *IPMA Level A*: Certified Projects Director manages complex project portfolios and programs.
- *IPMA Level B*: Certified Senior Project Manager manages complex projects—minimum five years of experience.
- *IPMA Level C*: Certified Project Manager manages projects of moderate complexity—minimum three years of experience.
- *IPMA Level D*: Certified Project Management Associate applies PM knowledge when working on projects.

IPMA uses a very distributed model of organization from its site.

"Each IPMA Member Association has its own explanation, process description, and application process."

It is best to go to the specific country IPMA website to get more information about the exam for your location. Table 7.6 summarizes the certification levels available from the IPMA.

If you would like to use IPMA certificates as an equivalency to PMP certification, we think that should be done by exception only, and should require the IPMA B or C Level certification, depending on your internal job profile structure (C would be appropriate for project manager, and B for senior project manager, for example).

PRINCE2®

PRINCE2 (PRojects IN Controlled Environments) certification should not be considered a *competitor* of either of the above certifications. While PMI is certifying knowledge of a framework (its framework) and three years of experience with its application process and exam, PRINCE2 is certifying the ability of a candidate to demonstrate proficiency with a particular methodology. On the PRINCE2.com website, it is described in this way:

"PRINCE2 is a de facto process-based method for effective project management. Used extensively by the UK Government, PRINCE2 is also widely recognised and used in the private sector, both in the UK and internationally. The PRINCE2 method is in the public domain, and offers non-proprietorial best practice guidance on project management."

There are two levels of PRINCE2 Certification—Foundational and Practitioner—with the Foundational level being a prerequisite for the Practitioner. The Foundational certification is meant to show that a candidate has sufficient knowledge and understanding of the PRINCE2 method to be able to *work effectively with, or as a member of, a PM team working within an environment supporting PRINCE2.*

The Practitioner level is meant to demonstrate that the candidate has achieved sufficient understanding of how to *apply* and *customize* PRINCE2 in their particular project initiatives. Candidates who pass the Practitioner certification are expected to begin applying the method to a real project at most levels of project complexity. To qualify for the PRINCE2 Practitioner, one of the following credentials must already be in hand:

- PRINCE2 Foundation
- Project Management Professional (PMP)
- Certified Associate in Project Management (CAPM)
- IPMA Level A (Certified Projects Director)
- IPMA Level B (Certified Senior Project Manager)
- IPMA Level C (Certified Project Manager)
- IPMA Level D (Certified Project Management Associate)

PRINCE2 is an excellent complementary (not competitive) certificate because of its methodological focus on *how projects should be run,* which is then supported by the framework-oriented certifications listed above.

Others: Watch Out!

For the very reasons we wrote this book—the need to identify and confirm PM competencies—credentials for project managers are a *hot* commodity. Year after year, the PMP and PRINCE2 certifications, for example, receive high ratings as *top certificates* in terms of their benefit for a career.

This demand, unfortunately, stimulates vendors to provide *quick and dirty* credentials for project managers that promise the same sort of distinction and accomplishment that the PMP, IPMA, or PRINCE2 certificates offer, while being much less expensive and easier to attain, thus fooling some candidates into paying for what is, in effect, a relatively expensive and useless piece of paper. Watch out for these, and consider the mantra: *you get what you pay for.*

PROJECT KPIs

Depending on the level of PM maturity in your organization, you may have (and use) KPIs for projects. Detailing these KPIs is beyond the scope of this book. For details on this subject, we highly recommend Dr. Harold Kerzner's *Project Management Metrics, KPIs, and Dashboards: A Guide to Measuring and Monitoring Project Performance.* You should see a change—over time—in KPIs if the competency program is working. There are a lot of dynamics working here at the same time so do not anticipate an instant or a one-to-one correlation between the effort expended in PM competency and your organization's KPIs.

When we attempted to do this correlation, we did see noticeable improvements in our organization's results, but the effect was delayed from the time when we implemented the competency development program. Despite this delay, the good news was that the greatest correlations were in the area of customer satisfaction and new business generating from existing projects.

To answer the question we asked at the beginning of this chapter— *how do you know if the bridge is working?*—ultimately, improved project results will speak for themselves. Interim progress, though, can and *should* be measured by looking at your achievements in terms of:

- Percent of PM population with a PMP certification (in large companies, this can be as high as 40–50%);
- Percent of PM population pursuing and achieving internal certification;
- Statistics related to attendance/subscription to PM learning events; and
- Statistics related to participation in corporate social media groups (members, activities, posts).

If these are high and increasing, your bridge is built and you are on the way to better results!

8

The Feedback Loop and Improving the Bridge

Remember the dotted-line feedback loops in Figure 7.1, where we were consciously and constantly looking to take wisdom from running the internal certification process back to improve the process? We're now going to take that same construct and apply it to the entire principle of bridging the gap in project management (PM) competency.

PDCA

The plan-do-check-act (PDCA) cycle, whether you know it or not, is woven into the *A Guide to Project Management Body of Knowledge (PMBOK® Guide)*. Just look at the process groups: Initiating, Planning, Executing, Monitoring and Controlling, and Closing. These are based on the PDCA concept. It's mentioned by name in the *PMBOK® Guide* under the chapter called *Project Quality Management*, and it's a fundamental tenet of quality management.

Its origins are traceable to Walter Shewhart, known as *the grandfather of quality management*, or the *father of quality control*. Shewhart was a strong believer in the value of information and its use in statistical process control. Noticing variations in his studies of manufacturing processes, he identified the importance of *special cause* and *common cause* variation, which in turn, inspired Kaoru Ishikawa to include major aspects of this work in his quality control tools, which are vital to the field of quality to this day.

The PDCA concept is sometimes called the Deming Cycle, after W. Edwards Deming who was a highly influential quality *guru* and preached the use of the PDCA cycle, but it is properly called the Shewhart Cycle.

How does this relate to competency management and this book? In Chapters 1, 2, and 3, we defined the problem at hand, looked at ways in which we could plan how to best proceed to address the PM competency gap, and assessed the community of project managers. This is the *plan* part of PDCA.

In Chapters 4, 5, and 6, we examined the tactical options available to implement our strategy (the overall *plan*), and explored ways to best turn them into a program of work to help us implement it. That's where the *do* part comes into play.

In Chapter 7, we discussed understanding and measuring success, and verifying that we are making progress as expected—the *check* part of PDCA.

Here in Chapter 8, we dive in a little deeper to take a longer term, more holistic view of our *bridge* to look at a wider set of influencers. This will let us truly determine if our bridge is serving our PM community and our organization properly, and how we need to *act* to continue to improve.

What is it that we'll check? We'll be checking for impacts to PM competency, the ways in which we assess this competency, changes in ways to improve competency, and even fundamental shifts in the required competencies themselves. These changes are often rooted in political, economic, social, and technical (PEST) changes that affect not only your project managers, but your organization's entire operation. Reacting to these effects will require considerable effort. It's sometimes even difficult to realize they're happening in the first place.

Even if you can realize a shift is taking place, it may be difficult to make the relatively large adaptations that may be necessary. How can you adapt as a PM community? To answer the question, we first model the entire system as shown in Figure 8.1.

The first thing to notice about the diagram is that the PM competency model you have developed can likely be preserved—which is a good thing because it is (as shown by its central location) somewhat shielded

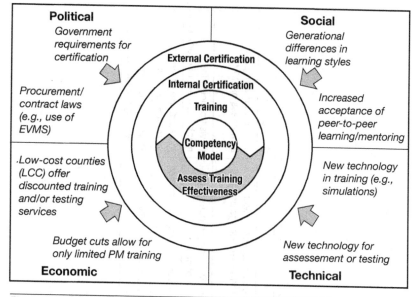

Figure 8.1   PEST influences on PM competency development

from the PEST forces (shown as arrows). You'll also note the connection to Figure 7.1, in which we illustrated the flow of internal certification. In that diagram, the foundational elements of the competency model and training are at the base of the work flow, whereas in Figure 8.1, they are at the center of the diagram. Your competency model is at the center of it all; it should be durable and needs to be considered stable by your PM community. It's going to be easier and more effective to change the surrounding elements of training and assessment as long as they remain logically tethered to the core PM competencies.

What are the PEST forces? We've summarized them using Table 8.1. We call this the *PEST-ACER* table because that's the acronym formed by the column and row labels—area, change, effects, and reaction (ACER).

In this table, we provide illustrative examples to help you populate your own version—for your own context—your enterprise environmental factors (EEFs) as the Project Management Institute (PMI) would call them. Once populated, you can use the change, the effect, and the possible reaction much like you would use a risk register, with the areas serving as risk categories. For example, if you foresee a significant increase in virtual employees, then this would have the effect of making on-site, instructor-led

Table 8.1 PEST-ACER examples

Area	Change	Effect	Reaction
Political	Revised government contract regulations require stringent use of Earned Value Management Systems (EVMS)	Government could assess project managers in EVMS knowledge and use	Increased training and awareness of EVMS
Economic	Accrediting body triples its fee for the credential exam/application	Sharp increase in funding required for professionalism of staff	Revisit policies for reimbursement of exam fees
Social	Significant increase in virtual employees	On-site, instructor-led training becomes impossible	Increase use of virtual instructor-led training
Technical	Breakthroughs in simulation and gaming for training	Radical new capabilities for PM curriculum	Revise curriculum to take advantage of breakthroughs

training very difficult—if not impossible—to employ, and you'd have the response of increasing the use of virtual instructor-led training.

Like a risk register, we urge you to consider both the threats and opportunities in your response to the change. In this case, that translates into:

- Threat: well-respected and popular instructor-led classes may be canceled or limited.
- Opportunity: with new technology, the classes could still be nearly as effective (or even more effective with millennials), and you could save significant travel and logistics costs.

A template to monitor and control your PM competency development program can be found in the Web Added Value (WAV)™ section of the J. Ross Publishing website at https://www.jrosspub.com/wav/.

While we are listing in this chapter the main areas to deeply dive into, we recommend practicing this approach on all the key elements you have chosen to use in your strategy and/or tactical approach as they all need to be reviewed periodically to ensure any EEFs have been considered.

CURRICULA UPDATES

Based on the previously mentioned advice and just on general principles, we recommend a yearly review of the curricula for your PM population. There are several motivators and drivers at work here:

- Changing media (e.g., books available via online systems).
- Corporate artifacts being collected all the time—new ad hoc training sessions become available and can be codified and made part of the curricula, as necessary.
- New PRINCE2, PMI, International Project Management Association standards may make whole segments of an older curricula obsolete.
- Grassroots demand from your PM community for different types of training or different areas of training. For example, there could be a groundswell of interest in agile methodologies, or understanding cultural differences; especially true when a company is going through a merger/acquisition.

In any case, a yearly review, done with representatives of the PM office, the training organization, and a team of representatives from the practicing PM community, will go a long way in assuring a match between the competency model and the PM practice. This is illustrated by the *chasing-tail* element of Figure 8.1, which you see illustrated in the inner circle—the continuous assessment of training.

CUSTOMER AND PM MATURITY ASSESSMENT SURVEYS

Customer (Quality) Surveys

If you have any input into your organization's customer surveys, here is a tip from us. Leverage the information you gain from these surveys! It's critical to determine how PM, and PM capability in particular, are being received by clients for two reasons:

- Reason 1: You *need to know* and *you can really use* verbatim information and raw data to see whether the changes that you are making are indeed helping.
- Reason 2: Your project managers are—or at least should be—intensely curious about how their work makes a difference in morale among your PM community.

Make sure that your customer satisfaction survey contains questions which specifically go after the quality of the customer's PM experience, asking about (in particular):

- The level of engagement by your project manager;
- The perceived level of expertise of your project manager;
- The perceived level of helpfulness of your project manager; and
- Specific areas for improvement from the PM aspect.

It is important to note that the customer, although clearly an important stakeholder, is not the only one. If the project manager has been too lenient, for example, in allowing new scope to creep into the project without commensurate additional budget or schedule, *a good score here may actually indicate a problem* for the project's other stakeholders—like shareholders and sponsors. Be sure to look at this feedback as part of a bigger picture.

PM Assessment

One choice for PDCA feedback is a PM assessment. This is not the set of PM assessments we described earlier in Chapter 7, but rather a more comprehensive *organizational* assessment. It is a review not of individual performance or even of individual project performance, but rather a maturity assessment of your current PM capability, which is usually done by an outside organization that specializes in this. There are dozens, if not hundreds, of consultancies that offer these services, promising (from a composite of these firms' websites):

- Increased credibility of your value, thanks to defined metrics;
- Support for budget approval;
- Accountability for project teams and team members;
- A disclosure of actual and intended behaviors;
- Observation of corporate culture;
- Next steps to increase your competitive position;
- Definition of efficiencies to save money;
- Empowerment of your staff members; and
- Help to end debates and speculation about the value of PM.

We agree that these can help; however, shop carefully. Be certain of the value that is brought by the consultant (previous experience in your practice area is helpful), and assure they have the experience to gather the right information accurately from the right people in your organization.

At the heart of most of these analyses is a maturity assessment tool which will apply an algorithm. As with any algorithm, even one sophisticated and generally relevant for your organization, with poor input, you could get misleading results.

CAREER PATH

From time to time—most likely every three to five years—it makes sense to step back and assess the job titles you use in your organization. Is *junior project manager, project manager, senior project manager,* and *project consultant,* or whatever terms you use, serving you properly? Has the context changed enough that it may make sense to shake it up a bit?

For example, perhaps your customers seem to be organizing their projects in terms of programs and portfolios—or your own organization has started to line up this way. Perhaps it's time to look at a career path that goes more like this: *project manager, program manager, program director,* and *portfolio leader.* It's worth the effort to investigate this periodically.

This can be a pretty heavy exercise for a large organization because of the involvement of the global human resources organization and perhaps government/union regulations. This is why we recommend a longer (three to five years) review cycle for such a momentous change.

Speaking of a feedback loop, how about the competency of closing projects and doing project reviews? Can that competency be improved? One of our colleagues, Mel Bost, PMP, author of *Lessons Learned: Taking Project Management to a New Level in a Continuous Process Improvement Framework,* thinks so. We've included a story from Mel that encourages the entire process of collecting lessons learned, improving processes, and working toward continuous improvement.

A Little Mood Music, Maestro!

As project managers, we have all participated in project reviews and project close out sessions that looked and felt more like inquisitions than positive, healthy, and constructive reviews. What went wrong? Who is to blame? Who was responsible for these outcomes and results? These actual results were not expected, and we are going to get to the bottom of the story.

There is a certain *mood* created by reviews such as these that perpetuates similar behavior in subsequent reviews. They take on a habitual characteristic. How does this happen and how might we, as PM practitioners, change these practices to improve our PM processes in a positive, sustainable, and constructive way?

Each of us has found ourselves *whistling* or *humming* a tune that has gotten stuck in our heads. You could be walking through a department store or grocery store with some background music softly playing and suddenly you are humming or whistling it too; or you could see a musical performance that really struck a *resonance* in your heart or mind.

We often say that this music sets the *mood* or *tone* for our behavior and actions. For example, I can recall as a young child hearing my mother softly singing . . .

> O what a beautiful morning,
> O what a beautiful day.
> O what a beautiful feeling,
> Everything's going my way.

I didn't think much about it at the time but, as I grew older, I began to recognize that what she was singing actually represented her philosophy or attitude and approach to life. The more she carried this tune with her throughout the day and week, the more her behavior and actions and those of people around her mirrored that tone.

I would say that there is something *infectious* about the mood music you have in your head—so much so that I want to challenge each of you to find that mood music that improves your performance and that of your projects in every area.

Once you do that, you will realize that you can personally change the mood and tone of your project reviews and close outs to reflect your own philosophy of what a successful project should look and feel like.

For project managers who are familiar with the older ways of conducting project reviews, there exists an opportunity to completely change the mood music of these reviews. *You can break the habit.* Focusing on project lessons learned in a positive manner establishes a mood or tone for all project managers in an organization, which they can then emulate as they go about their daily project manager tasks.

Is this thinking too radical for the project community to embrace and use as a new standard for conducting *actionable* project reviews? I really think not. We have all been impacted by mood music in all facets of our lives and this is just another application of that concept.

You, as an active project manager in your organization, can help ingrain this thinking and approach in your project practices. You can forge a new philosophy and approach to your PM career going forward by embracing these ideas.

There is an article in the June 2014 issue of *Scientific American* called "The Neuroscience of Habits." One of the major recent findings is that short-term decisions and judgments are often directed by *habit* rather than by rational and reasoned study of all the issues. Mood music works the same as habits. So, if we can get project managers to embrace project lessons learned as up-to-date mood music, they will begin to use it in their habitual thinking going forward.

Before his death, noted leadership development teacher Louis Tice of The Pacific Institute often stated that "people act in accordance with the truth as they perceive it to be." What if that *truth* was guided by mood music that valued lessons learned as a contributor to advancement of processes and procedures? When I was a project coordinator with ConocoPhillips, we initiated some project lessons-learned reviews to give our project managers some experience at identifying, capturing, and sharing lessons learned from projects. We established a Microsoft SharePoint database for storing these lessons learned for future reference. In doing so, I would like to think that we started the mood music for project managers to follow going forward, which focused less on who was to blame for project shortfalls and more on the improvement of the project process going forward for the entire organization.

So, what is the bottom line here? If you ensure that your project environment is providing the right background and mood music to your project managers, you can cement the habitual reactions that will lead to identifying, capturing, and sharing project lessons learned for continuous improvement to your business.

So, come on Maestro . . . a little mood music if you please!!!

In our case, the mood music to which Mel refers should be playing in the background as you and your organization build longer and better bridges to span the gaps in PM competency. This is important work, after all. You are strengthening the capability not only of your project managers, but of your organization for the long term. Let the band play on!

9

Leveraging Expert Judgment

In this book we have discussed our opinions on project management (PM) competency development, and have shown you many examples from our own experience in industry, as well as from our peers. We've done research, looked at statistics, talked to practicing project managers, and have shared our discoveries in PM competency based on:

- Our own decades of industry experience;
- Conversations with project management office (PMO) directors at medium and large organizations;
- Participation in academic institutions as course developers and instructors;
- Contributions and participation in Project Management Institute (PMI) Congresses and as officers in PMI Chapters;
- Questions from our survey (over 250 practicing project managers); and
- Research from PMI and others who study PM for a living.

Having said that, the most frequently mentioned tool and technique in *A Guide to the Project Management Body of Knowledge (PMBOK® Guide)* is *expert judgment*. With that in mind, we decided to provide our readers with the expert judgment of a variety of PM leaders who are authors, bloggers, consultants, podcasters, and professors. You may recognize several names here because many of them are highly visible contributors to PM media (books, blogs, podcasts, training, conferences). We asked these experts three thought-provoking questions and were delighted with their responsiveness—so delighted, in fact, because it shows how PM competency development is considered by these thought leaders as a critical element for successful project delivery.

Here are the questions we asked them:

1. What are the warning signs that a gap in PM competency exists?
2. Which one or two PM competencies have become more critical to project success over the past ten years, and which will gain importance over the next decade?
3. What solutions do you envision for the development of these PM competencies?

The following are the responses we received in order of arrival in our inbox. You will see a variety of opinions, not all necessarily aligned with each other's and/or with ours, but in a sense, converging to some of the focal points that we have discussed throughout the book.

HAROLD KERZNER

Dr. Harold Kerzner is Senior Executive Director with International Institute for Learning, Inc., and a globally recognized expert on project, program, and portfolio management—having authored numerous well-recognized books on these topics.

PM Competency Gap Warning Signs

PM competencies arose because companies did not know how to create job descriptions that differentiated between pay grades for project managers. While this seems like an easy thing to do, it is actually very difficult as the U.S. government and the private sector found out. You cannot use age, dollar value of the project, or years of experience as you would with traditional career paths in a discipline because a 25-year-old project manager can have better PM skills than a 50-year-old project manager with 20 years of experience. The 25 year old can be managing a $4 billion project today and a $200,000 project next year. The solution was to create competency models and then have the PMO work with educational providers to provide training that supports the competencies. Look in my *Best Practices* book because there is a great model in there that Eli Lilly developed when they fell into this trap. They created three competencies: technical, leadership, and (PM) processes. Then they developed training programs to support each competency.

Sometimes it is easy to develop job descriptions when there is a great deal of similarity between projects. But for large companies, with diverse projects, job descriptions must be replaced with competency models.

PM Competencies Now and in the Future

Eli Lilly included technical competencies because of the research and development (R&D) requirements in their business pipeline. But for the traditional company, technology can be purchased or, if the project manager has only an understanding of technology rather than being an expert, he/she can rely upon the technical expertise of the assigned team members. So, using the Eli Lilly model, it would be a close tie between *process knowledge* and *leadership*. However, process knowledge includes business processes as well as PM processes because most PM methodologies and frameworks today have business processes included. This is something the *PMBOK® Guide* does not address well. Today, project managers should not view themselves as simply managing a project, but should realize that with each project, they are managing part of a business. They are being transformed into business managers.

How to Develop PM Competencies

The biggest mistake I see is that too many companies design competencies based upon what skills they want the project managers to have today. I believe that good competencies should be forward looking and also address the skills needed for the company to survive 10–20 years rather than just this year.

> Project managers are being transformed into business managers.

ANDY KAUFMAN

Andy Kaufman, PMP, is an international speaker, author, and executive coach and is president of the Institute for Leadership Excellence & Development Inc.

PM Competency Gap Warning Signs

At a macro level, perhaps the most obvious warning sign that a gap in PM competency exists is related to project success rates. If we struggle to deliver projects successfully, there's a gap. Though this is a trailing indicator, it's the ultimate dose of reality that there are problems with how we are leading our projects.

The more intriguing challenge is to identify leading indicators—warning signs we can detect before the mushroom cloud of project failure emerges. Here are two examples of warning signs I look for:

- How and how often are risks talked about? If risks are rarely reviewed and discussed in meetings with the team, sponsor, or other stakeholders, that's a warning sign. If risks are talked about but the reaction is more along the lines of, "Hey, don't be so negative," or "Don't be Danny Downer!"—it's a warning sign.
- How much cognitive or affective conflict is there? In his book, *Why Great Leaders Don't Take Yes for an Answer*, Michael Roberto discusses the difference between cognitive and affective conflict. Cognitive conflict is about the ideas and approaches. It's our most idealistic view of conflict, in that it helps us get to better outcomes by having potentially difficult, even vigorous, discussions without getting personal. Affective conflict crosses the line of respect. Cognitive conflict is needed, and if there isn't enough, it's a warning sign. It could be an indicator that people don't care or at least aren't engaging. Affective conflict can be deadly to teams, and it is certainly a warning sign to address.

PM Competencies Now and in the Future

Increasingly project managers are required to influence without authority. I would expect this only to increase in importance as a competency as organizations get flatter and more *matrixed*.

Related (to this competency), it is critical that project managers build and maintain effective relationships. As Dan Shapiro told me in our discussion about his book, *Negotiating the Nonnegotiable*, we seem to be tribal in nature. We cluster in our groups and often don't sufficiently build bridges to other tribes. Herminia Ibarra is even more direct; she says our networks are lazy and narcissistic. In our discussion about her book *Act Like a Leader, Think Like a Leader*, Ibarra explains that we tend to build relationships with people who are easy to network with because of proximity (e.g., we go to lunch with people who sit near us in the same building). Also, we tend to network with people like us (e.g., we build the strongest relationships with people in our department or in the same profession).

Whether due to continued globalization, outsourcing, or increased diversity in the workplace, project managers will continually be required to build and maintain relationships beyond their natural organizational tribes.

> If we struggle to deliver projects successfully. . . . it's the ultimate dose of reality.

If I could throw in a third competency, it would be related to learning. There's little reason to think the pace of change is going to slow down. An oncologist in an MBA class I teach told me, "Everything I learned in med school is irrelevant now." He was learning PM because he sees that beefing up his business focus is increasingly critical to his ability to succeed in the future. Similarly, project managers need an insatiable hunger to learn and grow just to keep up and be relevant a decade from now.

How to Develop PM Competencies

In a recent interview with Jim Kouzes about his book, *Learning Leadership*, he emphasized research that indicates challenge to be the best way to develop our ability to lead. Books and classes are helpful, but ultimately, we learn best by doing. To that end, my favorite way of developing competencies is a combination of:

- Education, including simulations;
- On-the-job challenge; and
- Ongoing mentoring and coaching.

Any one of those can be helpful, but the three together are a powerful combination to develop the knowledge and skills to grow as a project professional.

WAYNE TURMEL

Wayne Turmel is cofounder of the Remote Leadership Institute, a podcaster, and an author of both business books and historical fiction (*The Count of the Sahara*, 2015).

PM Competency Gap Warning Signs

Often the first signs of trouble are ignored. With communication, especially in remote and virtual teams, those problems are seen as minor annoyances. E-mails don't get returned, people get tired of trying to get an answer and start excluding team members from the conversation, or the manager gets copied on every e-mail correspondence, creating a lot of rework and sucking up mental energy.

When teams aren't sharing updates and communication in an honest, proactive way, very often you don't know there's a problem until deadlines are missed or it's too late to correct a mistake before the client sees it.

By carefully monitoring both the content and tone of e-mail and meeting conversations, and allowing everyone to be heard and contribute, a good project manager can see the warning signs of conflict, misunderstanding, lack of trust, or misalignment. By only paying attention to data, we're at grave risk of seeing the flashing alerts that we would pick up if we were all in the same room together.

PM Competencies Now and in the Future

Without a doubt, PM competency will involve the ability to communicate while being mediated (and mitigated) by technology.

The need for good communication skills has always been there; the great management guru Peter Drucker pointed out that the greatest PM job of all time was building the pyramids—and we've just been trying to live up to that standard ever since. That's true, but the guy in charge of the pyramids wasn't trying to flog people over a conference line and a crummy speaker phone. So the need for competent communication is at least as critical as it has ever been.

Added to this is the notion that there are additional skills required when new technologies are involved. For an example, when asked if tools like Skype for Business, Slack, and other technology was important to the job, 80% of managers said they were *mission critical.* Yet fewer than 15% of managers said they were *competent and confident* using those tools to their best advantage. Even in highly technical fields, team members tend to use fewer than 25% of the features of these communication tools. In highly technical fields, the assumption is that these folks understand the technology and have no fear of it, but reality shows that not to be the case.

Project managers in the future have to understand:

1. The communication skills necessary to build good human working relationships and information pathways;

2. The tools available to them; and

3. How to choose the appropriate tool and leverage its power to overcome the challenges of working remotely and get the most from them. The more things change. . . .

How to Develop PM Competencies

Funny enough, the first step—and it's not a minor or obvious one—is to acknowledge how the way we work today (distributed, remote, and virtual teams) impacts the dynamics of a team. When highly competent people work remotely from each other, there is often a tendency to look inward and tend to our own work; silos form.

As communication tools are introduced, the training and learning needs to come in both the tool itself (How does this work? Why use this tool versus something else?) and in the work demands that create context for that tool or best practice (How can using a webcam, even if it's personally awkward, be used to build team relationships and enhance productivity and work quality? How does this tool fit into the workflow?). Many project managers, because they start as subject matter experts or individual contributors, sometimes ignore the interpersonal, turning communication into mere data transfer which, no matter how efficient, is not nearly enough.

Developing communication and technology skills in tandem will be critical. By definition, if we only use self-directed, asynchronous methodologies, it will play into the isolation and silos. Dare we say, we may have to have group (in-person or live online) interaction to help model skills and have crucial conversations.

> When teams aren't sharing updates and communication in an honest, proactive way, very often you don't know there's a problem until deadlines are missed or it's too late to correct a mistake before the client sees it.

GINA ABUDI

Gina Abudi, MBA, is president of Abudi Consulting Group, LLC and author of *Best Practices for Managing BPI Projects*, *Implementing Positive Organizational Change*, and former long-time president of the PMI Mass Bay Chapter.

PM Competency Gap Warning Signs

I see warning signs in:

- Continued project failures with an inability to reflect on those failures;
- Inability to engage team members and stakeholders in the project;
- Failure to accept responsibility for the project;
- A lack of understanding of the vision for the project and its alignment to corporate strategy; and
- Insufficient and/or poor communications with stakeholders.

PM Competencies Now and in the Future

The ability to effectively communicate with and engage stakeholders in a variety of ways have been critical to project success over the past ten years, especially with the continued growth of global initiatives (emotional intelligence).

As projects have become more complex, as well as the increasingly differing needs and wants of stakeholders, it has been essential for project managers to communicate with and engage stakeholders in a variety of ways to keep them interested and involved in the project. Without this engagement, it is unlikely that the project will be deemed successful by stakeholders.

Benefits realization is becoming increasingly important. This requires project managers to focus more on strategy rather than solely the day-to-day work of the project. It requires project managers to work closely with key stakeholders to identify, plan, and track the project against realizing benefits to the business. This certainly requires project managers to think more strategically and critically about the projects they manage, as well as make connections to projects launched and their impact on/benefit to divisions and departments. I am certainly seeing this as an essential competency for project managers at my own global clients.

Simply having technical knowledge and even basic leadership skills is insufficient. My global clients want project managers who are strategic in the actions they take and can think critically through how to ensure benefits realization from every project that the organization undertakes.

How to Develop PM Competencies

The best solutions to develop these competencies include exposure through practical experiences. Looking at PM from a strategic viewpoint enables for more focus in developing PM competencies. It matters more when it is tied to organizational strategy.

For my clients, a path to development of PM competencies includes, at a high level: identify gaps in competencies → develop a plan to reduce those gaps (training, coaching, practical experience) and tie them to performance management → measure success in increasing competencies.

> PM matters more when it is tied to organizational strategy.

JIM DE PIANTE

Jim De Piante, PMP, is Executive Project Manager Emeritus, De Piante International, LLC.

PM Competency Gap Warning Signs

Taking the long view, projects that fail to live up to expectations are a pretty big clue that there is a problem. Competent project managers deliver the right scope, on time, and within budget.

But why wait until the project is delivered late and over budget to see that there is a problem? You will know immediately that something is wrong on the very first day that the project begins. Is there an agreed-to and formally approved statement of requirements for the project? No? Well, there you go. You will fail.

PM Competencies Now and in the Future

What does ten years have to do with anything? PM competencies don't change with the zeitgeist. Notwithstanding all that we have learned, we haven't gotten much better at delivering projects successfully. How about we master the competencies we haven't mastered from 10 years ago before we start looking at the novelties?

How to Develop PM Competencies

The three most important things in PM don't have anything do with the project manager or PM. They have to do with the business analyst and the systems analyst (called by different names in different domains). Those three things?

1. Requirements
2. Requirements
3. Requirements

Apart from that, we need to never lose sight of the fact that PM is not a technical discipline. It is fundamentally a people discipline. The essence of PM is leadership (which implies extraordinary skill in relationships and communications—where the project managers spend 95% of their time).

Assuming you are properly managing requirements (business and system), in order to implement them properly, you do not need technical skills, you need leadership competencies. So the next three most important things in project management are:

1. Leadership
2. Leadership
3. Leadership

Do the basics right and you will succeed. And it all begins with knowing what you are supposed to make. Requirements. And then leading your team well. Requirements. Leadership. Everything else is superfluous.

PM is fundamentally a people discipline.

ELIZABETH HARRIN

Elizabeth Harrin is a popular blogger (GirlsGuideToPM.com) and is the author of *Collaboration Tools for Project Managers* and *Social Media for Project Managers*.

PM Competency Gap Warning Signs

Project performance is the main warning sign. It's not often possible to benchmark the performance of project managers against each other because the projects they are working on differ so widely. And if a project is stopped prematurely or canceled, you can't immediately assume it had to do with the project manager's poor performance. More and more we need to be reviewing and closing down projects that are not meeting their business case goals. It's no one's fault a lot of the time, it's just the way that the business has evolved around the project.

I mention all of this just to set the scene that it's hard to define what a project manager's performance should be when it comes to project results, and that's often why competency gaps go unnoticed.

The best thing to look for is projects that skip between green and red, projects with a lot of *surprises* and a long list of risks and issues that don't seem to be managed. And complaints from customers; that can be very telling!

PM Competencies Now and in the Future

The most important competency is definitely *soft skills* in its widest form. More specifically, I would say stakeholder engagement. As we are seeing more projects being affected by community action and involvement, it really is possible for a project to get stopped because the wrong people were engaged (or overlooked). After all, problems don't stop projects, people do.

We've already seen *stakeholder management* evolve in the PM language to *stakeholder engagement* and we've seen a new chapter appear in the *PMBOK® Guide*. I think the area will grow in importance over the coming 10 years.

How to Develop PM Competencies

Understanding what project managers need to work on to improve their skills is the first step in working out how to develop them.

Peer reviews, project audits, and quality reviews can be ways to identify project performance that might be an outlier due to project manager competency. Then you can follow up with conversations: you may find that the project manager in question is perfectly aware that they don't have the required skills but no one has offered to help them do anything about it in the past.

Training is the obvious answer, but I don't think this alone can really change competency. So much of *competency* is tied up in long-term behavioral shift, understanding workplace culture, and lived experience. This is hard to get in a two-day training course.

Supporting project managers with mentors and coaches is a more practical way to effect long-term change and to really grow the skills of your PM team with any depth.

> It's hard to define what a project manager's performance should be when it comes to project results, and that's often why competency gaps go unnoticed.

MARK REESON

Mark Reeson, M R Project Solutions, is a PM consultant, trainer, blogger, speaker, and coach.

PM Competency Gap Warning Signs

There seems to be an endless run of projects that still seem to be failing and yet an increase in the number of people that are being labeled or titled project managers. There still seems to be a focus within the industry that getting a qualification is the answer when we all know that simply passing an examination or an assessment does not mean you can do the job in hand.

This approach then misleads the community as a whole into believing that more can be placed on a project manager almost immediately after qualification, when the individual needs help and support more. It is the interpersonal skills that will help them grow, not simply the technical skills they learn in the classroom through processes.

PM Competencies Now and in the Future

Two competencies that have been and remain critical to be a successful project manager are those of scope management and understanding the real workload and effort required to deliver the project, i.e., the ability of the project manager to contextualize their project by having the self awareness of what it takes to deliver the project in the manner and environment in which it needs to be delivered.

As the industry moves forward, the competency of leadership will take greater hold and will need to be advanced both as part of leading the team and also as being part of the team.

I believe the second of the two, which will take on greater significance in the coming years, will be the ability to manage time more efficiently as the demands on everyone's time becomes more precious as we move into a world where demand and demand now seem to be the new norm.

How to Develop PM Competencies

I believe the solution to these continuing problems starts with the *training* companies, but then the responsibility also belongs to the workplaces to continue the learning.

This learning should now start to involve more scenario-based physical activities that are relevant to the organization in which the work is being done, which allows the project manager to make the mistakes in a safer environment and to take the learning of the sessions into the workplace.

In addition, these approaches to learning allow those involved in projects on the outside to gain a greater understanding of the project manager's expectation and vice versa.

The problems will continue to grow until recognition for application of skills is given the same (if not greater) importance than the theory and the examination.

> As the industry moves forward, the competency of leadership will take greater hold.

SUSANNE MADSEN

Susanne Madsen is an internationally recognized project leadership coach, trainer, and consultant. She is the author of *The Project Management Coaching Workbook* and *The Power of Project Leadership*.

PM Competency Gap Warning Signs

There are many different warning signs, with the most obvious being that projects aren't on track as they are either late, over budget, or not producing the output that was expected. In many cases these warning signs are directly related to how well we perform—or don't perform—the traditional PM disciplines in terms of defining, planning, executing, and controlling the project.

Another warning sign—which is equally if not more alarming—is when a project delivers roughly the output it was expected to, but without producing any material benefit or value add as a result. In the PM industry, benefit realization is traditionally the responsibility of the executive sponsor, but this view can be problematic as it decouples the project manager and the project team from one of the most important aspects of the project—the value the project will ultimately bring.

Everyone has to step up and take responsibility for the project's benefits. It isn't until the intended outputs, outcomes, and benefits have been delivered that the project team can claim to have done a great job.

But there are other signs too that a gap in PM competency exists, and some of them, unfortunately, seem to have been accepted as the norm on many projects. Some examples would be: teams that work long hours, regular meetings that frequently get canceled, conflicting views and opinions that are suppressed rather than explored and resolved, misunderstandings that occur at all levels due to insufficient communication, and only a few people on the team who take responsibility and make decisions while the rest are largely disengaged.

These signs are evidence of an underlying competency gap, not in traditional PM planning skills, but in interpersonal and leadership skills.

PM Competencies Now and in the Future

In the past 10 years, there has been an emphasis on the hard PM skills, acquiring the right tools and defining the best processes. In many ways, that's a good thing as project managers have needed this foundational knowledge in order to successfully deliver their projects.

This trend will probably continue for a while as more and more people run projects in parallel with their day jobs and are in need of understanding the basics. These people aren't necessarily career project managers. They may be sales and marketing staff or have an operational role, and part of their job is to also run projects.

What we're also seeing, however, is that hard skills aren't sufficient to be successful. The hard skills don't help project managers to engage their teams, to become better communicators, or to get better at resolving conflict. And they don't help project managers focus on the business and ensure that benefits are delivered. That's why we'll experience a growing emphasis on leadership, interpersonal skills, and business acumen.

In the next decade, projects will continue to become more complex, be more interdependent, have more stakeholders, and be delivered by distributed teams and people who expect to be involved. The requirement for the project manager to be a leader in addition to a manager will therefore gain importance in the next decade.

When I say *leader*, I mean someone who can navigate complexity, who can speak and understand the language of the business, and someone who has the emotional intelligence to engage and motivate the team. That might sound like a tall order, but it's very possible and absolutely essential for the project manager to acquire these skills if projects are to be delivered successfully.

How to Develop PM Competencies

That's a very good question and one that I'm continuously working on!

To improve the project managers' leadership and interpersonal skills, we need to train them in a different way to what we typically do today, and over a longer period of time. Traditional classroom training works well when teaching hard skills, but is less effective when it comes to soft skills.

Soft skills have to be taught in a very practical and interactive way that focuses on behaviors. The training has to enable the participants not just to reflect on existing behavioral patterns but to also practice new behaviors that help them overcome their day-to-day challenges. This could, for instance, be to practice how to have a conversation with a team member who is not taking responsibility, or how to converse with a stakeholder who is critical of the project.

The training also has to help the project managers increase their self-awareness and understand what their triggers are, and how they can get better at managing their emotions under pressure.

Developing a project manager's leadership skills is an ongoing process that can't be learned from theory alone. People have to work with it at a practical level through role-plays and interaction with others. They have to get feedback from peers and on-the-spot mentoring from their managers as this will ensure that they continue to learn and minimize their blind spots.

Professional coaching, peer-to-peer mentoring, and shadowing someone in a business role are also great tools for development.

> Training must enable participants not just to reflect on existing behavioral patterns, but to also practice new behaviors that help them overcome their day-to-day challenges.

STEPHEN LEYBOURNE

Dr. Stephen Leybourne is a professor at Boston University and the author of *Learning to Improvise, or Improvising to Learn: Knowledge Generation and 'Innovative Practice' in Project Environments*.

PM Competency Gap Warning Signs

I think that we have moved from a situation where tools and techniques were seen as preeminent in project-based management, to an emerging—maybe even *emerged* paradigm that supersedes the *plan then execute* with *the minimum of deviation* model.

We have now accepted that there is no *silver bullet* in PM that projects—and particularly *interlinked* programs and portfolios of projects—are much more complex than the earlier academic and practitioner literature suggested, and that projects are operating in increasingly complex and turbulent environments.

When a shift like this takes place, the competencies that we felt comfortable with—i.e., planning tools like Gantt charts, work breakdown structures, the calculation of earned value, etc.—suddenly seem inadequate to the delivery of projects in the new PM landscape.

There has been a shift toward *behaviors* and the acceptance that people construct and deliver project deliverables, and the PM domain has to adjust to this new reality.

PM Competencies Now and in the Future

Leadership and the ability to manage and inspire project workers, and the effective use of emotional intelligence (EI) are the two competencies that I see as vital to the effective delivery of projects in the current project landscape.

Good leaders make things happen, and utilize behavioral concepts such as motivating; building commitment and trust; and ensuring that project workers deliver.

EI is an essential skill for those leaders, as an understanding that we are all different and perceive not just project issues but *all* issues differently, and will enable empathetic leaders with good EI skills to succeed and deliver.

In the next decade the issues of ambiguity, uncertainty, and complexity will rise to the fore since PM is not going to get easier. The PM landscape is likely to become more challenging, and the ability to make decisions based on incomplete information and to deal with uncertainty in requirements for potentially changing deliverables brought about by the aforementioned *turbulent* environments and the complexity of interlinked projects will become desirable skills.

I also see linkages with improvised work here, as rapid delivery to meet emerging and changing requirements becomes more important and a reliance on creativity and intuition—used in a controlled manner—opens up the opportunity to use less planned interventions to resolve project issues around changing requirements.

How to Develop PM Competencies

I think that the first thing that has to happen is that people working within and around projects—and this includes project sponsors—may have to step away from a complete dependence on *process* and following the PM procedures laid down by the organization. This means building trust in the abilities of project-based workers to use experience and tacitly built

knowledge competencies to resolve project issues and emerging requirements as they arise.

Obviously, the degree of project maturity within organizations varies
significantly, but I see most organizations having to accept a greater degree of uncertainty, and this means that effective project managers with a
reputation for effective *delivery* will be more in demand than ever.

DAVID SHIRLEY

David Shirley, PMP, is a professor at Boston University, the Cleland
Award-winning coauthor of *Green Project Management* (with Rich
Maltzman), and the cofounder of EarthPM, LLC.

PM Competency Gap Warning Signs

There are subtle warning signs, like stakeholders (internal and external)
losing enthusiasm for your project, and more obvious ones like getting behind schedule, and/or over budget, and/or product and processes failing.

There is no doubt that there are *hard* competencies and *soft* competencies. Like Maslow, there is a pyramid. The hard competency, project
planning (which in itself can be decomposed into several steps up, going
up the pyramid), has to be there to be able to achieve the softer of the competencies toward the top. Gaps can exist anywhere along the continuum.
Gaps in the hard competencies are easier to spot.

PM Competencies Now and in the Future

I'm not sure that the competencies required in the past and today aren't
the same ones that will be critical to PM success in the future, only altered
somewhat. What I mean is that they will change in structure, and they
already have. I wouldn't go so far as to say drones will be delivering project
status to stakeholders, but communications, my number one future concern, will continue to evolve.

Of the personal competencies, verbal and written communications
will be critical to project success. While project managers will have to continue to talk to people, more and more communications will be through
social media or alternate type communications. Without this knowledge

and expertise in these *new* communications, the project manager will be at a disadvantage, probably putting the success of the project in jeopardy.

How to Develop PM Competencies

I've always thought that the practice of educating project managers is a little like trying to turn a supertanker. Once started in a particular direction, it is very difficult to redirect it.

However, in order to properly arm the project manager with the ammunition he or she needs to successfully manage projects, we must be willing to change directions quickly as new communication methods emerge.

Thought leaders in this field, like Elizabeth Harrin, are on the cutting edge of this technology (if I can use the word technology). Perhaps a more Agile approach, rather than a traditional one, needs to be undertaken to both identify and educate project managers.

Either way, the supertanker needs to be more of a speedboat and be able to *turn on a dime* but without tipping the boat!

> Educating project managers is a little like trying to turn a supertanker. Once started in a particular direction, it is very difficult to redirect it.

MEL BOST

Mel Bost is a PMO expert, a principal with BOT, and is the author of *Lessons Learned: Taking Project Management to a New Level*.

PM Competency Gap Warning Signs

Lack of clear, concise communication with and/or commitment of the project team, stakeholders, or sponsors is a first sign of a PM competency gap.

PM Competencies Now and in the Future

Development and execution of a robust project risk management plan for the highest priority risks has become essential for project success over the past ten years. Also, development of third-party procurement/services plans has become essential.

Over the next decade, more projects will contain a *technology development* aspect and an infusion of *information technology* which will require new competencies in understanding and managing new technology introductions. Project managers must learn to manage new technology development.

Project managers who are competent in *risk management* will apply new concepts such as *controllable* and *uncontrollable* risk to successfully manage new technology introduction.

How to Develop PM Competencies

For the single PM practitioner, benchmarking and best practice identification and utilization can provide new PM competency development. For project managers within a PMO setting, the PMO must provide leadership in identifying, introducing, and teaching new PM competencies.

> Over the next decade, more projects will contain a *technology development* aspect and an infusion of *information technology* which will require new competencies.

ROBERT WYSOCKI

Robert Wysocki, Ph.D., has more than 40 years of experience as a PM consultant and trainer, information systems manager, systems and management consultant, training developer, and provider. The founder of Enterprise Information Insights, Inc., he has written 20 books on project management, business analysis, and information systems management; one of which is the widely used textbook *Effective Project Management: Traditional, Agile, Extreme.*

PM Competency Gap Warning Signs

Project managers who have not made a commitment to business strategic goals and their reliance on established processes tells me they are not a team player. Complex PM requires a holistic view of the organization and that is missing in most project managers.

PM Competencies Now and in the Future

Flexibility and creativity in process execution are at the top of my list. I firmly believe that both of these are driven by the characteristics of the project, the internal organizational climate and culture, and the external market conditions. Furthermore, since these are dynamic, the management process must also be dynamic.

How to Develop PM Competencies

I would argue for a seat at the strategy table for PM. Project managers need a vested and recognized role at the corporate level, and they don't have that today.

> Complex PM requires a holistic view of the organization and that is missing in most project managers.

MOIRA ALEXANDER

Moira Alexander is a blogger and the author of *Lead or Lag: Linking Strategic Project Management & Thought Leadership*.

PM Competency Gap Warning Signs

Aside from the obvious missed objectives, communication breakdowns can be the first, more subtle, but key signal that competency gaps may exist. It can be an indicator that not everyone has a clear understanding of expectations, roles, processes, stakeholders, or even the intended goals.

That said, sometimes signs don't present themselves in this manner, but rather through small process-based glitches along the way. Although these may seem small or isolated, once consolidated they can create an extensive disconnect that can compromise efforts. In tandem with communication breakdowns, they can create high risk and even spell project failure.

PM Competencies Now and in the Future

As I've previously maintained, I believe in many ways the term project manager is somewhat misleading, as the role ideally requires individuals who are thought leaders and strategic thinkers in every sense. Because of this, I often refer to project managers as project leaders and believe their true value lies in the ability to focus on high-level aspects like strategic alignment and leadership.

Leadership abilities as a core personal competency is critical for success and should encapsulate a high degree of accountability and transparency, as well as the ability to mentor new leaders who offer the same potential. This requires a project manager who, as Peter Drucker so famously said, ". . . not only does things right all the time, but also does the right things."

Cognitive abilities are another core personal competency I believe to be critical to project success, now and into the future. This ability enables project leaders to see well beyond just the obvious. Instead, they are able to adopt more of a *holistic* view and approach when dealing with project obstacles and achieving goals. They can stretch beyond limitations and continually seek hidden opportunities and better value.

How to Develop PM Competencies

Today's leaders will need to make a conscious and deliberate effort to highlight and demonstrate the benefits of these nontechnical high-value competencies. They will also need to invest significant time and effort in mentoring tomorrow's project leaders in this regard.

Additionally, more focus should be put on developing these personal core competencies in future PM training and development programs around the world, whether internal or external to organizations.

> In many ways, the term *project manager* is somewhat misleading since the role ideally requires individuals who are thought leaders and strategic thinkers in every sense.

DAN PICARD

Dan Picard, Mindedge, is a seasoned PM trainer and content provider.

PM Competency Gap Warning Signs

Aside from the obvious signs that people have talked about for years (poor communication, missed deadlines, budget overruns, etc.), I'd be a little concerned if I noticed a lot of workarounds and hidden factories in use, or a lot of waste in reaching project objectives.

Workarounds and hidden factories would suggest that maybe the project manager didn't have a good grasp on project scope, quality, or risk, and waste would imply that costs may have run higher than they needed to.

Unexpected procurements halfway through a project might indicate that the project manager may have had to *buy talent* from outside of the project team, which would make me question his or her HR (human resouce) and work assignment capabilities.

And while surprises on the project may be a red flag to many people, I would also be concerned if no surprises occurred. In a perfect world, a project manager would be prepared for every possible contingency, but in the *real world* we know that things occur on projects that we couldn't be ready for.

I'm reminded of the Lean saying that *having no problems is the biggest problem of all*; if the project managers in my organization told me that they hadn't seen any project issues that they weren't ready for, I'd question whether they were truly in touch with the details and finer points of their projects. I'd also question their approach to continuous improvement and would worry about the quality of the lessons learned they'd captured.

PM Competencies Now and in the Future

Two competencies that have grown in stature over the last decade or so are the ability to strategically align projects to overall organizational objectives and a focus on interpersonal skills to enhance project success.

We've all learned that for our projects to be of real value to our organizations (and to continue to be funded), they need to support the mission and vision set forth by senior management and corporate executives. And while technical skills continue to be an important factor in project results, the *soft skills* employed can have just as big an influence.

Looking forward, I would counsel people to strengthen their transitioning, influencing, and complex decision-making abilities.

Project management seems to be moving toward a melding of Agile and Waterfall techniques, but this can be difficult—and in some cases, scary—for many people to adapt. A project manager who can guide his or her team through this transition (or others like it) would be a tremendous asset to an organization.

The rate of collaboration, partnerships, and interdisciplinary engagement continues to increase at a staggering pace, so an ability to influence others that you may not have authority over can quickly set you apart as a highly capable project leader. And because clients and stakeholders now expect practitioners to be able to achieve results at top speed, the power to process complex information and make effective decisions quickly and efficiently will help to ensure that a project will remain on track to meet its goals.

How to Develop PM Competencies

The most important solution would be some sort of updated scenario-based approach to mentoring and training. The approach will need to avoid the *sage on the stage* technique that simply lectures people on the benefits and merits of a long list of possible solutions.

Instead, an innovative approach will need to be created that allows learners to work through *real-life* narratives, analyzing problems and synthesizing a response that takes into account all of the tradeoffs that need to be made to come to a reasonable result.

This *immersion approach* would prepare practitioners to pick out the important artifacts that will have the greatest impact on their situation and to deal with them in a realistic way. The mentoring/training will likely need to incorporate some sort of technology that allows all involved parties to work together in a convenient location (whether it occurs in a physical or a virtual environment), at a beneficial pace, and at a favorable time that does not interfere with their *regularly scheduled* duties and responsibilities.

But the most powerful aspect of this approach will still need to be the capability to teach effective ways to dissect important information from complicated situations and to synthesize appropriate yet realistic responses.

An innovative approach will need to be created that allows learners to work through *real-life* narratives.

KIMBERLY WIEFLING

Kimberly Wiefling is a global business leadership consultant, the author of *Scrappy Project Management,* and an entire series of very scrappy books.

PM Competency Gap Warning Signs

According to some fascinating research published in the MIT Sloan Management Review, over 80% of global teams are failing for entirely predictable and avoidable reasons. Among the most common are:

- A lack of trusting relationships among team members
- Failure to overcome communication barriers—and these are not exclusively language-related, but include the inability to make decisions and problem solve as a team
- Misalignment between individual goals and team goals—basically a lack of shared priorities
- Unclear goals

These are the warning signs that a PM competency gap exists, and that the team is destined for another round of *lessons not learned.*

PM Competencies Now and in the Future

Globalization in today's business world is rapid and inescapable. As a result, many projects these days involve geographically dispersed teams comprised of members from a wide variety of countries and cultures.

While language barriers, decision-making style, and time zones are well-recognized challenges, the positive benefits of global teams continue to drive this trend. We must be able to collaborate across borders and boundaries of every kind. In addition, teams frequently include members who do not all work for the same company, and who may not have access to a common IT system.

As a result, the competencies that have become most critical to project success, and will become increasingly important as globalization continues, are:

- Global mindset: globalization in today's business world is rapid and inescapable. Even if you only do business in your home country, you still are likely to face growing competition from abroad. In 2011, Pfizer—a non-Japanese company—became the biggest pharmaceutical company in Japan, which is even more amazing because it is in a regulated industry! My definition of a global-minded person is someone who behaves as if they are a citizen of the world in addition to a citizen of their home country. The Thunderbird School of Global Management has a more detailed definition that includes important qualities like exceptional open-mindedness, cultural curiosity, and a willingness to experiment. Although working in another country is an incredibly valuable experience, you don't have to be assigned to work abroad to achieve a global mindset. There are plenty of opportunities to expand our awareness of what's happening on a planetary level via the www (world wide waste of time).

- An understanding of perceptual biases and cognitive distortions: human brains are the same all over the world. Working in global teams, I'm constantly searching for commonalities among people beyond the barriers of language and culture. While there are certainly plenty of differences between people from different countries, the unconscious workings of the human brain unite us. It seems that the way we evolved assures that everyone tends to fall into these same cognitive traps. In my experience, understanding and overcoming these common cognition vulnerabilities leads to dramatic improvements in the way we work together and the results that we produce. Awareness leads to clarity, and clarity leads to higher quality choices, which increase our chances of project success.

- Cultural intelligence includes the ability to build trusting relationships and work effectively with people who are culturally different from us. But it's important not to rely on stereotypes in relating to people from other cultures. I've found the *Island Model of Culture* an effective metaphor for establishing common ground with project team members regardless of their origin. The obvious traits we associate with *the norm* of a particular culture are those that an outsider can easily observe. Walk down a busy Tokyo street during lunchtime and you can't help but notice that they're a sea of dark suits, white shirts, and dark ties. In the evening, you might wonder how such *shy and conservative* businessmen can keep so many karaoke joints in business. Only a peek below the surface could resolve this seeming contradiction. Below the water level you'll find the unobservable influencers of behavior—factors an outsider would likely miss in a casual encounter. These are the values, beliefs, and norms driving the observable behaviors. As far as I can tell, these influential factors and their observable characteristics are what cross-cultural experts refer to as a country's *culture*. Beneath all of the obvious and obscure differences lies the bedrock of shared human being-ness (except perhaps for sociopaths).

- Team collaboration tool mastery: successful project leaders must be adept at sharing information online in ways that are useful and accessible to team members globally. My favorite information sharing tool is a Google Site (their version of a wiki) with a Google Drive folder to store files. These tools enable a group of people to share responsibility for creating, modifying, and growing the content of the electronic project notebook, and serve as a team memory—vital to avoiding amnesia in project teams. The benefits of a shared computer space, where groups of people can collectively create, access, and edit information are undeniable. There's no better way to get everyone on the same page than by having just one—and only one—page that everyone is looking at. The problem is getting them to look at that page! When we're working in the same building, we can always call a meeting and force people to look at the same documents together. When we're spread all over the world, it's not so easy. Sending an e-mail doesn't guarantee that the e-mail is read, and creating a wiki doesn't guarantee that anyone bothers to visit it. But I'm not giving up, mind you! While it's been challenging to get people to adopt new tools and new ways of doing business, the alternative—returning to a blizzard of disorganized e-mail and overstuffed computer folders—would be like giving up my iPhone in favor of a landline.

How to Develop PM Competencies

Knowing how to do something is not enough, it is the discipline to DO that is required. But how to develop discipline? One way is to commit to a checklist.

A checklist can be thought of as a set of operating guidelines that remind us of what we should do even when we don't feel like it. It's a rock in a sea of flotsam and jetsam. It's the next best thing to being lucky.

I know a pilot who has flown 7,000 hours. I asked him the other day, "Chuck, the next time you fly are you going to use your preflight checklist?" "You bet!" he replied. Now why would an experienced jet pilot with that much experience use a checklist? Because that's what professionals do. Professionals know that, in the heat of battle, much of our blood rushes to our arms and legs where it's useful for the flight or fight response, leaving little to nourish the one major advantage we have over monkeys—our frontal lobes.

As professionals, we need to do what needs to be done, regardless of whether we have time to do it (there's never enough), regardless of whether we think other people will like it, and regardless of how we feel about it. Our feelings are not a reliable guide to what needs to be done to guarantee project success.

> There's no better way to get everyone on the same page than by having just one—and only one—page that everyone is looking at.

TODD WILLIAMS

Todd Williams is president of eCameron and an executive consultant, author, instructor, and keynote speaker.

PM Competency Gap Warning Signs

The book I am currently writing (*Filling Gaps in Strategy and Project Execution: What Executives and Project Managers Need to Know to Execute Strategy Successfully*), which I hope to get to the publisher in January, is on the gaps in project execution. The problem, and how I read your question, is people keep focusing on the project manager. Granted they have issues, but many of them cannot resolve the grander problem. The gaps are that they are:

- Not leaders. . . nor are many of the people above them. . . nor are they allowed to be, as the *leaders* above them see project managers as managers.
- Unaware of how their project fits in the grand scheme. They are not given the visibility into the corporate direction, so they cannot see what is important and how to maintain alignment.

- Provided with executive sponsors that are ineffective. The sponsors know little about PM and are incentivized on other successes, not the project's.
- Governance (if it exists) is so overbearing that it is surprising any projects start.
- Project managers and the rest of the organization know nothing about adoption or organizational change management. . . yet projects deliver change. I am totally baffled by this lack of connection.
- Last, there is the language gap. Projects are tracked for success by measuring scope, schedule, and budget. But you can hit or miss those targets and be a total success or abject failure. The real measure is value (to the delivering and receiving parties).

This is just one example of many areas where executive PM gaps exist. The genesis is that executives come from sales, marketing, or operations and have never run a real project. Project managers never make it to the CEO seat. This gap in understanding is huge and a continual problem.

Executives speak about initiatives, goals, and execution while project managers talk about projects, tasks, and implementation. They talk right past one another.

What I am saying is that we keep looking at the competency of the project manager as the competency required to run projects, when we need to be looking at the competency of the organization to run projects. As Peter Senge says, it is more complex and we need to look at the system, not the operation.

PM Competencies Now and in the Future

Leadership and adoption/change management (not project change control).

How to Develop PM Competencies

As you can infer from my answer to the first question, these are large organizational changes, and they have to be addressed from the top down. They need to be tackled with education throughout the organization.

I believe it starts with defining the executive sponsor role with accountability for the project's success (for both the delivering and receiving end) based on value. This action alone keeps projects aligned to corporate goals, creates minimal viable products, and requires a focus on adoption.

This pushes executive sponsors into a *right-sized* governance role. They cannot levy too much governance or they will collapse under the weight, but they need enough to keep this tied together. This is much like how a classic product manager role works. It also means that the project manager role elevates to a greater leadership role that has to mind the details of adoption (using someone on the project). It automatically switches the focus to value.

In the long run this might give the project manager a career path into the *professional executive sponsor* role, but seems a little farfetched at this point.

MARISA SILVA

Marisa Silva is a PMO Analyst, competency center manager, consultant, and blogger (The Lucky PM).

PM Competency Gap Warning Signs

To hold (or not) the necessary level of competencies highly influences the outputs and outcomes produced, thus, a key warning sign that a gap in PM competency exists is poor performance and its immediate reflection on the project. This gap is mainly demonstrated through delayed and/or unclear deliverables, entangled communication, unclear responsibilities, a dissatisfied client, and a de-motivated team.

PM Competencies Now and in the Future

Over the past ten years the world of PM has considerably changed and nowadays PM is starting to be perceived as not just an instrumental, execution-oriented discipline, where project managers are expected to simply *get the job done*, but as leaders who must hold more than just technical competencies if they are to deliver projects with a positive and sustainable impact.

In the past years, two closely related PM competencies gained a new attention as critical to project success: leadership and stakeholder engagement management.

It is now acknowledged that leadership is much more than good management and is a foundational competency for project managers, since it includes elements such as the ability to communicate effectively or to motivate teams, both essential to project success.

Considering the current panorama where projects have become bigger, more complex, and involve a wider number of stakeholders—such as happens with infrastructure megaprojects—another key competency that has become critical is stakeholder engagement management. No longer can the project manager afford to only communicate with the sponsor or client; there are a number of stakeholders with different interests, needs, and attitudes that need to be identified and whose engagement has to be continuously managed throughout the project. To neglect this competency can be, nowadays, the difference between a successful or a failed project.

The future is always uncertain but it is reasonable to suggest that competencies such as change management, business awareness, and systems thinking will gain importance in the universe of PM.

While it is accepted that projects introduce change, and that people perceive change in different ways, this is rarely addressed consistently by project managers. To effectively manage change is thus not just important, but needed, and it is my hope that project managers will start paying more attention to this subject in the future.

Projects are also vehicles of strategy; they are created to put business strategies into action. For this reason, project managers cannot afford to manage their projects in isolation, without considering, understanding, and challenging the business context in which projects exist.

In fact, no project is an island. Linked to this idea is also the concept of systems thinking, which I believe will be in high demand since projects are becoming more complex than ever. To this end, to be able to explore how the different parts of the project interact and to make sense of chaos is likely to be a valuable PM competence in the future.

How to Develop PM Competencies

The conscious-competence learning model reminds us that there is no easy or fast-track way to develop a competency in individuals.

Competency development is a personal and individual journey. Nevertheless, there are suitable solutions out there. Coaching, project-based learning, and reflective practice are methods to be considered since they are highly practice-oriented while at the same time providing an opportunity for reflection and improvement.

Finally, although some may find it obvious, learning from experience continues to be one of the best ways to develop new competencies.

> No longer can the project manager afford to only communicate with the sponsor or client.

VIJAY KANABAR

Dr. Vijay Kanabar, PMP, is the coauthor of *Project Management MBA Fundamentals* and *The Art and Science of Project Management*.

PM Competency Gap Warning Signs

You must have heard of the *cause and effect* principle. Let me use this as an example to answer this question. A couple of years ago, I set out to study posted job descriptions for PM positions. While researching the competencies carefully, I found a list of attributes that did not surprise me:

- The new project manager will make sure that project schedules don't slip
- The new project manager will make sure that the project stays on track financially

But what took me by surprise, however, was the strong emphasis on behavioral competencies. It was as if frustrated senior executives, reflecting on failed project managers, chimed in that the next project manager better be good at:

- Effectively communicating relevant information to superiors
- Demonstrating leadership
- Evaluating and resolving issues in a timely fashion
- Managing conflicts
- Negotiating with stakeholders and influencing them successfully
- Demonstrating very good interpersonal skills

Reflecting on the cause and effect principle here, the *effects* certainly are missed schedules and blown budgets, but the real *cause* could be a lack of competencies in communication and stakeholder management.

One could surmise that while missed schedules and cost overruns are noticeable symptoms, the causes are the *invisible* competencies such as being a good communicator or negotiator.

PM Competencies Now and in the Future

For several decades, the entire portfolio of behavioral competencies was underrated across industries. An individual who is technically competent in their application domain will soon disappoint their stakeholders if they do not have sound behavioral competencies.

Behavioral skills, also known as soft skills, can be regarded as skills associated with a range of topics from leadership, emotional intelligence, communications management, and stakeholder management, to promoting ethical behavior and working effectively in a global cultural mix. Conflict management and negotiation is a core component of this list.

Within this context, I believe the ability to *set aside differences quickly and communicate well* will gain importance over the next decade. We all recognize that there is politics in every reasonably sized project, but if a leader is unable to quickly *forgive and forget* and move over quickly to resolving the *real task* at hand, a project will fail!

How to Develop PM Competencies

While I am a practitioner, my career is in academia. Sitting from this vantage point in a reputed research-oriented university, I appreciate the value of research and envision that we will see a substantial growth in the nascent field of PM.

Educators, practitioners, and professional PM organizations are going to work together and come up with solutions and best practices for today's increasingly complex projects.

PMI needs to be commended for the substantial investments they are making in research and revolutionizing undergraduate PM education. As a member of the Task Force of Global Academic Volunteers, I have seen the fruits of their substantial sponsorship in education. Graduates and eventually practitioners will possess ideal skill sets in the technical and behavioral areas as well.

> *Effects* certainly are missed schedules and blown budgets, but the real *cause* could be a lack of competencies in communication, leadership, and stakeholder management.

NAOMI CAIETTI

Naomi Caietti, PMP, is a blogger, consultant, and author, of *Get Unstuck...Transform Your Leadership* and *The Vision Project.*

PM Competency Gap Warning Signs

Project failure is still one of the most talked about subjects in major sectors and industries of PM (i.e., information technology, healthcare, and construction).

Several years ago I weighed in as an expert on the topic of project failure for a PM Network article titled "The Blame Game: It's Not Always the Project Manager's Fault." Here are excerpts from the article regarding the top warning signs that a gap in PM competency exists:

"The project manager can still make poor decisions or exhibit behaviors that inevitably lead to project breakdown—even when executive leadership does exactly what it should. Several clear signals on a troubled project indicate that the project manager may be letting things slip and necessitate intervention on the part of senior management or the sponsor:

- Lack of Leadership Skills: "Some project managers lack the maturity, thoughtfulness, and leadership skills necessary for their position," says Naomi Caietti, PMP, enterprise architect, State of California, Sacramento, California, USA. "Not listening to all the information being given and not delegating tasks are just two indicators that leadership is lacking," she says. When that starts affecting day-to-day project execution, it's time for a change.
- Poor Ongoing Planning: Though the project manager may not be involved in the initial planning, he or she is responsible for keeping the project on track. Setting unrealistic expectations and showing a lack of foresight can steer a project toward trouble.
- Tunnel Vision: Like falling into the planning trap, some project managers focus too much on one facet of the project, losing sight

of the big picture and end goals. That makes it almost impossible to respond appropriately to changing factors or new ideas.

- Incompetence: This may be the most obvious one to detect—and the clearest example of when failure should be placed on the project manager.

If a project manager is deficient in basic management capabilities, he or she has no business being in that position. If the project manager is indeed at fault, the next step is determining a course of corrective action. In less extreme cases, Ms. Caietti suggests mentoring and coaching. "Executive management needs to show support to the project manager," she says. "There has to be a conversation, and then the project manager needs to get some training."

Companies invest a lot of time and money in their project managers, so it's in their best interest to look at failure as a learning opportunity, rather than a reason to terminate. "Failure is one of the hardest things that a project manager will face," says Ms. Caietti. "Executive management needs to be supportive of project managers when this happens."

PM Competencies Now and in the Future

Leadership; direct and indirect management of people and emotional intelligence; and influencing and developing relationships are the top competencies that have become more critical to project success in the last decade.

Several years ago, a study was done by the PMI Leadership Community of Practice and identified competency, leadership, and emotional intelligence as the top three indexes that project/program managers need to excel in to be successful in their projects.

As project/program managers, we need to recognize that what made us successful today may not make us successful in the future. Project managers should continue to focus on personal growth and development as we move forward in the 21st century.

Trends like digital futures, internet of things, and big data are bringing about change and complexity which will be the only constant. It will be important moving forward to focus on the new project complexity, shifting into a 21st century project leader to reduce project failure and increase value through innovation.

How to Develop PM Competencies

Today we have choices to navigate and accelerate our career path; it is the choices we make along the way that will guide us to reach our greatest potential and our lofty goals. We can only realize these choices if we embrace a leadership mindset to reflect to move forward. There is nothing more powerful than to take stock of what you've accomplished to begin the next chapter of your life. You must be willing to step outside your comfort zone to grow.

PM learning is gained through time and experience; how can these results be achieved faster? Here are my recommendations for accelerating your growth to be a more strategic leader:

- Raise your self-awareness through assessment and reflection. You must focus on your individual personal growth and development. There are several assessment tools out there today; take an assessment of your behaviors to receive a detailed analysis.
- Create opportunities to leverage your strengths and minimize your behavioral gaps. As a project/program manager, you must understand your career path and position yourself to take advantage of these opportunities.
- Identify mentors, coaches, or sponsors inside or outside your organization with similar behaviors. Check with your internal organization to determine if they have a mentor program. Many PMI chapters now have mentor programs to help mentee/protégés. You may have more than one mentor for specific areas of focus, i.e., process, business, politics.
- Work with your mentor/sponsor to select projects and programs to lead that provide opportunities to build targeted skills. You may have to do this internally and externally. Choosing projects that align with your goals may be challenging; it requires support from human resources, management, and your PMO. A career path inside your organization is critical to achieve this; however, this can also be achieved by pairing a project manager with a senior project/program manager to shadow a medium or large project with a key role on the team.
- Attend targeted training that will enhance the desired behaviors. You must not wait too long to apply what you have learned; pair

the training with a project or initiative. You may have to do this internally or externally.

- Learn more about change, stakeholder engagement models, and breakthrough PM.
- Create an action plan to minimize your behavior gaps and facilitate improvement in your delivery of projects/programs in your organization. This is your responsibility and your mentor can provide feedback.

RON ROSENHEAD

Ron Rosenhead is a PM consultant, blogger, training director, and author of *Strategies for Project Sponsorship* and *Deliver That Project!*

PM Competency Gap Warning Signs

There are actually several:

- Performance reviews reveal that the individual does not feel comfortable with a skill or some knowledge. Performance reviews are very good learning experiences when done correctly; however, they rarely are and competency gaps are being lost because of poor arrangements in this area.
- Complaints or general moaning from stakeholders about someone. I have seen this in several projects and this manifests itself in discontent among some of the stakeholders.
- De-motivated staff—this is usually the project team not pulling in the same direction. One example I saw was several team members asking to be taken off the project while one left the company.

PM Competencies Now and in the Future

This is linked to the first question—people skills. This is so wide, however, for me it covers areas such as:

1. Listening
2. Questioning

3. Motivating others

4. Negotiations

5. Being open and honest

6. Giving and receiving feedback

For me they cover the basics. Let me expand on what I mean below, and to do so I have chosen one of the six areas: listening skills.

I ran a PM course a few years ago where I included *soft skills* as defined above within the materials delivered. The room was really buzzing with people engaged in PM activities: scoping, stakeholder management, risk, etc. I then changed direction and introduced some simple people skills activities.

The change in atmosphere was amazing. From being really engaged and well involved, the group looked away from each other, no one spoke—and there was a *clear atmosphere*. I paused and asked what was going on, citing how engaged they were before and compared it to now.

Silence! I pointed out that this often seems to happen when soft skills are discussed. People were reluctant to speak until one person told us that his team had taken him to the side and told him he did not listen! He said he was shocked and thought long and hard about it and concluded they were right.

He said he worked on this area for around 12 months and slowly started to improve, and after 18 months he received positive feedback from the same people, alongside others who told him that he had changed (for the better). I wonder what they were saying behind his back!

How to Develop PM Competencies

I mentioned performance reviews above. I believe these are not as effective as they could be. Over the years I have asked project managers (full time and those who are also managing business as usual) about performance reviews. I have not had much positive feedback.

I have also spoken with HR professionals and mentioned that performance reviews do not seem to be doing their job, which is why we have introduced 360-degree review into the portfolio of services from Project Agency.

Until we have proper reviews (however you define one), then PM competencies will suffer. Linked to this will be a need for a more flexible development process; e.g., the training of one project manager may be totally different from another.

ROGER WARBURTON

Dr. Roger Warburton is a professor at Boston University and coauthor of *The Art and Science of Project Management.*

PM Competency Gap Warning Signs

There are more and more projects, and so, more and more people are working on projects with no formal training—a growing population of accidental project managers.

Stage #1: People think they understand projects, but don't know the fundamental definitions. Two examples:

"My project this week is to make 100 widgets" (not unique and, therefore, not a project).

"You mean a risk can be positive?" (Yes, and enhancing the positive risks can make a huge difference.)

Stage #2: People take a PM Class: Charter, Scope, Plan, Network. . . . OK, I've got it! Then they write a Charter and realize it's really hard. And, since they were only doing a simple party project, they begin to realize it will be much, much harder for their real project. That's only the Charter, wait until they get to the Scope.

Stage #3: They estimate the future cost and schedule and think that it is quite difficult. But, in reality, it is only a percentage calculation. You can calculate a percentage, right? The bad press for Earned Value leads people to think they don't need it and/or can't do it. OK, so you don't want to know the final cost and schedule?

Stage #4: The customer knows. You regularly report the planned work, the accomplished work, and the cost. Therefore, your customer already has the data to predict the final cost and schedule, and with no help from you. The increasing sophistication of customers in PM means that many companies don't have the required skills.

PM Competencies Now and in the Future

For a while now, people have been talking about how important *communication* is to successful PM. But there are few cases and fewer examples of what that actually means.

How do you communicate a cost overrun? It is now possible to accurately calculate the cost and schedule after about 20% of the project. This has two consequences:

1. You need to know how to communicate this. Your customer needs to know.

2. Do you understand the political and ethical implications of the cost and schedule overrun? Do you tell the truth? Does the customer have the funds? How acceptable is the delay? Will your project get canceled?

These examples show that PM skills are inextricably intertwined. Therefore, future PM will emphasize that you need both technical skills and communication skills. Learning one without the other is pointless.

How to Develop PM Competencies

Relentless education. But, I admit that I am biased. After all, I am a teacher.

BARBARA TRAUTLEIN

Barbara Trautlein is the creator of the CQ® System for Developing Change Intelligence® and the author of *Change Intelligence: Use the Power of CQ to Lead Change That Sticks.*

PM Competency Gap Warning Signs

My coaching advice is to *use your own and others' emotions as data*. That is, emotions and emotional reactions are data that a savvy project manager should pay attention to as critical inputs to diagnosing the state of their projects—as well as of their competencies.

Looking internally at one's self, a warning sign would be frustration and stress. This may signal that *what got you here won't get you there*, as Marshall Goldsmith says, and that there is an opportunity to build advanced skills to meet new and increasingly demanding challenges.

Looking externally at one's stakeholders, warning signs would be that they are expressing what may be interpreted as emotional reactions toward the project manager or the project, which may also manifest as frustration and stress, or behaviors such as lack of sponsorship, lack of engagement, and lack of responsiveness—bottom line, a lack of meaningful traction and positive connection.

PM Competencies Now and in the Future

Engaging stakeholders has become and will continue to be increasingly vital for project managers in this complex world. And I do not mean merely *managing* stakeholders—rather, I mean genuinely *engaging* them.

The amount of information we are bombarded with on a daily basis is shocking and won't slow down any time soon. Project managers need to be able to cut through the noise and connect with their stakeholders.

Project managers must be able to engage upward to influence sponsors and business leaders; across—inside and outside the organization—to work effectively with their partners; and with the *targets* of their projects—the impacted workforce, user community, etc.

How to Develop PM Competencies

As the authors have astutely explained elsewhere in this book, project managers today need to build their Change Intelligence® (or CQ®) to equip themselves to engage for change. CQ is the awareness of one's Change Leader Style, and the ability to adapt one's style to be optimally effective across people and situations.

So often, what looks like resistance in others is actually what we as *change leaders* (and since every project is a change, every project manager is a change leader) are not giving our stakeholders—what they need to *get it*, *want it*, or be able to *do it*. By building CQ, project managers develop competency in the three critical styles of leading change, namely inspiring the *head* (so people *get it*), connecting with the *heart* (so people *want it*), and helping the *hands* (so people can *do it*).

After all, what can a project manager control? Only one's self. Yet, by building the critical competency of CQ, project managers can greatly expand their ability to positively influence others and impact objectives, greatly enhancing the probability of joint collaboration and mutual success.

> Project managers need to be able to cut through the noise and connect with their stakeholders.

LILIANA BUCHTIK

Liliana Buchtik is the award-winning author of *Secrets to Mastering the WBS in Real-World Projects*. She is also a keynote speaker and a consultant.

PM Competency Gap Warning Signs

There may be several warning signs that a gap in PM competency exists, but I will specify three of them. One is the inability of meeting project objectives. For example, when there is a key project deadline or target budget to adhere to and the individual is unable to meet it, it may indicate a gap in PM competency exists. It could also indicate several other reasons for that inability, for example, probably the problem is not PM competency, but the reason is that the target budget or date established in the project charter was determined by a different individual and was unrealistic, but again.

Being able to meet project goals in accordance to the plans is one of the core competencies a project manager must have. That implies many other competencies that the project manager must have in order to reach goals; for example, being good at managing teams, at managing stakeholders, at communicating, and so on.

A second warning sign could be poor performance. For example, a project promised certain benefits to its sponsors or investors and there is a lack of benefits management or benefits monitoring, or due to several reasons, the project manager and/or the PM team is not performing well in that regard. Poor performance could apply to any PM knowledge area, it could be poor performance at cost management, quality management, risk management, or at other aspects such as logistics management.

A third warning sign could be an increase of conflicts on a project team or among project stakeholders. This could indicate that there is a lack of PM competency regarding soft skills, leadership, team development, negotiation, communications, etc.

PM Competencies Now and in the Future

One of the critical PM competencies to project success, I believe, is flexibility. Being flexible and adaptable is a PM competency that not every project manager has. PM competency is simply not easy to find sometimes. And this competency is even more important in certain areas or regions of the world, more so than in others.

For example, in the culture and countries belonging to Latin America, this competency is probably more important than in the United States. By definition Latin American countries are more informal than countries such as the U.S. or Canada. As a result, things in an informal culture tend to be more challenging sometimes; things typically take longer to be finished; bureaucracy in some governments is more challenging; not all the people possess the needed discipline in PM; PM maturity is not as high; economies sometimes are more unstable; and resources are more scarce than in other countries. Therefore, the project manager has to have different skills with one of them being flexibility. Flexibility to find optimal solutions despite the context; flexibility to adapt to constant changes in the environment, politics, economy; and so on.

In the next decade, the PM competencies that may gain importance will be related to areas of expertise, not necessarily related to core PM competencies. For example, stakeholder management has been more critical in recent years. In countries such as Chile, Peru, Colombia, and others, we have seen huge investments on hold and projects canceled during execution (e.g., as a result of the special interests of particular stakeholders that have placed so may barriers to the projects that those projects didn't succeed). In Peru, there is a million dollar mining project on hold as a result of a conflict with an environmental group. So for the project manager, it is not only important now to manage time and cost and a few other areas, but also to become experts at things such as stakeholder management. This is more important in some industries than in others (e.g., this is more critical for a project manager running an oil and gas, mining, or construction project than it is for an IT or financial project).

How to Develop PM Competencies

I do not believe in one size fits all. I believe that, to begin with, solutions are good depending on different factors, such as cultures, countries, and/or regions. With that I mean that a solution that may be good for project managers in the United States, may not be applicable elsewhere. For example, in North America it is more common to see programs recognize or reward individuals based on their performance; however, in some countries in Latin America, this could be perceived as an incorrect model since in those countries the recognition goes to the team and not to individuals.

Some cultures are team oriented while others are more individual oriented so the solutions should be for specific situations, cultures, countries, organization types, and industries. Another example, if you have a master's degree in the United States, you will probably be recognized or your salary will increase as a result of your MsPM or MBA achievement, but in countries in southern Latin America, I have heard stories of individuals not willing to pursue a masters degree because the company would not recognize it. The company thinks that *if this individual has better competencies, better titles and degrees, and is better prepared then he or she may leave our company sooner, so let's keep them as they are now. . . .* Sad to hear it, but it's true in some places.

We need to develop solutions for different realities. In realities like the ones I have mentioned here, it may be good to begin with programs to raise awareness of the importance of developing competency within the organization; to sell the value of it for the company and not just as a good thing only for the individual.

KATHY SCHWALBE

Kathy Schwalbe is a professor at Augsburg College. She is the author of the widely used textbooks *Introduction to Project Management* and *IT Project Management.*

PM Competency Gap Warning Signs

One obvious warning sign is that organizations cannot fill their project manager positions. Another is that organizations do not respect the project managers they do have, often due to the fact that they are not in tune with the needs of the organization and are not delivering positive results.

PM Competencies Now and in the Future

I believe that positive leadership is more crucial than its ever been and will continue to gain importance over the next decade. By positive leadership, I mean that a project manager should inspire others to do work that will impact the project, the organization, and perhaps the whole world in a positive manner. In order to do that, project managers must understand the big picture.

I have had people criticize my PM textbooks because I always addressed the concepts of strategic management and project selection. They say that project managers aren't involved in those areas. I say that they definitely should be! Project managers need to know what's really important to an organization and how their particular project fits into the overall strategy. Project managers and their team members can also be in a good position to propose new project ideas based on their past experiences.

Another important competency is perseverance. Project managers should only work on projects they believe in, and they should be willing to stand up for what is right to help their projects succeed.

How to Develop PM Competencies

Education is crucial to developing any skill, and people can learn to be positive leaders and to have perseverance. Personally, I was very shy growing up. I was lucky to have great parents, teachers, and coaches who pushed me to develop my skills, mostly in sports and academics.

Developing confidence is often more difficult. Once I realized I was blessed with several talents (at about age 16), I gained confidence by setting and achieving higher and higher goals for myself. I also had several mentors who encouraged me to do things I never thought possible. As parents, friends, siblings, coworkers, bosses, etc., we need to continue to develop our own skills and take the time to educate and mentor others.

> Positive leadership is more crucial than its ever been and will continue to gain importance over the next decade.

MENNO VALKENBURG

Menno Valkenburg, Agile PM, GPM-b, PMP, TSPM, is an Independent International Sustainable Project Pilot 1 Focus consultant and is coauthor of the upcoming book, *Five Frustrations of Project Managers.*

PM Competency Gap Warning Signs

Warning signs that a gap in PM competency exists include when the project manager:

- Complains that he/she has too little time to spend on PM activities;
- Is not meeting (simple) deadlines or targets;
- Complains about others and it's others' fault that he didn't meet deadlines;
- Cannot show an updated schedule;
- Does not know his main stakeholders;
- Is not communicating status or communicates late; or
- Talks more than listens.

Other warning signs include when:

- Team members start to get demoralized and demotivated;
- Team members start spending more time and focus on other *projects*;
- Stakeholders start to complain and ask why the project is taking so long to complete;
- The sponsor and/or steering committee starts to micromanage the project; or
- Too many other priorities get thrown on the plate.

PM Competencies Now and in the Future

Over the past ten years, projects have become more complex and include a broader variety of stakeholders. Stakeholders have also become more demanding and their expectations have increased. Management of stakeholders and appropriate communication have become more critical for project success.

In the next decade, flexibility and agility will gain importance. The agile approach to PM that started off with software development projects in the early 2000s is now moving into mainstream projects. More and more organizations are adapting agile principals in their PM practices, including non-IT/software projects. Alongside agility, it will be critical for successful project managers to adapt sustainability practices and further develop their behavioral competencies. This includes reducing the project's ecological footprint, adapting sound social and labor practices, and building a culture of improvement teams.

How to Develop PM Competencies

A solution for the development of these PM competences is *focus*. Project managers should ensure focus and streamlining of goals and objectives. The team will want to change strong ingrained old patterns into desired behavior patterns and actions that are necessary to achieve a challenging goal.

Besides focus and changing behavior patterns, it is critical for project managers to build trust. Trust in the project and project team can be built by showing interest and to quarrel. Yes, quarreling is fine, it really helps team development, building trust, and development of PM competencies. Make sure to continuously provide and receive feedback.

LAMBERT OFOEGBU

Dr. Lambert Ofoegbu is the Head of Research and Development at p3m global MENA. He is an OPM3® Assessor and is the publisher of *PMforesight Magazine—Project Management Perspectives in Africa*.

PM Competency Gap Warning Signs

I recognize PM competency as the interplay of outstanding and assessable skills, knowledge, abilities, and individual qualities that project managers use to deliver on their professional obligations in organizations. The gaps in PM competency connote the discrepancies between the organizational capabilities and the requirements toward sustaining positive corporate performance.

The warning signs of a difference in PM competency manifest as a progressive inability of the organization to meet strategic objectives. It starts by individual failures of various managers to deliver following deficiencies in skill sets. Nevertheless, there is a warning equally, when you start noticing that the organizational PM tools appear inconsistent and ineffective with the emerging dictates of the business environment. In these warning situations, whether personality or tools oriented, the mismatch you envisage might be because of incompetent managers that did not have the requisite skills to develop and use the tools, or inability of the managers to rightfully apply the existing tools.

PM Competencies Now and in the Future

I can broadly categorize PM competencies into four: core PM, organization and people, processes and procedures, and general management.

Following my 25 years of related scholar-practitioner experiences, I posit that each one of the categories has the same value of importance in shaping the success of projects. I equally envisage that this assertion will remain valid in the next decade. The emerging business environment that is characterized by continuous demand by the customers and corresponding innovation by the organization requires the full activation of all the categories of PM competencies to cope with the developmental surge.

How to Develop PM Competencies

I recommend competency gap evaluation at regular intervals. This periodic assessment will enable the consistent identification of PM competency gaps that might ensue initiating the process of bridging the gaps. The results of the assessments should expose the nature and dimensions of the subsisting PM competency gaps, developing a road map for the capacity building and bridging of the identified gaps.

Structuring the bespoke competency development framework for individual players might be a step in the right direction. Eventually, process improvements to accommodate the emerging dictates of the market environment will be desirable. Ultimately imbibing the precepts of continuous improvement (plan, do, check, act) will help in ensuring that PM competencies are up to date.

The emerging business environment that is characterized by continuous demand by the customers and corresponding innovations by the organization requires the full activation of all the categories of PM competencies.

TIM WASSERMAN

Tim Wasserman is the Chief Learning Officer and Program Director of the Stanford Advanced Project Management Program.

PM Competency Gap Warning Signs

Project performance data continues to be largely unchanged and suggests that roughly 1/3 or more of initiatives fail to meet their initial targets. While some of this can be attributed to gaps in the foundational and technical skills required to plan and manage project execution, a large reason is that many technically competent managers and leaders still do not have a strong personal skill toolkit that allows them to effectively manage the *white spaces* in their plans. Study after study consistently reports that senior executives feel their organizations are poor at aligning strategy with execution, and they lack the associated skills required to achieve improved project and initiative performance.

PM Competencies Now and in the Future

As a broad category, the need is for individuals and teams to be much better able to adaptively execute their work. From a leadership perspective, a tolerance for ambiguity, and the ability to manage without formal authority will continue to be critical to individual effectiveness and project success.

These key relational skills must be developed on top of a strong foundation of technical skills, which must be much more varied than in the past, to reflect the need for planning and execution in a much more adaptive manner. Leaders of project-based work must have the ability to apply techniques that bridge the continuum from traditional, waterfall approaches, to those that are truly agile. They must be able to pivot without much advanced notice. They must develop a strategic perspective and the ability to understand the larger context; this focus on thinking strategically and understanding the linkages that lead to improved alignment between organizational contributors will also lead to better decision making. Adaptive execution must be the mantra of the future in order to achieve sustainable success in a world that is increasingly volatile, uncertain, complex, and ambiguous.

How to Develop PM Competencies

Practice, learn by doing, and most importantly, coaching. . .

> Many technically competent managers and leaders still do not have a strong personal skill toolkit that allows them to effectively manage the *white spaces* in their plans.

ANDY CROWE

Andy Crowe, PMP, is the founder and CEO of Velociteach and is the author of *Alpha Project Managers* and *The PMP® Exam: How to Pass on Your First Try*.

PM Competency Gap Warning Signs

Whether it is an individual or an organization, the warning signs are usually the same: a recurring issue, problem, or deficiency occurs two or more times consecutively. Every project is going to have its challenges, but organizations and project managers should learn. When the same problems repeat, it is a sign that there may be a larger competency issue. The root causes can take some skill and insight to identify, and they are often challenging to address.

PM Competencies Now and in the Future

Over the past ten years, we have seen conflict resolution become highly important to project success. Roger Fisher, in his book *Getting to Yes*, points out that conflict is a growth industry, and that prophecy has proven true for anyone delivering projects. But healthy conflict resolution requires a lot of skills, including leadership, negotiating, and emotional intelligence, just to name a few. These can often be taught or improved, but they also require growth and change on the part of the project manager; and not everyone is necessarily motivated to change or is capable of growth at every point in their career.

In the next ten years, technology will continue to evolve at an unprecedented pace. Project managers are going to have to be able to anticipate the future and get better at delivering rapid value. Very few products, services, or results are standing still. This will require project managers to embrace change, which can go against our DNA. After all, we have been taught our entire careers to protect the project from change and to influence the factors that cause change. We need to migrate our perspective to look at change as more of an opportunity than a threat.

How to Develop PM Competencies

Any PM competency is developed deliberately and with practice. They simply do not happen on their own. Real growth occurs in community. Organizations need to model and champion good conflict resolution and openly welcome change. It starts from the top. Challenging senior management to embrace these values, model them, and incorporate them into performance reviews and everyday practice is a great place to begin.

ELISE STEVENS

Elise Stevens is a blogger and podcaster, and founder of Fix My Project Chaos.

PM Competency Gap Warning Signs

The warning signs that there is a gap in competency are:

- Bluster—lots of bluster and noise to cover the skills shortage
- Poor behavior, such as shouting in the open plan office
- High levels of visible stress
- Stress leave
- Being absent (there in person, not in spirit)

PM Competencies Now and in the Future

The two PM competencies that have become critical to project success are:

1. Focus on leadership—it is not just about the process. It is all about how we lead our teams (direct, virtual, stakeholders, and vendors)

2. Adding business value through concentrating on benefits realization (ensuring that the project actually delivers value to the organization)

The competency that will gain the most importance over the next decade is being a trusted business partner. Bringing our skills in PM, lean/agile, and business experience.

How to Develop PM Competencies

I would like to see more value placed on other skill development (business, innovation, lean, etc.) not just on PMI certification. Online learning offers a great opportunity to grow these skills. Having mentors from other professions is an additional way to grow PM competencies.

AMY BAHEN

Amy Bahen is a PM training business development consultant and a long-time coordinator of large PM training programs.

PM Competency Gap Warning Signs

From my experience, a clear warning sign would be an organization not laser focused on the execution of business priorities; the absence of clear alignment between strategy and the portfolio of programs and projects that support the strategy; and onsite client teams missing milestones impacting the top and bottom line.

Research shows that executives across industries feel as though their top leaders and enablement teams are not focused on the right work at the right time to achieve business initiatives. Program and project managers are accountable for the execution of work that will either increase operational efficiency or increase customer base and market share. If we fail to provide talent development programs for these leaders that will enable them to think more strategically and influence their client and teams to reach a win-win scenario, we are failing to recognize the full potential the employee base can have on the business.

PM Competencies Now and in the Future

Strategic thinking and influencing without authority. These are two skills program and project managers face on a daily basis. If we can help provide behavioral training that will better enable these leaders to work smart with their clients, we will see an impact in business performance and employee productivity as well as engagement. Moving into the next decade, I think it will be imperative for program and project managers to have a better grip on business acumen and how their work impacts the financial statements of the organization. If we can enable project and program managers to build on their technical skills with strategic and more real-time thinking, we will see organizations working smarter and not harder.

How to Develop PM Competencies

I think this is twofold:

1. Technical solutions: what tools/methodologies is an organization following that seem to best execute their project-based work?

2. The gray space tools or critical thinking skills: these are what we commonly call the soft skills of program management. They are critical in my mind, you can have the best functional SME and trained project manager on the job, but if they cannot politically navigate through the organization and gain trust and buy in from their stakeholders (internal and external), they will inhibit themselves from achieving their business objectives. Part of this arena will include the heart of the organization becoming more flexible/agile and nimble. We need to adapt to changes that are happening in the external environment that encompasses the inner working of the organization. Technology is driving many of our business decisions and business models as organizations reinvent themselves to compete in the 21st century, have the right talent in the right

places to help drive the organization forward, and adapt to a higher level of customer satisfaction since clients are more equipped to make decisions while demanding higher value with lower cost.

JEANNETTE CABANIS-BREWIN

Jeannette Cabanis-Brewin is Editor-In-Chief for PM Solutions and is co-author of *The Project Management Handbook.*

PM Competency Gap Warning Signs

Naturally, all the usual missed targets as to schedules, budgets, and scope/quality point to deficits in PM competency, but it is important to remember that these may also be caused by other problems that are more systemic or structural in nature. Even competent project managers will struggle within an organizational structure/culture that does not support effective project planning and execution. Project targets can be impacted by, for example, conflicting priorities introduced by executives who have not bought into the portfolio planning process/criteria or by poor demand management by the PMO. I think my bias when identifying the root cause of project failures is to look first at systemic ills, then second at the individuals within the system.

PM Competencies Now and in the Future

I think all the business-related competencies have become more important: project managers can no longer work in ignorance of their organization's primary business goals and metrics. The *soft skills*—which are actually harder to employ!—support these business skills. In particular, all aspects of stakeholder coordination (I dislike the idea of *managing* stakeholders) are key to, for example, identifying and delivering on business benefits.

Over the next decade, I would look to see project managers playing more and more strategic roles in organizations. Our newest State of the PMO study indicates that about half of PMOs now report to the C-Level and a majority engage in strategic-level functions, such as participating in strategic planning, portfolio selection, and organizational risk management. I expect to begin to see the PMO viewed as a source of C-level talent in the near future.

Thus, today's project managers should be preparing themselves to lead not just projects, but organizations. Higher-level skills in performance measurement, strategy management, risk management, and benefits realization should therefore be on their to-do list.

How to Develop PM Competencies

First of all, something that I fear is very much going out of fashion: reading. There are excellent resources online to educate yourself about leadership topics, but in my experience, people no longer have the attention span for digesting serious material and—even more crucial—the time to reflect on it. That said, because organizations are not focusing nearly enough on mastery-level skills, instead offering primarily basic PM training (and that for only an average of six days a year, according to The State of the PMO 2016), the onus is on the individual.

Project managers who aspire to leadership roles on programs, in PMOs, or beyond, will have to search out opportunities to lead. Sometimes this just requires taking on work that is a stretch beyond the comfort zone. Or, if the workplace does not present such opportunities, there are volunteer roles that can give us practice in leadership. Online learning and certificate programs now abound for skills where knowledge is lacking. But, to reiterate, the role of reading widely in the business press and applying what you learn cannot be underestimated.

> Today's project managers should be preparing themselves to lead not just projects, but organizations.

RICARDO VARGAS

Ricardo Vargas, PMP, is a podcaster (the 5-minute Podcast) and the author of 15 books about PM. He is a past Chairman of PMI as well as Director for Infrastructure and Project Management at the United Nations.

PM Competency Gap Warning Signs

Failing projects, cost overruns, and delays: these are the obvious warning signs that things are not moving the way they should be. All project results are a clear consequence of the way it was planned and managed and the way the external factors evolve during the project time frame. It is important to highlight that PM only exists as a profession because projects are hard, complex, and really *serious business*. Being very direct and honest, if the results are not achieved it is because the competency was not there to apply the technical and *soft* skills to understand the project context and environment.

PM Competencies Now and in the Future

If we go back in time, most of the competency developed around PM was related to tactics and operational approach. Tools like earned value management, critical chain, and quantitative risk analysis were on the top of the agenda of every single project manager. Nowadays, the challenges are different. With the complexity of the environment and the extreme volatility of today's world, the new project manager needs to develop several nontechnical skills like leadership, conflict management, political awareness, and change management. The biggest challenge today is to adapt this new set of skills with the current mindset of the project managers. It is a big challenge that organizations need to overcome.

How to Develop PM Competencies

The development of these *soft* competencies is a very different challenge if compared with technical skills. It is a much more *behavior* development than anything else. Developing outstanding communication skills, including active listening, is something that is very poorly learned by reading a book. These skills are only developed if you practice them. The best way to develop this critical thinking is by doing and applying on the day-to-day work and for me, the best way to do that is by developing a very strong mentorship program, where project managers at a more junior level can improve their understanding by practicing. It takes more time and this is the challenge.

> PM only exists as a profession because projects are hard, complex, and really *serious business*.

PAOLA MORGESE

Paola Morgese is a blogger and is the author of *The Handbook for Sustainable Projects*.

PM Competency Gap Warning Signs

Warning signs that a gap in PM competency exists could be a lack of coherence and discrepancies between words and actions. For instance, if a practitioner shares concepts about team building or emotional intelligence, and then fails while applying these topics to his or her own team and in relationships with colleagues. Or, other red flags could be contradictions and the use of words in a wrong context. For example, if a project manager is confused about processes and knowledge areas or on the phase where his/her project currently is. Also, copying the work of colleagues could show weak PM competencies.

PM Competencies Now and in the Future

I think that the two PM competencies that have become more critical to project success over the past ten years are the same as those which will gain importance over the next decade, and they are: knowledge building and sustainability.

Knowledge building is key because knowledge management and knowledge sharing are no longer enough in a world where change happens quickly and continuously. With knowledge building, I mean knowledge creation. It is a dynamic process linked to innovation and creativity, driving towards better solutions both technically and economically speaking. Knowledge management is static as it moves information that already exists and doesn't put innovation in motion.

Sustainability gives a comprehensive view on the project, from the beginning to the end, and beyond. With sustainability, I mean economic, social, and environmental values and principles permeating a project and flowing from a global organizational strategy. Sustainability provides a deeper analysis of the characteristics of a project and of its context. Sustainability is not only the future of PM and of project managers, but also the only way that we have to live in the future.

How to Develop PM Competencies

The solutions that I envision for the development of knowledge building and sustainability are development, improvement, and investment in research in both these fields—and professional training, of course. Solutions can also be developed by project managers in their daily work. Competence and knowledge are connected to each other since the first is based on a deep knowledge of a discipline.

Competence in PM derives from knowledge in PM. A competent practitioner shows ability, authority, problem-solving skills, culture, and experience. But he or she can go a step forward, beyond lessons learned and best practices of acquired knowledge. Their PM competencies allow them to create new, useful knowledge content, tools, and techniques in their area of expertise for the progress of their own projects and of PM itself.

SHAI DAVIDOV

Shai Davidov, PMP, is a project, program, and portfolio management expert. She is the founder and principal of PMT, Israel, a longtime PMI Israel VP/Board Member, and a Senior Teaching Fellow at Edinburgh Business School, Scotland.

PM Competency Gap Warning Signs

Better to focus the question—warning signs to whom? the organization? the individual? in what level? senior? junior? manager? team member?

Anyway, warning signs for lack of competency are there all the time. Even before a project starts (or initiates), a seasoned project manager will be able to identify gaps in another colleague while drinking tea together—it is the approach, the mindset, that gut feeling which tells you—*this guy just does not have it* . . . Then you start to rationalize it. You start evaluating their commitment to project values and concepts (can time be compromised?). You can see how they interact on a personal level. Are they *people people* or *process people*?

Then of course you check the alignment between execution and the process/task that was defined. The warning sign can be small (like tiny cracks) but unless spotted, they'll widen. This is the same for the organizational level when you start to see that opportunities do not materialize, or integration/understanding/execution is somehow not as anticipated.

You (the organization's management) should start asking the WHYs. Is it the environment? Is it us? Could be both, but the idea is to be able to analyze the operation/project/strategy. If we need someone external to do any of the work—Houston, we have a gap in competencies. It could be a lack of professional knowledge, or personal ability. I always ask myself if I can grasp the big picture and if I can drill down simultaneously—the PM competencies are stretched between those two.

Needless to mention that the signs are also a function of the project/organization maturity level/complexity of the project/constraints/other stakeholder involved.

PM Competencies Now and in the Future

Data analysis and manage uncertainty.

How to Develop PM Competencies

Decision-making supporting tools are already out there. I believe project managers and other managers will be using scenario planning techniques on a daily basis. I think that efforts will be put into trends analysis (based on big data analysis) and the quantification of phenomena that are still considered qualitative—benefits, success, leadership.

JOHN TODD

John Todd is the Principal of Downtown Recruiting and former VP at the PMI Mass Bay Chapter.

I'll combine my answers in a single response, as follows. The PM profession has changed and matured over the last decade. Project managers are expected to act as leaders who understand the business and how their projects support the mission of their company. We have seen an increase in requests for project managers with strong leadership skills and who are strategic partners to the business.

After surveying company leaders in the Greater Boston Area, these two areas have been identified as gaps in the current PM community. These can be difficult competencies to train and coach. Many companies have mentorship and leadership programs that pair senior and junior project managers together in the workplace. This approach allows the junior project manager to be coached in real-world situations and see firsthand how their actions influence those around them. For new project managers and business analyst hires, larger companies have rotational training programs to allow the new hire to rotate through different departments and business functions. A formal training program using in-house or outside vendors is another popular approach. In many cases these training programs are tailored to the specific needs of the company or industry.

For project managers looking to develop these skills outside the workplace, local universities, training vendors, and your local PMI Chapter offer programs in these areas. Given the nature of these competencies, in-person courses with role play exercises, real-world references, and active learning techniques are a recommended option. Networking with peers and finding a mentor group are also good options. Finally, stay abreast of what is happening in the business community by reading business journals and industry-related articles.

> We have seen an increase in requests for project managers with strong leadership skills who are strategic partners to the business.

MARK PHILLIPY

Mark Phillipy, PMP, is a podcaster and blogger (The Sensible PM).

PM Competency Gap Warning Signs

Businesses that win in today's fast moving environment are those who can deliver what the customer needs when they want it. This is accomplished by identifying the customer's needs quickly and delivering innovative solutions faster than the competition. Since these solutions are delivered via projects, today's project environments must be able to deliver at light speed and pivot on the proverbial dime.

Project managers that are not able to execute projects in this fast-paced environment should begin to evaluate their PM competencies. Do you find that your projects are slow to deliver? Are the products or solutions that are delivered not quite what the customer needs? Does your project feel more like a slow-moving train or one that is difficult to change to another track once the train gets moving? These are all signs that you as a project manager need to learn new PM competencies which will allow you to deliver the right solutions to your customers when they are needed.

PM Competencies Now and in the Future

In the past decade, the world has experienced a challenging financial slump in which we are still recovering. This combined with continued emergence of economies throughout the world and the fast paced needs of worldwide customers are highlighting the need for businesses to be lean and reactive to their customer's needs. There are two key PM competencies that have become critical in this environment, and I believe they will become even more essential for all project managers to develop proficiency.

Business acumen: Companies need to have project managers who understand the business and their customers. Project managers need to be able to clearly understand the mission, vision, and values of the company and how to execute projects which strategically align with business goals and objectives. We must understand the priorities of the business and work with upper management to keep projects in line with those priorities.

Agile mindset: Delivering the right solutions to our customers as quickly as possible is critical in today's business environment. Project managers must have an agile mindset and develop the skills required to deliver solutions quickly and pivot as the customer's needs change.

How to Develop PM Competencies

Continual development of your PM competencies is critical to keep your career vibrant. An increased focus on your personal development in these areas will help you be a leader in your business and in the PM community.

Business acumen: Project managers should continually develop their business acumen. PMI has led the need by identifying in *The PMI Talent Triangle*® an emphasis on *Strategic and Business Management*. PMPs are required to have at least eight business management PDUs as part of their continuing education. I recommend much more. Additionally, project managers should utilize training classes, books, and online sources to increase their business acumen.

Agile methodologies: There are several agile methodologies available, which will continue to evolve and develop to be even more reactive to customer needs. Scrum, Kanban, Adaptive Software Development (ASD), Lean Development, Extreme Programming (XP), Agile Modeling (AM), and Feature-Driven Development (FDD) are all lean approaches to PM. PMI has developed the PMI Agile Certified Practitioner (PMI-ACP)® as a certification that can be acquired.

> Continual development of your PM competencies is critical to keeping your career vibrant.

GREAT MINDS THINK ALIKE

As mentioned at the beginning of this chapter, we were thrilled with the volume of responses to the request for answers to our three questions on PM competency, and maybe even more with the speed and *enthusiasm* of the responses—many of them came with cover letters that said, in effect— "I've been thinking about this lately, I'm so glad you asked for my opinion," and "I realized that I needed to do this to clarify my thinking, thank you for asking!"

To us, it shows that this was something that our thought leaders cared about—deeply.

However, even more important than the simple volume and intensity of the responses, what was fascinating to us was the way they aligned in theme. Of course, not everyone agreed with everything we've asserted in this book, nor did they necessarily align 100% with each other. But there were so many key threads that we thought it was worth studying them because they have value in and of themselves, and it helps pull together what you have read in our book.

We note that, almost uniformly, the thought leaders believe in the relative importance of leadership, communications, soft skills, and business acumen. In fact, we studied the thought leaders' responses in a unique

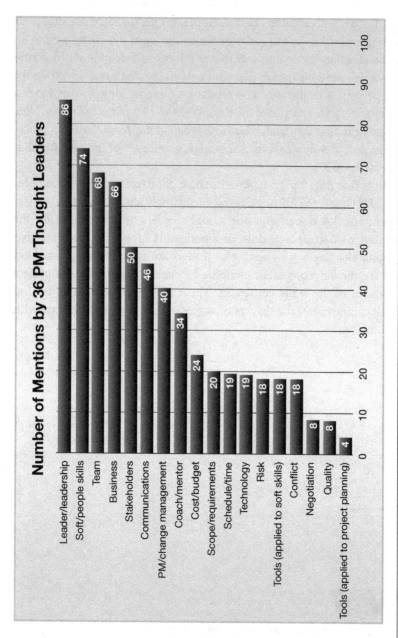

Figure 9.1   Terms mentioned by 36 PM thought leaders

way—we looked at *mentions* of key PM words and phrases, such as *soft skills, communication, requirements, risk, quality, time,* and *schedule*. We carefully took into account the context of their use, to eliminate situations where the meaning was negative or where the word was being used in an expression (such as *time* in *will not give you the time of day*). In Figure 9.1, you will see a histogram that summarizes the number of *mentions* for these key words or phrases. The results are quite striking. In fact, here's a quick Pareto-style analysis of the data. We have 18 types of *mentions*. Note that only the first six (*leadership, soft/people skills, team, business, stake-holders,* and *communications*) encompass about 63% of the total number of mentions (620).

Note that the *Iron Triangle*—the triple constraint—of PM (from pre-*PMBOK® Guide, 5th Edition* days) is surprisingly absent from this top tier of mentions. We don't think our thought leaders meant to diminish the importance of scope, schedule, and budget; they're just expressing that the competencies of (for example) leadership, team building, and soft skills are the key competencies needed to *achieve and drive* the project efficiencies of the triple constraint. These are the competencies behind the triple constraint, the drivers of success—and that's right in line with our thinking.

Selected References and Useful Links

INTRODUCTION

Heitkamp's office, quotes from: http://www.heitkamp.senate.gov/
public/index.cfm/2016/10/heitkamp-ernst-announce-house
-passage-of-bipartisan-bill-to-improve-federal-efficiency

Henry, Lindsey K. *The Multi-Cultural Identity of Medieval Sicily:
William II's Complex at Monreale*, research paper posted on
academia.edu, May 2015: http://www.academia.edu/12294486/The
_Multi-Cultural_Identity_of_Medieval_Sicily_William_II_s
_Complex_at_Monreale

Hoffman, Dr. Edward. *A Brief History of Project Management at
NASA*, NASA APPEL (Academy of Program/Project & Engineering Leadership) online magazine article, September 1, 2008, http://
appel.nasa.gov/2008/09/01/a-brief-history-of-project-management
-development-at-nasa/

Jarus, Owen. *Hagia Sophia: Facts, History & Architecture*, online Live
Science article, March 1, 2013, URL: http://www.livescience
.com/27574-hagia-sophia.html

Kozak-Holland, Mark. *Lessons from History: History of Project Management*, presentation to University of Virginia CMIT (Center for
the Management of Information Technology) Charlottesville, VA,

September 16, 2011, URL: http://www2.commerce.virginia.edu/
cmit/activities/Kozak-Holland_Sept%202011.pdf

Monreale, URL: https://en.wikipedia.org/wiki/Monreale

Moskowitz, Clara. *The Secret Tomb of China's 1st Emperor: Will We Ever See Inside*, online Live Science article, August 17, 2012, http://www.livescience.com/22454-ancient-chinese-tomb-terracotta-warriors.html

Online Etymology Dictionary, *competence*, http://www.etymonline.com/index.php?term=competence

PMI Press Release on S.1550: https://www.pmi.org/about/press-media/press-releases/senate-program-management-act

Schiro, Giuseppe. (text), *Monreale-City of the Golden Temple*, F.lli. Mistretta Publishers, Palermo, Italy, 1990.

Standing on the shoulders of giants: https://en.wikipedia.org/wiki/Standing_on_the_shoulders_of_giants

Terracotta Army: https://en.wikipedia.org/wiki/Terracotta_Army

CHAPTER 1

The DIKW Model: http://www.systems-thinking.org/dikw/dikw.htm

CHAPTER 2

Binder, Jean. 2007. *Global Project Management*, Gower Publishing Limited, Hampshire, England.

Hillson, Dr. David and Dr. Ruth Murray. *Scaling the PEAKS of Competence*. PM World Journal. Vol IV. Issue IV. April 2015.

Pellerin, Charles. 2009. *How NASA Builds Teams: Mission Critical Soft Skills for Scientists, Engineers, and Project Teams*. John Wiley & Sons.

Pulse of the Profession report from 2015 from PMI which focuses on knowledge transfer: http://www.pmi.org/-/media/pmi/documents/public/pdf/learning/thought-leadership/pulse/pulse-of-the-profession-2015.pdf

The value of building a community for knowledge sharing:
http://www.providersedge.com/docs/km_articles/Managing
_Knowledge_for_Advantage_-_Technologies.pdf

CHAPTER 3

Cohen, Allan and David Bradford. *Influence with-
out Authority*, https://www.amazon.com/
Influence-Without-Authority-Allan-Cohen/dp/0471463302
http://www.hrvoice.org/9-ways-to-influence-without-authority/
https://hbr.org/2008/02/exerting-influence-without-aut.html
Cohen, Yuval, the Open University of Israel, Raanana, Israel; Hana
Ornoy, the Lander Academic College, Jerusalem, Israel and the
Open University of Israel, Raanana, Israel; and Baruch Keren, SCE—
Shamoon College of Engineering, Beer-Sheva, Israel. Personality
Types of Project Managers and Their Success: A Field Survey. *Proj-
ect Management Journal*. 44(3). June 2013.
Kiersey Test: http://www.keirsey.com/sorter/instruments2.aspx
Millennial reference: https://www.entrepreneur.com/article/243862
Thomas-Killman Conflict Mode Instrument: https://www.cpp.com/
products/tki/index.aspx

CHAPTER 5

Saladis, Frank. IPM day: http://internationalpmday.org
Trautlein, Barbara. Change Quotient: http://changecatalysts.com/
resources.html

A2

A Competency Survey of 250 Project Managers

While preparing to write this book, the authors launched an informal survey on what their peers in the field of project management (PM) think about PM knowledge and competency. There were only a few questions, with room for personal comments, if desired. At the moment of publication, there were 253 responses. The outcome data of the survey are interesting in and of itself, but it's our intention to advance the DIKW model (see Chapter 1) and transform that data into information and knowledge, and perhaps even wisdom.

We provide both the data and our observations here in this Appendix.

QUESTION 1—WHICH IS MORE IMPORTANT: WHAT THE PROJECT MANAGER *KNOWS* OR WHO THE PROJECT MANAGER *IS*?

Figure A2.1 shows that the result is centered evenly between *what you know* and inherently—*who you are*. This significant sample of project managers finds that it's really almost exactly an even mix of the skills and knowledge you can gain through training and experience; and the person's characteristics and traits.

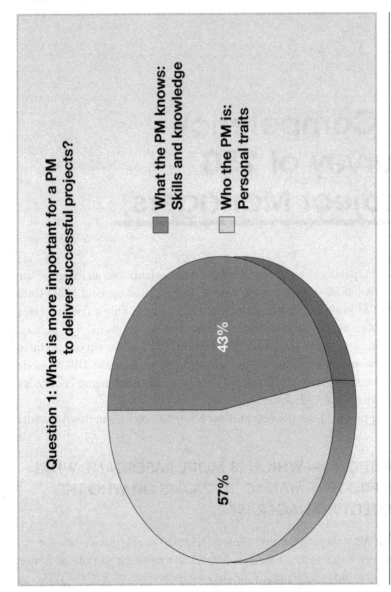

Figure A2.1 Responses to Survey Question 1: What is more important—what the project manager knows or who the project manager is?

Observation 1. No matter what you do for your PM population, there will be individuals who won't be as successful as others in performing as a project manager due to their inherent traits and characteristics. Training alone might not be enough to compensate for attitude. Coaching, training, simulations—they will help, for sure—but don't be surprised if they do not yield radical improvement in the capability of your project managers or in your organization's project success rate. You will need to balance the selection of candidates for project manager positions—starting with those who have the right behavioral strengths and attitude, and then developing a strong PM community with the efforts to build an extensive training curriculum.

Observation 2. Project managers with personalities not favorable to PM work can learn enough skills to help them deliver projects effectively. Example: assertiveness in people who are naturally shy—they can learn to communicate more efficiently and rely on professional allies and champions to help them escalate. Although this seems at odds with Observation 1 (and it is, to some extent), we're saying that the survey and accompanying feedback shows an optimism for building skills and capabilities in project managers even if their traits are not perfectly aligned with the required traits of a project manager. It's just going to take more time, more training, and a more extensive support structure—including a special focus on mentoring programs.

QUESTION 2—WHAT PERSONAL TRAITS ARE MOST IMPORTANT FOR A PROJECT MANAGER?

We have seen the importance of traits in the answers to Question 1. So let's dive deeper into those traits (see Figure A2.2). Which personal traits are most important? Our result is symmetrical—about the same value for each of these 11 key traits. Note that all of them were considered important—not a surprise, since we drew these 11 traits from significant project research that had already identified these particular 11 as important.

Observation 1. There was one minor spike for the trait of *strong commitment to project*. We think that is a symptom of the fact that a project needs a *cheerleader*—someone who is constantly keeping the team's eyes on the prize. This is one of the distinguishing factors, after all, of a project throughout the day-to-day operations. Interestingly, *propensity for details,*

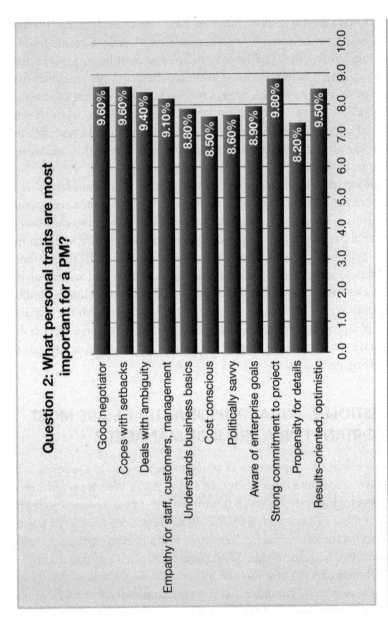

Figure A2.2 Responses to Survey Question 2: What personal traits are most important for a project manager?

which is a trait that is commonly associated with project managers, is the one with a slightly lower score. We think that is an outcome of the fact that project managers need to consider the *pareto principle* regarding the data they process. If they are lost in the details, they're likely missing the top 20% of project detail that is posing 80% of the weight in terms of threats or opportunities that affect project objectives.

Observation 2. Project managers recognize (in themselves and in colleague project managers) that there are more than just one or two personal strengths or traits required to be effective and efficient at PM. Several *layers* of personal commitment, social interoperability, and business focus are considered equally important, and among these 11, there are only a few that have even a moderate deviation from that very high level of importance.

QUESTION 3—WHAT KNOWLEDGE AREA IS MORE IMPORTANT FOR A PROJECT MANAGER?

Using the 10 knowledge areas (KAs) of *A Guide to the Project Management Book of Knowledge (PMBOK® Guide)* as a basis, we asked individuals to choose between these in terms of priority. We fully realize that this is a theoretical and somewhat frustrating exercise because of its forced choice between vital elements of our profession—any of which could admittedly rise in criticality and urgency at any given time in a project's life cycle. But actually, we did it for that reason—to force a choice between these KAs at a visceral level. So here's the 10,000-meter version of what we found: communications, scope, and stakeholder management are higher than the others, but still in a similar range of importance. (See Figure A2.3.)

Observation 1. Communication, scope, and stakeholder management represent a considerable portion of responses. If we further consider that stakeholder management was drawn from the communications management knowledge area, starting in the 5th Edition of the *PMBOK® Guide*, it further supports the importance of the *soft-skill* areas of PM—which is one of the reasons our book dives deeper into soft-skill competencies. This can also be seen in the work of Dr. Charlie Pellerin after he discovered that project managers working in large tech projects (such as the launching and deployment of a space telescope) need a significant shot in the arm when it comes to these skills. Improving the skill sets of

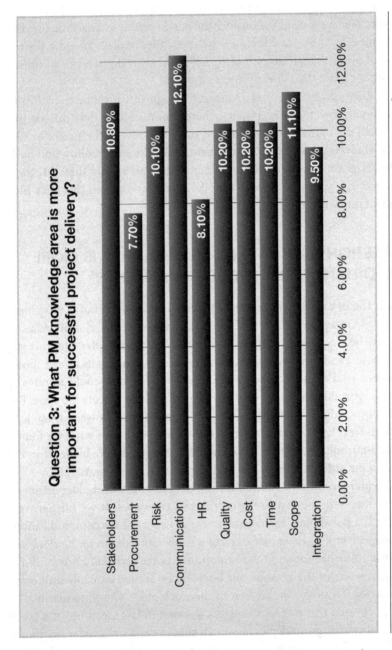

Figure A2.3   Responses to Survey Question 3: What knowledge area is more important for a project manager?

project managers in this area should be a priority, and results in a higher return on investment. Spend your training dollars wisely by focusing on these areas.

Observation 2. Effort spent in these two areas will also yield results in improving personal strengths for some individuals—increasing their sense of empowerment. We'd further assert that the skills that your project managers learn in this area are exceedingly worthwhile (as long as you can retain these employees) because they become an excellent *feeder pool* for your organization's senior leadership positions. After all, if these folks can communicate, influence, and control scope on projects for which they're not officially *the boss*, imagine their capability and potential if they were to get full authority and power!

QUESTION 4—WHAT ARE THE MOST IMPORTANT PERSONAL COMPETENCIES FOR A PROJECT MANAGER?

For this discussion, see Figure A2.4. One main result is that communication is considered to be nearly twice as important as cognitive abilities, and leadership is considered as important as communication.

Observation 1. Both communication and leadership are one-and-a-half times more important than any other competency. Once again this reinforces the concept that money spent in improving these skills will likely yield the best return.

Observation 2. Cognitive ability is the lowest of all of these personal competencies. Really? What this survey says (taken to its extreme) is that the project manager does not have to be a deep thinker—does not have to *know a lot* to get the job done. It sounds vaguely insulting. But is it really? Upon some reflection, this is actually demonstrating the true, more fundamental value of a project manager—a person who connects team members to tasks and resources to team members. If we allow ourselves a musical analogy, he or she is the person conducting the orchestra. So indeed, the project manager does not need deep knowledge of any particular instrument, his or her skill is getting just the right sound (or proper outcome) from the orchestra. That's what these 253 people seemed to be

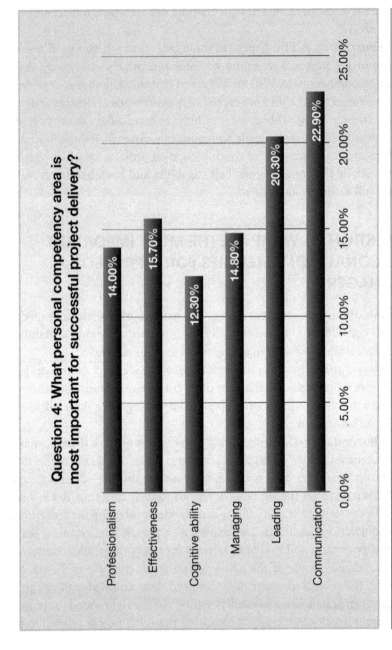

Figure A2.4   Responses to Survey Question 4: What are the most important personal competencies for a project manager?

telling us when they ranked cognitive ability the lowest—at least that's our interpretation, and luckily, it's reinforced by the verbatim comments.

QUESTION 5—WHAT ARE THE MOST IMPORTANT ASPECTS OF PM SKILLS FOR SUCCESSFUL DELIVERY OF PROJECTS?

This result surprised us because of the low ranking of the *financial* aspects (see Figure A2.5). Financial aspects received a score of fewer than 14%, while the *planning and executing* and *leadership* skills at the other end scored about ten points higher.

Observation 1. Leadership and people management is considered slightly more important than actually planning and executing the project. Both are at the top of this ranking, but it's interesting that leadership skills get this sort of attention and scoring by our sample of project practitioners. It corroborates well with the answers we saw in the previous questions, but it's more directly stated when we directly contrast planning and executing with leadership.

Observation 2. The relatively low rating for financial aspects of PM skill may stem from the fact that, in many cases, the project manager is somewhat isolated from day-to-day financial management of the project. Both authors have encountered telecom projects in which the project manager counted on a product manager or other sponsor to take on this responsibility. We've also seen that as the organization matured, there was a move toward giving the project manager the role of overseeing the project's income statement. In our population of 250 survey takers, we had a mix of maturity levels, and that's how we interpret this score.

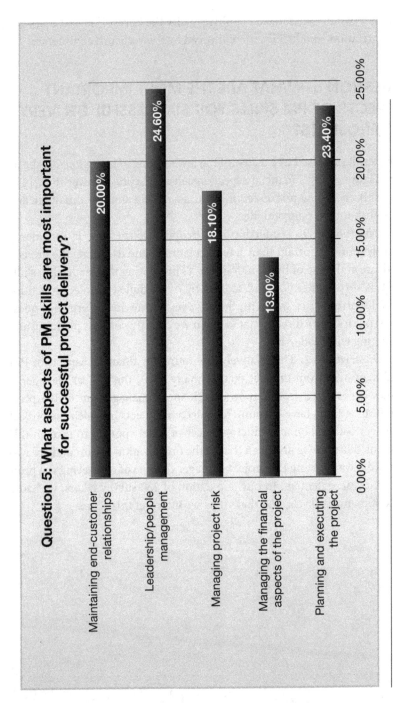

Figure A2.5   Responses to Survey Question 5: What are the most important aspects of PM skills?

QUESTION 6—FREE TEXT COMMENTS

We were happily shocked at the number of comments that people took the time to write, some of them rather lengthy and thoughtful. We think that this is a sign that the subject hit a nerve in the PM population and that they agree with us—that competency is key. Since the feedback was so insightful, we felt compelled to share some of these comments with you here about PM and the role of the project manager.

The ability (of the project manager) to be a trusted advisor to the real project owner.

—Anonymous

Real-world project management experience and the innate ability to lead through a shared vision, with people that WANT to follow you, not have to follow you.
—Darla Howard-Ramirez, MBA, PMP, Virginia, USA

Great people skills—able to extract commitment from others. Great communication skills—keep stakeholders happy and clear on the path ahead. Remember to value everything against the benefits that the project is supposed to deliver.
—Aaron Pacifico, Head of Project Portfolio
Management, RSPCA, England

The ability to visualize the big picture from the business drivers down to the details of the execution. The ability to distill what really matters and prioritize which issues to press to resolve and identify what can be allowed to take their own course.
—Howard M. Wiener, MSIA, PMP, New York, USA

Effectively communicating with ALL stakeholders. Being able to "fly with the eagles" (seeing the big picture) as well as "burrow with the beavers" (knowing the details). But it is not just competencies that make a project manager more successful; it is also personal traits such as integrity and honesty.

—Anonymous

I'm a firm believer in the soft skills, the value of human interaction, and empathy over those harder or technical skills. Provide me with the right person—someone who is emotionally intelligent, reasonably competent, open minded, and adaptable—and I can teach them the technical skills that they need to succeed as a project manager. Provide me with a technically accomplished person with a very solid knowledge base, but very limited soft skills and they will most likely never become a phenomenal project manager.

—Sloan Miller, Philadelphia, USA

Communication and the art of building strong relationships are vital. Project managers can surround themselves with technically savvy people at the heart of the project. The ability to keep everyone together and in sync is the best way a project manager can assure success.

—Anonymous

The ability to communicate is paramount. The ability to work with all stakeholders is a close second. Everything else is more or less the same.

—Anonymous

The two most important and versatile competencies are negotiation and communication. These are useful even when other competencies are also in play (for example, in navigating HR issues, these two complement and build on any available HR knowledge). The most underutilized skill is risk management; the ability to anticipate and plan for risks and have contingencies ready when risks become issues is typically not prioritized, and a key reason projects come off the rails.

—David F. Vincenti, PMP, New Jersey, USA

Leadership, communication skills, ability to suggest/discuss alternative solutions (in other words flexibility), and, finally, a good sense of humor.

—Anonymous

Projects are all about people, processes, politics, and everything in between. Project managers can't just rely on their tacit knowledge of project management; they must be better leaders who are mindful, open, flexible, empathetic, communicative, and engaged. Project management is both an art and a science—a blend of hard and core skill sets. If you just focus on managing a process, you'll be missing the big picture aspects of project management today—people.

—Naomi Caietti, California, USA

It's more important to be adaptable than predictable as complex systems are always(!) unpredictable. Managers should deal with it by using agile management and development. And do things because of passion, not because of money.

—Anonymous

Aside from the PMBOK® competencies and EQ/people skills, successful project managers are usually knowledgeable about the project subject matter. Someone who only has experience in civil engineering won't be effective in leading a pharmaceutical trial or a software development project, for example. We need to be able to hold up our end of the conversation.

—David A. Gordon, PMP, Nevada, USA

Know the specific industry in which you as a project manager operate is integral. Know what to expect in terms of pitfalls to avoid, common problems, contractor capabilities versus cost, good and bad actors in your market, and developing relationships with dependable materials and service providers is key to bringing a project home successfully.

—Anonymous

Understand the project and the people doing the project.

—Anonymous

CONCLUSION

We think you can see that the verbatim comments are very much in line with the data recorded from the survey. Communications and leadership skills and traits dominate in terms of what practicing project managers think will yield effective and efficient PM, although there were several practitioners who stressed the importance of *PM science* (use of Gantt charts, Monte Carlo analysis, earned value) and the importance of practice area knowledge (pharmaceutical, telecom, construction, finance). With regard to *what one knows* versus *what one is*, there is a balance between having the appropriate traits or characteristics and learning the proper PM skills—you cannot get away with only one *or* the other. The results from data points and the significant verbatim comments match quite well—your colleagues have spoken!

Web
Added
Value™

This book has free material available for download from the
Web Added Value™ resource center at *www.jrosspub.com*

Details of the 4-D Approach Applied to PM Competency

PROJECT TEAMS TAKE ON THESE MINDSETS—AND IT CAN BE A PROBLEM

The focus of this book is competency *gap filling* for the project manager and project management (PM) populations. But let's not forget that they get their work done through others. So, we devote a little time here to some particular differences between blue and orange project teams (see Chapter 3). It's important to note that—especially in technical project teams, which make up the majority of projects—the project team's mindset can be an accelerator or a detractor for project success. Since we're talking about the technical, the focus is on the *logical* side of the 4-D matrix and we are dealing with blue and orange project team mindsets.

Let's take a look at both, and see how this can yield improvement in your projects if you can detect and repair mindsets that are mismatched with the objectives. We'd assert that one competency that project managers should have is to recognize the makeup of their project teams.

The orange project team mindset will see project success as meeting cost and schedule commitments. They will be willing to trade off scope and performance elements of the project, perhaps too easily, to stay true to budget and schedule constraints. They will have very disciplined processes for team communication—sometimes at the cost of the conveyance of the information itself.

The blue project team mindset puts performance and meeting scope above all else. They'll value the information itself over the mode used to convey it—because they value the content so much—and therefore, there may be a lot of casual and pairwise communication, which means the team will not be able to count on the fact that everyone routinely receives the latest and best information.

Refer to Chapter 3, and in particular Tables 3.5 and 3.6, which provide guidance on how you can help shift the mindsets between blue and orange for better project effectiveness and efficiency.

LEVERAGING AND COMPLEMENTING OBSERVED TRAITS

As project managers who are familiar with *A Guide to the Project Management Book of Knowledge (PMBOK® Guide)*, you should recognize much of this from the theories referred to in Chapter 9. For example, one key tool that project managers use (hopefully) is a responsibility assignment matrix (RAM), which is meant to graphically display responsibility, accountability, who to consult, and who to inform (the responsible, accountable, consulted, and informed [RACI] code that populates the RAM). We noticed a striking connection between the 4-D approach, the tools and techniques promoted in the *PMBOK® Guide*, as well as the skills listed in its Appendix X3, such as leadership, team building, motivation, communication, influencing, decision making, political and cultural awareness, negotiation, conflict management, and coaching—and this is no coincidence. As far as personality typing, you are likely to be familiar with Myers-Briggs Type Indicator (MBTI) or DISC® (dominant, influential, steady, conscientious) personality typing. Both are very valuable. We think this one is particularly good to help project managers understand and take advantage of their own and others' personality types.

By understanding where you fit as a project team leader (gaining self-awareness) and, just as important, by understanding your team members' propensities among these four dimensions, you can gain power and authority on a project team. To understand this, let's look at Dr. Pellerin's definition of a team:

> *A group of people, under a leader's influence, interacting sufficiently to develop common behavioral norms.*

If you accept this definition, then the leader's influence is key. And the leader gains the most influence when he or she understands the forces (motivations) behind the behaviors of his or her team members. As a physicist, Dr. Pellerin explains (paraphrasing here) that if you imagine a large collection of project team members as individual iron filings, it is going to be a lot easier to get them aligned using a magnet rather than tweezers, individually forcing them to be in the right place at the right time. The argument here is that understanding the social aspects of your human contributors is like gaining the ability (a *force of nature, if you will*) to change behavior efficiently and effectively. As Dr. Pellerin found out through hard-earned experience, competency in the soft skills and being aware of the characteristics of project team members (and how to best respond to them) increases your capability as a project manager and increases your chances of project success—on the first try.

COORDINATING EXPERTISE, ESPECIALLY IN HIGHLY TECHNICAL PROJECTS

Certainly not all projects are NASA space telescope launches, like that of the prior section. But almost every project does have a technical component of some sort, and one of the things that PM must do is to coordinate the expertise in a project. This idea of project manager as *expertise coordinator* was recently featured in PM Journal Magazine (*Expertise Coordination in Information Systems Development Projects: Willingness, Ability, and Behavior*, PM Network, August/September 2016, Volume 47, No. 4). The article studied:

- Expertise in coordination ability;
- Expertise in coordination willingness; and
- Expertise in coordination behavior.

It also considered the effects and interactions of the aforementioned aspects on the important outcomes of a project when it comes to:

- Project performance;
- System quality (we would say, *the final deliverable* or *the project outcome*); and
- Personal work satisfaction.

What this research team determined was that coordination behavior is a function of both the willingness and the ability to coordinate, and that the expertise coordination behavior mediates the other two aspects. In other words, the project manager should seek to increase the willingness and ability of the team members to share their expertise as part of the environment they instill when they take on a project—and that will improve project success.

A4

Case Study: Philips Excellence Project Management

In Chapter 6 we discuss Philips' project management (PM) program, and in this appendix we provide, courtesy of Philips, the survey results to which we refer. We do so in an interview format, with questions being posed to Helen Bull, Head of the Philips Excellence Project Management Practice. The responses she received are summarized in Figure A4.1.

RATIONALE: WHAT DROVE YOU TO DO THE SURVEY?

The rationale for the study was driven by a need to better understand what our PM community felt about the quality of the tools and training in place to support them in their day-to-day jobs. From a practical perspective, these are standardized, yet tailorable tools, approaches, processes, and formal and informal training programs. We did not want to implicitly assume that they were valuable commodities to our community without eliciting their feedback on fit-for-purpose.

We also felt this was the right time to connect due to the many upgrades made to our tools and training assets in 2015, and together with the significantly increased and global personal connections made in 2015 to senior leaders and the global PM community in Philips. We widely use social media in conjunction with other more traditional styles

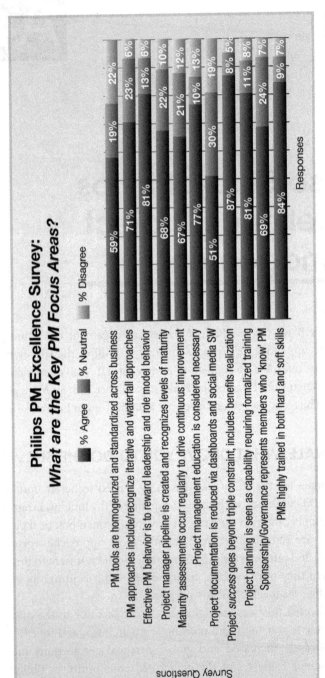

Figure A4.1   Philips PM survey extract

of communication, but were keen to formalize all PM related feedback through a more structured avenue, hence the survey.

MEANS: HOW WAS THE SURVEY EXECUTED—OVER WHAT TIME FRAME?

The two-week online survey was completed during May 2016, and was sent to our PM community and to their line management. A limited number of questions ensured that the survey was not onerous, which we mentioned in the e-mail introducing the survey to each participant. From the respondent pool, 86% were titled program or project manager, and of this group 73% had managed projects for six or more years.

Analysis of the feedback took a further two weeks after closure, with results published in two tranches. The first tranche addressed the eight closed questions with results released in early June 2016. The second tranche looked at the open-ended question whereby analysis took considerably longer due to the nature of the answers. These results were released in early July 2016.

SPONSOR(S): DID YOU HAVE AN EXECUTIVE SPONSOR?

Senior leadership in Philips (especially our CEO) are huge proponents of the Project Management Practice and recognize that strong project management is a core capability for our business. The survey was sent out under the banner of the Philips Excellence Project Management Practice, with results released to the organization via various media.

RESULTS: HOW DO YOU INTERPRET THE RESULTS? WHAT MAJOR FINDINGS WERE THERE?

The results provided insightful and valuable information to both the global project management community in Philips, and to the Philips Excellence Project Management Practice.

Project management courses in Philips University (click not brick), and the Philips Project Management Certification programs were rated as the most used by respondents. This was further supported with project management education delivering the highest satisfaction result by users at 77%.

In relation to tools and methods, a small percentage of users still did not fully use the tools and methods available to them. While the bulk of this group did, we still see a need to connect with our user base to encourage more frequency and with more of the assets in the practice (with standardization also comes tailoring to one's needs).

For the future of project management, 87% of respondents saw a key area of focus to be on the competing constraints of time, cost, scope, reputation, quality, risk, and value—especially in relation to the creation of business value.

A strong message was evident when three topics directly related to project management training and education entered the top five key areas of focus in relation to project management in the future. It was clear to us that our community should consider that project management education is not a *nice thing to have*, but rather a *necessity*.

Project approaches contributed to most of the comments related to tools and methods. A significant number of comments received were about the agile ways of working and also about waterfall approaches. This was not unexpected, as a lot of discussion is underway in the company about hybrid approaches.

SURVEY RESPONSE: WHAT DID YOU DO IN REACTION TO THIS, RIGHT AWAY, IN A WEEK'S TIME, IN A MONTH'S TIME, AND SUSTAINABLY OVER MANY MONTHS?

We were able to address a number of areas within the month. One example was a new coaching program for project management that was launched within a month of the survey publication date. In addition, in the same period we were able to address a number of questions in relation to how users could gain more professional development units (PDUs) for Project Management Professional (PMP)® certification retention. We will continue to use focus groups to be the eyes and ears of the organization in relation to what our community needs to both hone their skills and make their projects successful. Some topics will require more investigation with user groups in the organization. Where there is a valid case for change, we create formal avenues for adaptation or roll out.

The Project Management Practice can only be considered as *value-added* when it listens and responds to its users, who are not only the program and project managers of Philips, but all employees of Philips. Projects affect us all, no matter where we sit in the organization; and without a strong project management discipline and exceptional project managers we fail both as an organization, and as an employer—it is as simple as that.

INDEX

Note: Page numbers followed by *f* and *t* indicate figure and table, respectively.

·